New Ground

01 02 03 04 05 23 22 21 20 19

Caitlin Press Inc.
8100 Alderwood Road,
Halfmoon Bay, BC V0N 1Y1
www.caitlin-press.com

Text and cover design by Vici Johnstone
Family edition typeset by Bill Horne
Printed in Canada

Caitlin Press Inc. acknowledges financial support from the Government of Canada and the Canada Council for the Arts, and the Province of British Columbia through the British Columbia Arts Council and the Book Publisher's Tax Credit.

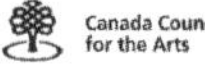

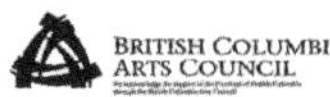

Funded by the Government of Canada | Canadä

Library and Archives Canada Cataloguing in Publication

Kujundzic, Ann, author.
New ground : a memoir of art and activism in BC's interior / Ann Kujundzic.

ISBN 9781773860015 (softcover)

1. Kujundzic, Ann. 2. Women artists—British Columbia—Biography. 3. Artists—British Columbia—Biography. 4. Feminists—British Columbia—Biography. 5. Women political activists—British Columbia—Biography. 6. Political activists—British Columbia—Biography.

N6549.K85 A2 2019 709.2 dc23

New Ground

A Memoir of Art and Activism in BC's Interior

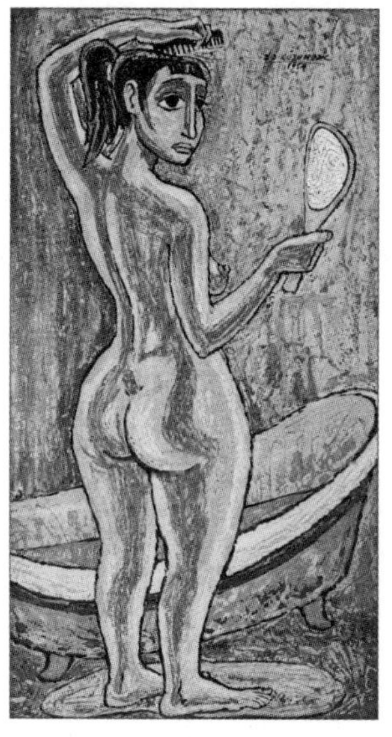

Ann Kujundzic

Caitlin Press

To my children, grandchildren and all those others who come after me

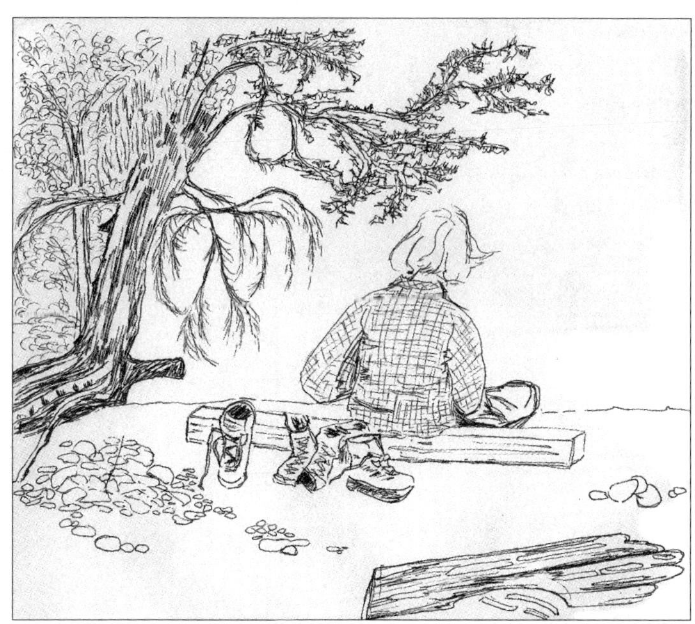

Drawing of Eleanor Knight on Haida Gwaii.

Contents

Foreword

Within a few pages of Ann Kujundzic's candid and engaging memoir, *New Ground*, the reader realizes that this woman's first ninety years just happen to have coincided with some of the most profound shifts in technology, culture, communication, family life and identity politics the world has ever seen—and that she has gladly thrown herself into the fray.

Ann was born in 1929, the year of the Stock Market Crash, in a small Scottish town where milk was delivered by horse and cart. She grew up in a home rich with books, music, art and ideas. At age fourteen, as the Second World War raged, Ann persuaded a friend to sneak away with her, leaving their rural English boarding school to visit the big city (Oxford). At age nineteen, while working as a sculptor's assistant in Edinburgh, she met and married Zeljko, an artist; their first child was born just a few months after the National Health Service (NHS) was founded. They moved often, renting small home/studio spaces (one of which was reached by climbing ninety-two stone steps!) and were always in the company of artists, writers and philosophers, amid clean diapers hanging here and there to dry. The family grew steadily in those days before safe, reliable birth control for women, and Ann made most of the family's clothes and took odd jobs, while Zeljko did artwork and taught classes.

In the late 1950s it was time for a change, and the family—now two adults with three kids and another on the way—moved to the Kootenays in southeastern British Columbia. There they founded the Kootenay School of Art in Nelson in 1960. Ann did the lion's share of looking after the home and children, but she made time to assist Zeljko and also to join the Voice of Women, writing press copy and speaking to parent and teacher groups. The family moved several more times, building an A-frame, taking on fixer-uppers, adapting a disused church and welcoming another child. And they continued to live among artists, writers, thinkers and musicians. (Yes, there were hootenannies!)

When Zeljko got an offer to teach at an American college, Ann chose not to move. She put in some intense years living and working on a communal farm, then set out to fulfill another dream—to study at the College of Massage. She moved to Vancouver to put her new skills to work, amid heated political activity stirred up by the Vietnam War, the women's movement, the civil rights movement and other causes. Ann found time to join the ranks of concerned citizens working for social justice. In January 1986 she spoke out candidly and confidently at a pivotal rally in support of Dr. Henry Morgentaler's campaign to give women access to safe, legal abortions, simply by telling the truth of her own struggle for reproductive control of her body. The sure, calm, measured text of her talk is reason enough to read this inspiring memoir.

Ann Kujundzic has taken on many more challenges, all her life—ethically and joyfully, with a rock-solid sense of responsibility to the human community. From start to end of this extraordinary memoir, the reader is in the presence of a warm, smart, funny, truly adventurous woman, who instinctively chose to make a difference.

–Mary Schendlinger

PREAMBLE

Throughout the many moves I've made, I somehow managed to hold on to my travel journals, as well as copious bundles of letters to and from family and friends. My typewritten ones on those old yellow carbon-copy sheets have become brittle, but they remain legible. I was surprised to rediscover many of the memories revealed in these epistles and wanted to explore them more deeply, so I started putting my stories together.

I've been fortunate to live through a lot of personal as well as social history: from Depression times during my childhood in Scotland, through the Second World War, and marriage at the age of nineteen to a remarkable artist who arrived in the UK as a displaced person from Yugoslavia. We spent our early married years together in Edinburgh, a somewhat tenuous city for artists, before immigrating to British Columbia in the late fifties. Five years after launching the Kootenay School of Art in Nelson, we moved to the Okanagan, where we opened an Art Centre in Kelowna. Together, yet in some odd ways separately, the two of us raised our five children in the incredibly rich and lively twenty years we shared together.

I lived in times when postal delivery came twice or three times a day, six days a week, and we sent handwritten letters frequently, knowing they would reach their destination within that day (or at latest the next morning)—a far cry from the instant, yet more impersonal, texting I now struggle with. On a more sober note those were also times when birth control was barely available, let alone reliable, presenting hazards that affected many marriages. Then came the Cold War with the threat of nuclear proliferation and fears of how strontium-90 could undermine the health of children being born. This was at a peak when we came to Canada, and I was surprised to find that Canadians were not as driven by political issues as those of us who had lived in Europe.

It may be interesting for my grandchildren, as well as others of their generation, to be able to read something of the variety of life that I've been so fortunate to experience, whether it was leaving my country of origin, operating an Art Centre, being part of a farm co-operative or, later, travelling on my own to China and the Middle East.

I have chosen not to include much detail about the thirty years I lived in Vancouver. I still grieve leaving my many good friends there, but after the occasional trips that I've made back to that remarkable city, I know I made the right decision. I thank my daughters and their families for welcoming me so generously to their homes here in Victoria.

My children played an essential role in my life and I am extremely proud of them all. They found their own ways through their share of unintended parental neglect. I always thought it safer to under-parent than over-parent, mostly because I feared my parenting might have the effect of messing them up. I have decided not to include much about them here, because I respect their choice to tell their own stories when they wish.

Although during my marriage I felt compelled on many occasions to put my husband's needs ahead of my own or my children's, it is only in retrospect that I question how much I really understood the driving passion of this man, an artist with whom I shared such intensity of life for twenty years. I thought, at the time, that I understood him, but there was no way I could possibly walk in his shoes; in reality I was still learning to walk in my own.

I have often felt I don't know myself in the way that others appear to see me. Yes, I feel very much here and now in this instant: my breathing, my posture, my pains and discomforts, and I certainly notice what is around me very clearly. I am to some extent unpredictable—to myself, anyway. Other people have described me as reliable and rock-like, which is not how I see myself. But I never had an image of myself in the way that I have an image of others, until writing this memoir. It has brought many memories to the surface, some pleasant, others unsettling.

When I reread letters my mother sent me in the months preceding her death, I was shocked to realize that she had indeed let me know that she was suffering some serious health problems. Her beautiful handwritten letters that came each week with occasional comments about her pain and lapses of energy should have given me cause for alarm, but at that time my own very busy and somewhat troubled life took all of my attention. I was looking for answers myself and was simply blind to the struggles she was facing. I had never known her other than in excellent health and just could not conceive of her being sick. I regret not having recognized her situation, spending more time with her or expressing more concern.

Because I am essentially shy by nature and don't care to be the centre of attention, writing about myself has not been a comfortable process. At times I've resisted the process of telling my own story, and revisiting some places has been hard, yet reclaiming others has brought rewards. And through the writing process, my several lives, which I often felt were completely disconnected, have now been gathered into a life of many chapters. My memoir has provided discernment and underlined connections I've had to many people who have been very dear to me. It's my privilege to share them with you in this, my story.

SCOTTISH ROOTS

My Parents

I've often wondered how my parents met—what prompted my own beginnings. There are a few things I know, and some of them are curious. My mother came from a working-class family in Stonehaven in Scotland, and my father from what was called an owning-class family in Rudry, a small village in Wales. I don't know what my paternal grandfather did, but it seems the family was comparatively well off. We certainly inherited a fair number of silver tea and coffee pots from them, together with hand-embroidered linen tablecloths, which my mother was very proud to own.

My father, William Herbert Johnson, the second youngest of twelve children, was forty years old, and my mother, Ann, the second oldest of eight children, was twenty-seven years old when I was born, the first of the five children they were to have. It seems strange to me now that my father had not married earlier, because after the First World War there was a dearth of young men. We knew so many single women when I was growing up, spinsters we called them. To me, as a child, they always seemed old. They had either lost their betrothed or never met an available man in the years following that war; it had taken its toll. My father was twenty-five years old when he enlisted and would therefore have been a prime candidate for the marriage scene when he survived the war. I know that he suffered greatly from the loss of his closest brother, Trevor, who died in the trenches. But it was to be another nine years or so after the war ended before he met and married my mother, and yet another three before I was born. My mother was a healthy, vivacious woman who enjoyed sharing life with him; whether on the tennis courts, where they both played a mean game, or in the kitchen, where he made superb raspberry jam; or playing cards, which was something they shared with us, as a family.

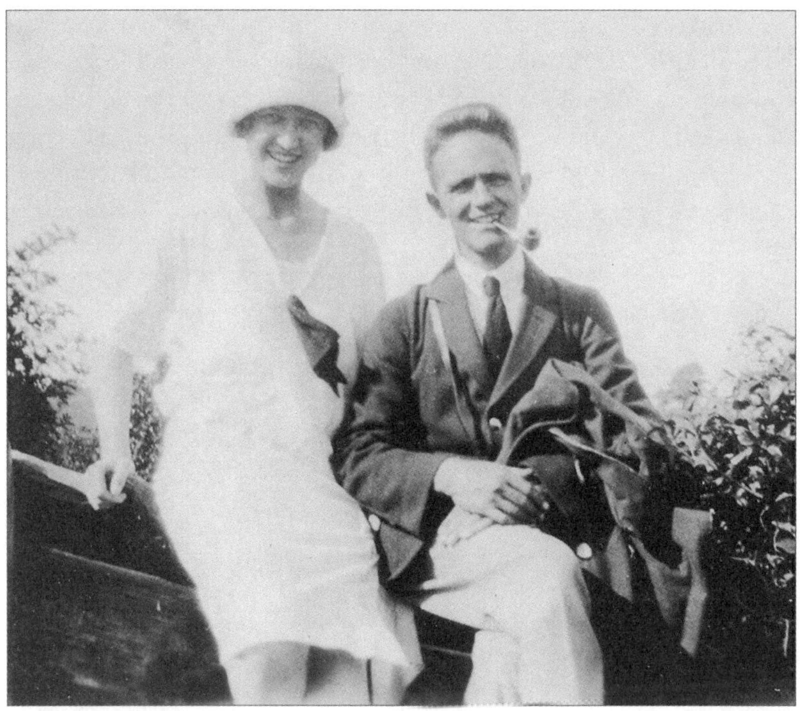

My parents, Ann Murray and William Johnson.

I remember them always being caring of each other, and there are two observations my mother made that have always stayed with me. The first was, "Your father was the first man I went out with who had clean nails." Working-class men didn't care too much about clean fingernails. The second came after observing my own somewhat volatile marriage, when she said, "Your father and I have never had an angry word in all the years we've been married." This statement might well be questioned as to its value in our present understanding of inhibition, but nonetheless it reflects something of their mutual caring and affection.

I was born in 1929, the Depression era, in Dysart, a small fishing village on the east coast of Fife. In those days we had horse-and-cart delivery of milk, bread and vegetables, and my father would be so delighted when a horse delivered its droppings on the street outside our house. He would immediately rush to collect this valued commodity for the garden. Those large, lovely, heavily shod, clumping Clydesdale horses worked daily and worked hard.

As I said, my father was one of those lucky young men who survived the First World War after serving the full four years. I have some treasured photographs of members of the battalion he served with in the desert. He would recount, with a smile, the experience of having all his teeth removed while on the North African front, to be replaced later with a set of dentures. But for years after the war he had inter-

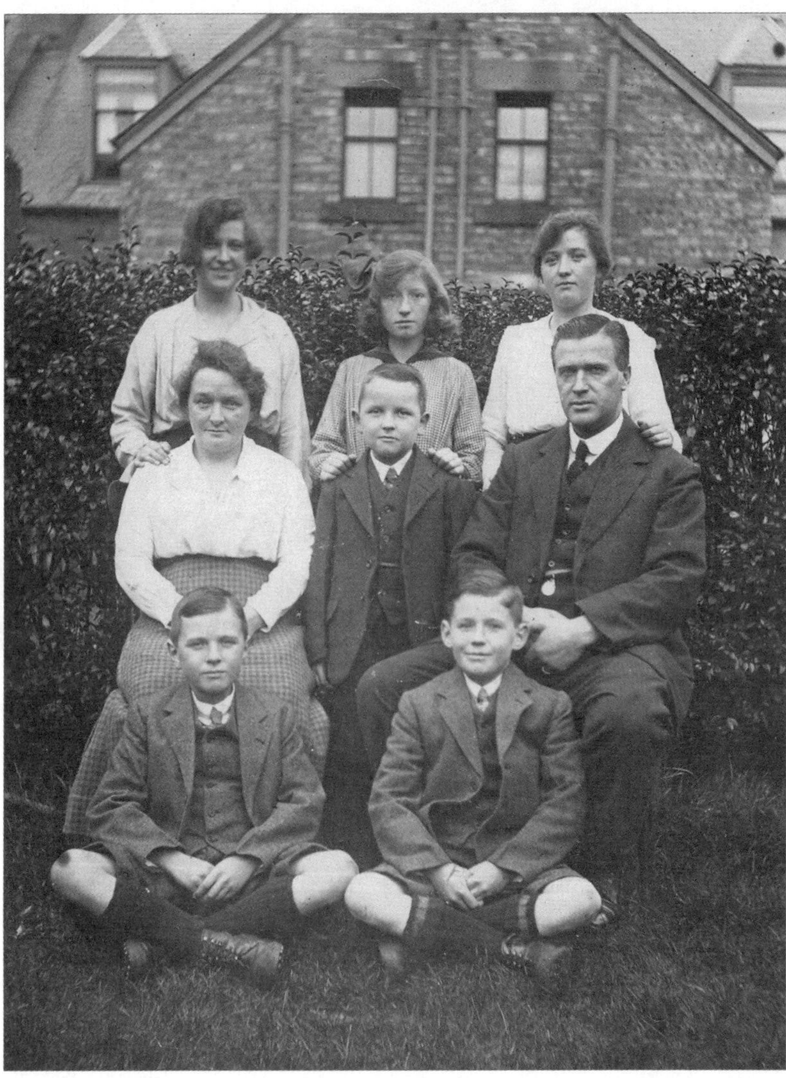

My mother's family.

mittent attacks of malaria, and my mother decided to take this on with naturopathic treatment. She had become interested in this approach to health through some enlightened friends who, like her, were health food addicts and avid hikers, and she was convinced of our body's ability to cope with illness without orthodox medical intervention.

I was probably six years old when she asked me to help when my father was stricken once again with malaria. She had wrapped his full body in cold-water sheets, compresses as they were called. His temperature was extremely high and I was asked to keep replacing a cold, wet towel on his forehead. I remember it so clearly: he was lying on a camp cot in the living room, mumbling incoherently from time to time. I don't know how many days my mother kept renewing the wet sheets that shrouded my father—they were replaced whenever they became dry—but I do know this was the last time he had malaria. On this occasion his body burned out the last traces of it. His recovery confirmed my mother's belief in a healthy treatment of cold-water compresses, combined with fasting.

Compresses became the standard remedy or cure that she provided for us all, as children, though they were limited to the neck and midriff in our case. These, together with bed and partial fasting, worked well for all the childhood diseases we encountered at school: from measles and mumps to scarlet fever and whooping cough. And

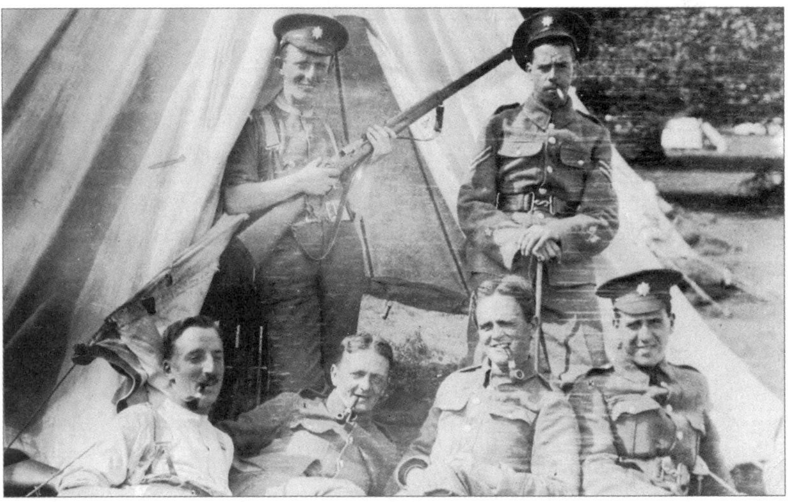

My dad and his brother, second and third from right in bottom row, First World War.

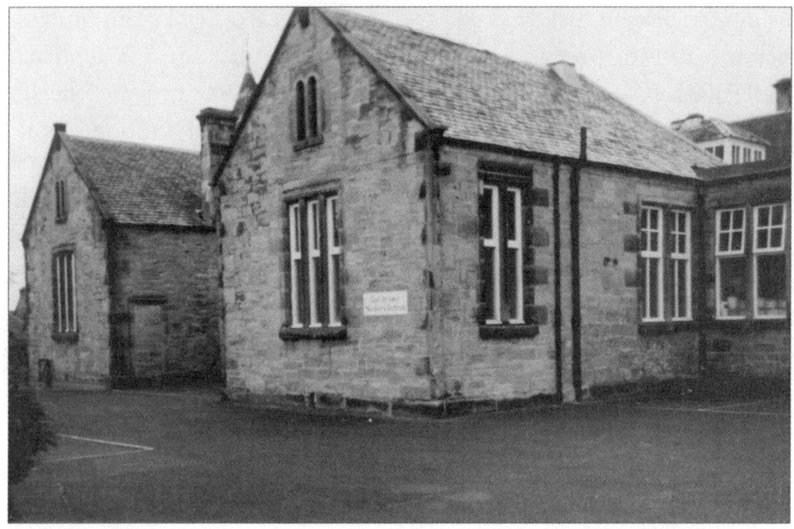

Gallatown Elementary School, which I attended in Dysart from age five to seven.

we all recovered in remarkably short time and were ready to return to school long before the allocated three weeks deemed necessary for any infectious illness. In those days there were district nurses who visited children who were absent from school due to sickness, and they would diagnose the problem and return later to observe our progress. They were always mystified when the spots had disappeared, the swellings had reduced to normal after only a few days, and there were no symptoms left to justify absence from school. It must have been a dilemma for them.

My mother was an unusual woman who questioned constantly, and I realize now that she was in many ways ahead of her time. With a working-class background and a father who drank heavily and was abusive to his wife and children, she had left home in her teens. She worked her way up until she became personal secretary to the manager of James Keiller & Sons, a well-appointed factory still famed for its Dundee marmalade. She investigated alternate health options and brought us up as vegetarians, not from a humanitarian or religious point of view, but purely because she believed that meat was not a very healthy or necessary food. She certainly fed us extremely well; we never lacked varied and delicious meals. Her homemade bread, soups and inventive entrees—such as lentil cutlets and parsnip pie—were widely

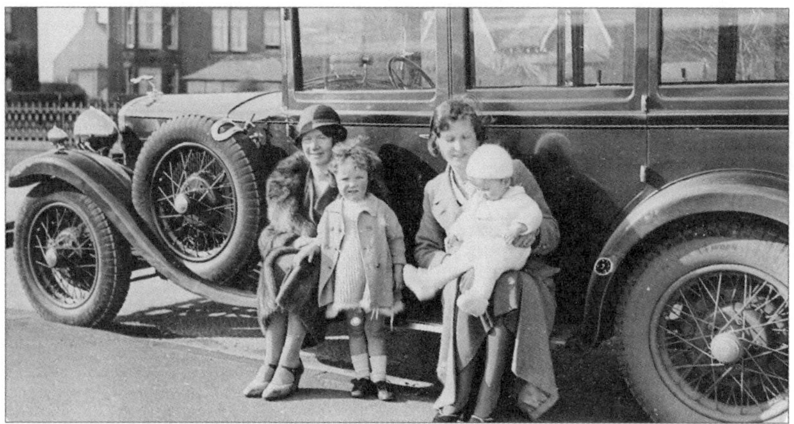

Left to right, Auntie Vie, me, Mother and baby Trevor.

appreciated. We all had our favourites. She would have qualified for entry amongst the many of today's gourmet health food caterers.

I wish I had paid attention to her culinary skills, but she encouraged me to take piano and violin lessons, to sew and read, all of which I was more than happy to do. "Anyone can learn to cook and do housework," she used to say. "Better you spend your time doing other things." Years later, when I was asked by my prospective husband if I could cook, I remember being sufficiently outraged by such a demeaning question that I answered, "Of course I can." I remembered my mother's words, "Anyone can learn," and, in time, I guess I did.

We moved up the road from the village of Dysart to a house on Windmill Road in Kirkcaldy and lived there until 1939. During that year, the threat of a second world war was becoming a daily preoccupation. Our neighbours, the Thompsons, thought it important to stock up on staples and advised my mother to do the same. But I clearly remember her saying, critically, "It's not good to hoard or stockpile. I won't do it. It's morally wrong." I've often wondered about that. In going through my father-in-law's small, well-stocked house after his death in Kelowna, we came across sack after sack of white sugar. He had come from Eastern Europe and had faced severe shortages during the Second World War. And I remember when I was first married, Zeljko insisted on having a small trunk, filled with dried and canned goods, under our bed at all times.

I never really got to know many of my father's family due to their distance from us; they mostly lived in the South of England and in Wales. I remember my father taking me to visit his sister, Millie, who lived in Swansea, when there was a big rugby match there. He loved rugby; it had been his sport as a young man. We went by train, and I must have been quite small, because he tucked me up for a while on the luggage rack high above the seats and told me to keep very quiet when the ticket collector came along, as he hadn't bought a ticket for me. I remember him bringing into the carriage a glass of beer with a lot of foam on the top and asking if I wanted to taste the foam. It looked remarkable to me, with an amazing colour and froth I'd never seen before, since we never had alcohol in our home. But I have no memories of anything about our time in his sister's home in Wales.

Two or three years after that, one of his older brothers, Jervis, came with his wife, Sybil, and their daughter, Audrey, who was just a year or so older than me, and they stayed with us for a few days. I didn't much enjoy their visit. Audrey was very prim and had to share my bed with me, which she didn't much like. Also, she had brought a lot of fancy clothes and just wasn't very friendly. Her parents seemed kind of formal, too, and came with a lot of luggage. I suspect they intimidated my mother. They were what she would have called upper class, and she admired the manners and the lifestyle this invoked: hand-embroidered linens, fine china and "good" silverware, which she loved to acquire.

They were indeed very different from my mother's family, who mostly lived in Dundee. I dearly loved all my Scottish uncles: George, Bert, Jock and David, who were full of fun and raucous jokes. They mostly lived in what were called housing schemes, which were low-cost square rental blocks, uniformly providing four family units, two on the upper floor and two at ground level, with small garden spaces around each separate block. My mother somewhat frowned on them and considered their lifestyle a bit infra dig. She aspired to something better for us. But my father was very much at home with her brothers; he enjoyed being one of the "boys" and would occasionally share a beer with them. This was something he never did at home, and I'm sure it was out of consideration for my mother's experience with an alcoholic father. And I came to realize that each of my parents had quite a strong attachment to their partner's family background.

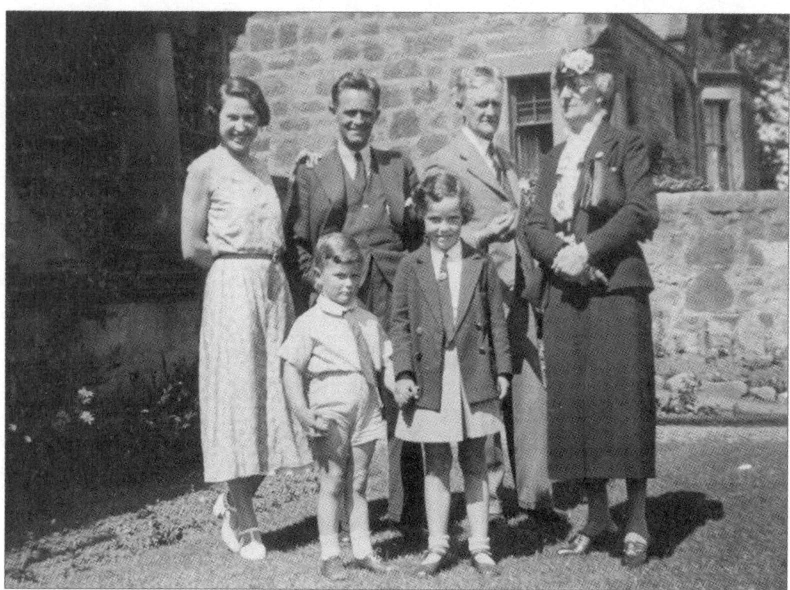

My father's brother Jervis, with his wife, on the right. Trevor and me in front.

Nonetheless, there was one way they both remained true to their roots; strangely, it was in political allegiance. When voting day came round, my father, who really didn't pay much mind to what was happening on the political scene, would not have bothered to go out and cast his vote had it not been that my mother was totally committed to voting Labour. He would say, "I guess I'll have to go and vote Tory to cancel your mother's vote for Labour." And my mother would say something like, "Och, you just don't pay enough attention to what's going on." Mother read avidly, and our house was full of good literature; my dad read only the football news. But they never argued about politics. I certainly never heard either of them speak a harsh or unkind word to the other, and neither would they countenance criticism of the other by anyone else.

Unfortunately, I had left for Canada with my husband and three youngsters and wasn't around when they died. I only know that my mother, who was extremely fit and healthy, shocked everyone by being hospitalized, at age fifty-seven. She died within two weeks from lung cancer that had eaten one lung and left only half of the other. She never smoked, exercised well and ate healthily, but was apparently very unhappy in her last few years. I believe she wanted to sell the small private hotel that they had been running for twelve years and have a different kind of life. I was told that my father was very worried about this. He didn't know how else they could make a living, and he had just turned seventy, which probably gave him cause for concern. No doubt they didn't find a way of resolving their differences, and I sensed my mother was greatly distressed over this.

The day I got news of my mother's death, I was living on this side of the Atlantic. A call came from my brother, Jerry, in Scotland, and I was standing in the hallway close to the front door, where our telephone was, when I lifted the receiver. It was the first time I'd heard from him since I'd left. His voice was unexpected and a trifle muffled. "I'm really sorry to have to tell you…Mum died yesterday. She died in hospital. She was taken in a few days ago. It was cancer. We didn't know."

Everything tumbled around in my mind. My healthy mother couldn't have had cancer. It didn't make sense: she'd always been exceptionally health-conscious. Moreover, this was certainly a big shake-up in my own plans. I was actually on my way back to visit her, with four young children and a fifth on the way. I was within a few days of leaving for this trip back to Scotland, mostly on the pretext of visiting her. She was greatly missing her grandchildren since our emigration two years previously, and this way I could quietly leave my artist husband in Canada and go back home. He seemed to be much happier in Canada than I was, and I wasn't sure I could keep on coping with his moods and constant restlessness. If I went back "home," I'd find a way of getting work. I'd always been able to get work in Edinburgh, and somehow I'd manage. But I would have needed my mother's assistance in this major move. She would undoubtedly offer to help with the care of my children while I figured things out.

Although my relationship with my mother had never been what you would call close, probably because I felt her expectations of me had always been uncomfortably high, I knew I could always rely on her. She'd played a huge role in my life, bringing into my childhood her love of books, music, theatre and dance, and a respect for political values. The Kingdom of Fife, where I was born and lived for the first ten years of my life, had elected a Communist member to hold a seat in the British Parliament, Willie Gallacher, a local hero. Fife was a county of coal mines, and one of them stretched for three miles out undersea. The coast harboured fishing boats that scoured the fierce waters of the North Sea. In this world, working folks took politics seriously.

My mother always had an overfull load of domestic chores. Washing all of our clothes and linens on a metal-ribbed scrub board at a deep scullery sink was hard, physical work. But she had boundless energy and always made time to take us for long hikes on a Sunday, or to go pick wild berries in the summer or hunt for those delicious little white button mushrooms on one of the golf courses nearby, or to organize and prepare mouth-watering foods for a birthday party. I was her first child, and four more were to follow me over the next eighteen years.

I remember that my father was very upset when I travelled back to see him some two months after my mother's death, and he wasn't able to talk about what had happened. I don't think he ever recovered from the loss, and he died within a few years. My two youngest siblings were still living at home. One was yet in school, and the hotel was sold within a couple of years of this happening. I regret that I wasn't around to say my farewells to either of my parents. Deprived of knowing anything about the situation leading up to their last years and of possibly being of any assistance, it is unlikely that I could have changed what happened. But I feel a loss in not knowing.

Now that I am getting closer to my own demise, I am very aware of how fortunate I am to have my own children close at hand, noticing my changes, my slower movement, my need for assistance, even though I often resist it. Who knows how it will be toward the end? It's a crapshoot and there is no point in getting too worked up about it. I often think of my parents with a questioning that cannot be addressed and with a sadness that lingers. Like so many things in life, it's about learning to make peace with the things that cannot be changed.

An Early Memory

Recently an unexpected image surfaced: it was of a little crib that I was given. I think it was a replica of the real one that the new baby, my little brother Trevor, slept in. But this one was very small, and a bit unstable. It was cobbled together with thin, flat, white enamel metal strips, with upright crossbars at each end. On its light frame, white muslin cotton flecked with tiny cotton burrs was draped and folded to hold a wee doll. I remember it didn't stand up very well and was always tipping over. In fact, it only looked pretty as long as I didn't touch it too much. I don't remember touching the real baby either. He slept in a crib right next to my parents' bed, on my mother's side. I was not quite three years old when he arrived and I was probably given the crib so that I wouldn't feel left out when the baby came. It was this image that took me back, and I'm a little surprised at the other odd pieces that come to mind.

I remember sleeping in the bedroom next to my parents, a room with eaves on one side and my bed tucked under the slope. It was a dark place for a bed, and there was something strange about the wallpaper. It had brownish patterns on it—sort of irregular, assorted shapes on a pale blue-grey background, with odd flesh-coloured spots scattered around. I could never make much sense of what the wallpaper was about, though I would study it endlessly, because I had to go to bed long before I was ready to sleep. Early to bed was the norm in those days: parents expected to have time for themselves in the evenings.

There was another room, which for a short time I used as a playroom, downstairs. It was a long, narrow room with very little light coming in. But this room had some magic in it. My worn-out orange teddy bear, with a few silky patches left on him, was always around. I can still smell him and feel his rough parts, and I don't remember him

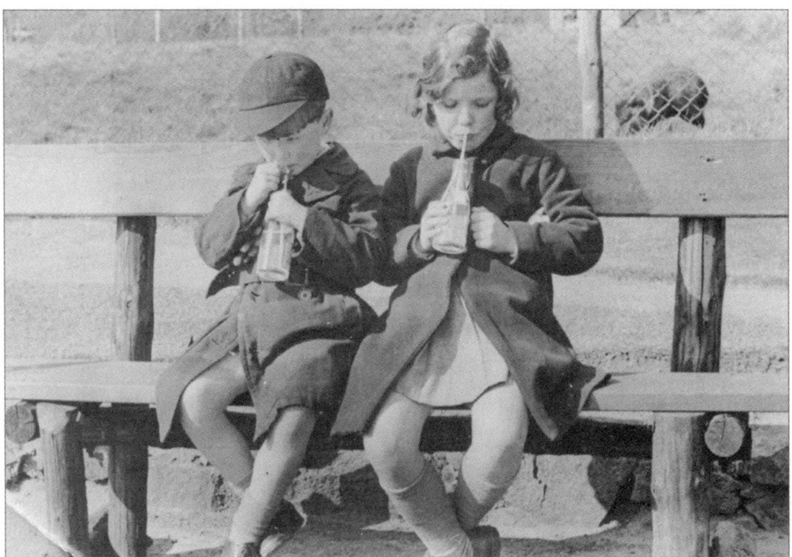

Me and my brother, Trevor.

ever being new. And I believe I had an Eeyore, a sort of grey, floppy stuffed animal that just wouldn't sit up straight, but I had mixed feelings about him. This room had a high shelf on one wall, with a curtain hanging from it, and when I was told to tidy up the nursery, I believed it meant hiding things behind the curtain. Or did it? Tidying seems the wrong word. Tidying seemed like not caring about them, stuffing them away like they were not real. Things had to be put in a safe place; that's where they belonged.

At this time we were living in Kirkcaldy, and it was a time before electricity had reached our home. We had gas lamps, one in each room, attached by an iron bracket to the wall. They had small, fragile mantles that looked as if they were made of stiff gauze, and they would burn away at the edges and sooner or later have to be replaced. A very unusual smoky kind of smell came from them, and the lamps had fluted, milky glass shades to protect them. They had to be removed before the mantle was lit. There was a tap on the side of the arm holding the mantle and shade, and turning the tap clockwise allowed the gas to come on. It was only then you could light the mantle, carefully, with a match. You had to be careful not to let too much gas out at first, or the sudden heat would harm the mantle, which cost a lot to replace.

My dad must have told me this, because I remember him lifting me up to see how it was done, but I don't think he ever let me do the lighting.

The kitchen was particularly memorable, with its huge black range up against the wall and a chimney behind and above. There was an ornate kettle stand attached at the front that could be partially swung off the stove, and it often had a soup pot simmering on it. The open-fire part was in the centre of the stove, with thick iron bars across it to keep the coal from falling out, and there were ovens on both sides. This must have been the source of heat for the whole house. I think we used to put our wet shoes, stuffed with paper, near the open oven doors when they needed drying out; I can recall the smell of drying leather. This was where we had our dining table and where we did most of our living. There was also some other furniture in this kitchen. The most impressive was a large, intricately carved wooden sideboard in a rich ochre colour. It had belonged to my Welsh grandparents and I've often wondered how we came by it. My mother gave it a place of honour.

I didn't like the scullery where the dishes were done; it was always cold. The stone floor was uncomfortable to stand on, and the sinks were too high as well as too deep. It was hard for me to turn the taps on and off. Those beautiful brass taps were quite small with handles that were very stiff, but so finely shaped. They are reminiscent of the house keys that we used, which were like little sculptures. They seemed to fit our hands well, or at least my hands, which have always been on the small side. I can feel those keys now—slender, shiny and very important.

We looked out onto the back garden from the kitchen, with steps leading from a door off the scullery. That garden has appeared in many of the recurring dreams I've had since we first owned a house with a garden. In the dreams I plant rows of seeds, but they don't come up, or they come up for a while and then disappear. I always wake up full of immense disappointment, or, more accurately, a feeling of failure. My father had a parsley plant near the back door, close to where my mother could use it for cooking. We ate in the kitchen. I have a recollection of a gas cooker in the scullery, opposite the sink, and most of the food was kept in a small pantry or larder at the far end of the scullery. Pantries and larders were the cool places where we kept dairy, produce and leftovers—when there were any.

Stone houses were often short on windows, and their thick walls didn't bring in much light. The kitchen window looked into the back garden, which had a low stone wall around it. The immediate area behind that was quite wild, with lots of gorse bushes, and, beyond that, a public golf course. I walked through it on my way to elementary school, but I don't remember ever seeing people actually playing golf on that course.

One of my unhappy memories is of blinking my eyes under cold water in a small tub in the scullery; it was part of the treatment I was undergoing for my poor eyesight. They found out about my short-sightedness the year I was five, when I first went to school and couldn't see the writing on the board. I managed to fudge it for a while, as I didn't want to have to sit at the front of the class. Very few kids wore spectacles in those days, but it caught up with me. This treatment was based on the Bates Method, popular at the time and endorsed by Aldous Huxley in *The Art of Seeing*. I was also told to go into the drawing room, which was always cold because it was seldom used, to do a series of eye exercises. I think I sat on the piano stool to do them. But I never really got into practicing those exercises; I found them very boring. My mother would get cross with me. She told me she'd come round, outside the house, and when she looked in through the window and saw that I wasn't doing them, she became upset. She always expected me to be a "good girl." Those expectations would haunt me for all of my growing-up years, though she probably never knew it.

I have a hard time remembering Trevor as really small. An image comes up of him crawling around the kitchen floor, and my next thought was, *He is in the way*, so I bumped into him and he began yelling. I wonder if that was the time when my mother said to me, "You should never make a boy cry." I remember how fond of me my dad was. He was probably as fond of me as my mum was of my baby brother. But my dad wasn't around as much as Mum, so it was always a treat when he was at home. My dad was an engineer who worked the night shift at the power station in Kirkcaldy, a sort of combination night watchman and skilled worker. I remember the wonderful replica he made of that power station and how much I envied my little brother that prize piece, because my dad had made it for him. However, I

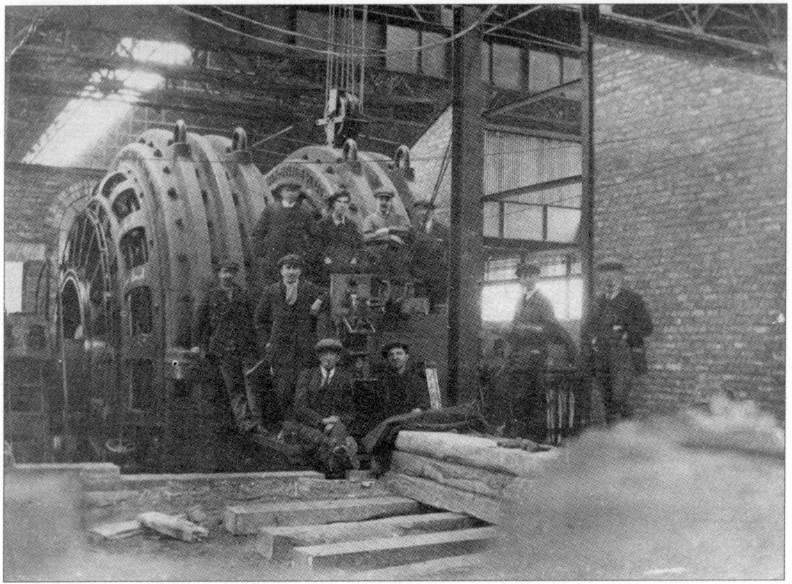

Workers at the Kirkcaldy power station.

don't think Trevor was ever too interested in it. It actually worked, and could pull things when you turned the handle, and it was made of very heavy, shiny brass and mounted on a sheet of wood.

I've already mentioned that my mother came from a working-class family, and she made an immense effort to rise above it. She was one of the hardest-working people I have ever known, but it wasn't the working part that bothered her. What she wanted to change for us was the vulgar or common aspects (her words) that are associated with the rough living conditions of the typical working-class family. My uncle George, her younger brother, who smoked and drank outrageously and whom I dearly loved, could easily get her goat by giving us treats, poking fun at our good manners and telling her she was "too stuck up." I remember going to his wedding when I was about four years old, primed to recite something, probably from A.A. Milne or perhaps from Robert Louis Stevenson's *A Child's Garden of Verses*. It was such a favourite way of showing your child off, and I hated it. I hated being shown off, I hated being laughed at, and I hated being the focus of attention. That was to be a recurrent theme in my years of growing up. But my mother needed to be proud of me, to show me off. It was the only wedding I remember attending, until my own, some fifteen years later.

Music played an important role in our house. My mother played the piano by ear and sang to her own accompaniment. When I was small I was in awe of her brilliance, although I was aware, even at that age, of something sounding not quite right. Later, I learned it was her chording. But she always had a nice touch. And my father built a gramophone cabinet with one of those megaphone attachments that you can still see on old advertisements for His Master's Voice, with a brown and white dog howling beside it. The first records we had were soft brown discs, playable on one side only, and they had to be treated with great care. They didn't lie flat on the turntable, but bulged up, and it was quite hard to place the needle with its heavy arm on the outer edge and not have it slip off.

I was fascinated with the whole process, and my father patiently showed me how to wind up the machine—the handle would not always stay turned straight out—and give it enough juice to last through the record. It needed a lot of turning, and as the record began to slow down I would rush back to give it some more. "Tiptoe through the Tulips" was one of my favourites, and I would play it over and over again, dancing all the while. This gave the drawing room a special excitement. The song I loved to hear my mother sing was "Love Is the Sweetest Thing." I always felt she sang it for my father. He would stand by the mantelpiece next to the piano, holding his pipe, which always looked as if it were dropping out of the side of his mouth, gazing at her with a lovely smile on his face. She would sing when we had company; these were always special occasions. We might be allowed to stay up a little later, and special guests could come and say good night to us when we were in bed.

One of these special guests was our dentist friend, Alan Mathieson. He would come up to say good night to me after the light was off in my room and quietly whisper, "What do you think I have for you?" and I would hardly dare answer in case it wasn't what I expected. But it was always the same: a small square of delicious, dark Bournville chocolate, which he would pop into my mouth; that taste is with me still. I was never sure whether he told my mother or not. My mother was very fond of Alan and talked about his bravery in going to Spain as a volunteer to fight in the struggle against Franco's fascism. What I don't remember is whether he came back. I only know that we never saw him after we left Kirkcaldy just before the outbreak of the Second World War.

Going for walks was often a Sunday outing. It was always cold; the North Sea brought chilly winds that blew in along the Fife coast. Sometimes we would walk from Dysart, the fishing village where we had first lived until I was about two years old. We went along the sea wall as far as Wemyss, the neighbouring coal-mining village. A horrendous landmark on this walk was the cliff cave, with a spiked iron railing cordoning it off, and a lifelike painted sculpture of a man's figure chained to the back wall of the cave. I never fully understood why, or what he represented. But I understood it to be a replica of a real historical situation. I was both fascinated and repelled by it, just as later, I would find myself looking at pictures of the martyred saints in one of the encyclopedias. I couldn't bear the horror of seeing their flesh torn by arrows but I somehow had to look, again and again. In fact, it is only in recent years that I have allowed myself to not look at torture scenes in films. It was as if I had to know, and face, the awful realities of what people did to each other.

Our stone house in Kirkcaldy was semi-detached, with an interesting porch that had pillars. It must have been quite a step up from the row house we previously occupied in the neighbouring village of Dysart. On the far side of our neighbour's house was a large cemetery with a high wall that bordered part of the golf course behind us. There was what was called a dove-house, a tall, narrow, round stone building at the top of the incline at the back of the cemetery. It might originally have been a windmill, and that's why our road was called Windmill Road. I went inside this old building and I remember its dampness, but it was not in use and had just the remnants of some flooring and steps. We were told not to go inside, and there was something ghostly about it.

Just down the street was the small local railway station. The tracks ran above street level; a railway bridge ran over the street and continued along a high embankment. We could hear the trains whistle as they thundered across the bridge and through the station; they stopped at the village of Dysart only once or twice a day. Most often they roared right through to stop at the main station in Kirkcaldy.

Once, I was accosted by big boys, who played in and around what was called the gravel pit, at the edge of the golf course, a scary place. I never climbed down into the pit, because it seemed hugely deep; the sides were steep, and gorse bushes were not the kindest of bushes to hang on to. The boys were probably all of six or seven years old, but to a five-year-old they were pretty intimidating, with their mocking shouts of, "Let's see your knickers, hen!" It puts me in a sweat even now. I seem to remember my mother asking who they were, but I didn't know. I probably couldn't see them all that well anyway, as my sight wasn't very good. I remember them only as looming figures, rough talking and noisy. She probably told me not to come back across the golf course, but I think I preferred to come home over the grass rather than down the streets. For a while I tried a longer route and crossed the golf course from another direction to avoid skirting the pit, for I wondered if they might be hiding in it, ready to pounce unexpectedly.

What surrounds us in our early years makes its own, deep-rooted connection and memory within us, whether good or bad, comfortable or uncomfortable, scary, difficult or tedious. We accept the perimeters of those experiences without question, for that's all that we know.

Elementary school was challenging. In Scotland we started full-time school at five years old. We sat in well-worn, marked-up double desks set up in rows, and it was considered best to be awarded a desk at the back of the room. This showed you were smart, as the "dummies" sat at the front. I shared a desk at the back with Annie Anderson. She was top of the class and I was second, and Billie Ritchie was a bit farther down. I had a crush on him because he was sweet-talking and had made a bit of a show by giving me a kiss one day. That was quite a bit of bravado, as the teacher would have strapped him had she seen it. I think I was really grateful to him for his boldness, but I was much too shy to ever talk to him. You talked to girls, but you didn't talk to boys; that was the way it went as far back as I can remember.

In those days, the school provided all materials: slate boards and chalk, pencils and erasers, and the teacher collected them at the end of the day. I won't forget the day when one of the erasers went missing, and the whole class had to stay in until the culprit was found. I remember the teacher sternly asking, "Who has it?" I blushed furiously, looking and feeling guilty, though I certainly didn't have it. I've often wondered where that feeling of guilt came from. It was before I knowingly did any of the things that I might have some reasonable excuse to feel guilty about.

I loved music class. We were taught Solfeggio right away, something I've found useful to this day in understanding chord structure, and we were given the opportunity to play tambourines, triangles and other percussion instruments that taught us rhythm. Scottish education certainly lived up to its reputation in giving us a thorough grounding, not only in the three Rs, but also in much more.

I have to confess that from an early age I felt different from the other kids. And although I feel very attached to my roots and to my memories of Scotland, I am not typical of Scottish women; in fact I've always felt somewhat isolated from my own breed. In some ways I'm a bit fearful of what I observe to be their more conventional and critical ways; perhaps it's because I am by nature a nonconformist. I guess I came by this honestly, because my mother was a good example of this. The Scots are often said to be stubborn, bold, individual, belligerent, adventurous, cautious and many other things.

Neither of my parents were churchgoers. I didn't enter a church to attend a service until I was about to be married. I was brought up as a vegetarian and didn't taste meat until I went to a Girl Guide camp when I was in my teens and had my first sausage grilled over a campfire. My four siblings and I all went to non-traditional schools as soon as my parents could afford it, although I spent three years before that in a Merchant Company girls' school in Edinburgh. And my mother was the principal income earner in our family at a time when it was unusual for a woman to be in this position.

A Confession

I don't remember there ever being a time when our home held only our family members. There were always boarders, "paying guests," as my mother liked to call them, who lived with us and brought in needed income. In fact, it later became our only income. My father, who'd been an engineer by trade, found productive work in cultivating a vegetable garden for year-round use and in doing all our home repairs and maintenance. Moreover, he was always ready to buckle down to household chores, whether this was washing dishes, making jam, cooking porridge, cleaning everyone's shoes or attending the coal fires that warmed most of our rooms for much of the year. My parents always shared chores and worked well together.

I clearly remember the first boarder who came into my life, an elderly woman we called Granny B, though her name was Barclay. She made her home with us in the early thirties, the Depression era in the UK. She had a particularly odd habit of standing, very determinedly, while eating. She would stand at the side of our dining table while the rest of us were seated. As she stood there, her long grey hair primly pinned in a bun, glasses falling off her nose, she would say, "A standing sack fills best." I realize now that she most likely suffered from Alzheimer's, and that makes me feel rather bad. I didn't much like her, especially the way she constantly clicked her teeth when she ate. I now begin to appreciate the limitations of false teeth, as I've had to deal with the indignity of a "partial" in my own mouth. I don't know how Granny B came to live with us, but I do know that my mother relied on her weekly pension of ten shillings to augment my dad's modest income. Thinking of her fills me with shame, because I have to confess to my first memory of taking something that was not mine.

Granny B collected her pension each week from the post office. Those were the days when the post office was the people's bank. Somehow I knew that when she came home she always put her pension money, consisting of a purple ten-shilling note, into a little black leather purse with a snib-fastener that she kept on the top shelf of the cupboard in her room.

Money was something we rarely had as children. When I was five years old I was given a halfpenny every Saturday as pocket money with which to buy a small, thin half-round bar of Cadbury's milk chocolate. My mother thought this was the least unhealthy of all the choices a halfpenny would buy. But other children at school all seemed to buy sweeties every day. I always envied them, and I guess at one point, when I was about seven years old, the temptation became too much. I crept into Granny B's room one day after she'd come back from the post office. I stretched up to find her purse and, scared as I was, took the purple note out of it. There was nothing else in the purse. I remember my mother asking her later that day for the money, and Granny B saying she must have given it to her; then my mother asking where she'd put it and helping to turn her room upside down to find it. My mother was really distressed, even quite angry with her. I can still feel my fear now. I knew I couldn't confess to having taken it; my mother just wouldn't believe I could do such a thing. I was her "good little girl" and I could never let her down. I was stuck with what I'd done and I would have to keep it secret.

I'd have done myself a favour if I'd taken the easy way out and just thrown away or destroyed that ten-shilling note. But there was some deep-rooted sense of honour—or could it have been retribution?—that forced me to spend it all. I had taken it and I had to deal with the consequences. And that wasn't easy. First I had to hide it, and I must have hidden it somewhere in my bedroom. It being paper money, I might even have put it in one of my library books until I could think of where I could get change for such a large note. Ten shillings was the same as having 240 halfpennies. I would have to take it far enough from where we lived so that I wouldn't be recognized; it meant I'd have to go out of our neighbourhood.

I realize how much freedom I had as a child. I was free to roam; the streets were considered safe. My parents didn't worry if I wandered. They knew that I spent a lot of time in the library. I loved the library and used it a lot even at that tender age; we started reading at an early age in Scotland. Even then, going away past the library, the shopkeeper in this unknown district still questioned me when I handed him a ten-shilling note. "Did your parents give you this, hen?" I remember telling him that my father had sent me to buy a bar of Fry's chocolate mint, which for some reason was what I'd chosen to ask for, probably because my dad had frequently sent me to buy him a pack of Wild Woodbine cigarettes and his favourite chocolate, a Fry's dark mint, from our nearby local store, on a Sunday. There were no restrictions on seven-year-olds buying cigarettes in those days. So I got over the first hurdle. But then I had this incredible amount of change: silver half-crown pieces, shillings, sixpenny bits and some of those tiny little silver threepenny pieces as well as copper pennies, halfpennies and even farthings.

When I came home with all this change, I knew I couldn't take it into the house. I had to hide it all somewhere outside. Our house had a big garden both front and back, and I looked around for a safe place. I decided on burying it in the dirt, in a corner of the front garden, close to the stone wall by the front gate, out of sight and the farthest place away from our front door. My father hadn't planted any flowers here; there was just a bush. But then I had to dig the money out to spend it, bit by bit every day, and my hands would get dirty even though I tried to use a stick. Fortunately my mother was always in the kitchen at the back of the house when I left for school in the mornings, and my father would be sleeping after coming home from the night shift at the power station. Of course I had to eat any candy I bought before I got home and make sure to get rid of any wrappings. With so much to worry about, I don't think I really enjoyed that candy. And what did we do with wrappings in those days? There weren't any garbage bins on the streets as we have them now. Yes, it took a long and uncomfortable time to spend it all.

As the year went on, I became increasingly worried that, although my parents hadn't found out about the money, Santa Claus would know. I really believed in Santa Claus, as did all kids in those days.

As the story went, "Santa Claus only fills the stockings of good children," and that would mean I'd be without presents when Christmas came that year. But not getting presents wasn't the big problem; the dreaded thing was that an empty stocking would show my parents that I'd done something very bad. And that's what was so hard for me to face. The nightmare built up till Christmas Eve, when my father left out a plate of homemade shortbread and a mug of milk, the usual preparation for Santa's visit, before he hung up our empty stockings over the fireplace. That was a very long night, and I don't think I slept a wink. However, I did hear someone coming in, very quietly, to lay a stocking at the foot of my bed, sometime during the night. I pretended to be asleep. But something felt strange—I just knew it wasn't Santa who had come into my room. This was to be the year I realized there was something very wrong with the story of Santa Claus. When morning came and it was time to bring our stockings down to the living room for all to see, I brought with me a stocking that was as full of treats as ever: a mandarin orange at the bottom, then an apple—a Delicious apple from Canada being the big winter treat—then some chocolate medallions in gold paper, and lastly the small wrapped "unknowns." And there were presents around the tree too, and yes, some with my name on them. That was the year my father made me a beautiful replica of a lighthouse: tall, slender and fluted, made of wood and painted white, with a tiny light bulb inside that I could switch on and off. It was a real treasure. The great relief, however, was that I hadn't been "found out." I had got all these presents even though I had been bad. Santa Claus apparently didn't exist. Sadly, I couldn't really tell anyone else why I knew that.

I paid for my theft in other ways. For many years to come I would have a recurring dream of surreptitiously finding piles of coins lying on the grass in the garden of whichever house we lived in, and I would always have to find a new place to hide them; no one had to find out. It wasn't a happy dream. This later gave me serious doubts about exposing my own children to the myth of Santa Claus, and friends often accused me of depriving them of something special. My intention was to save them from the trauma I went through. Why would I tell them lies about a fictitious Santa anyway? Although I have a suspicion I was guilty of pretending to be a tooth fairy. I also decided that I should never lay expectations on them.

All in all, what I came to realize, too late, is that my mother did her very best, which is what most mothers do. Having high expectations certainly wasn't the worst thing to lay on a child. The Santa Claus myth certainly wasn't her fault. If I had been able to confess my early stealing episode to her, it might well have made our relationship a very different one, and very possibly much better and closer. My great regret is that her early death meant I didn't have a chance to thank her for the many valuable qualities she demonstrated and the amount of work she put into raising us all. My appreciation for her has only increased with my years.

My mother appeared to be a free spirit in the way that she tackled much of her life. But one thing that didn't work was her need to prove her worth by turning us into visible products of her unusual energy and direction. One of the saddest things that I ponder over now is that she died so young and without warning, and at a time when she was at odds with my father. I suffered greatly, during my childhood, from her imposition of an upbringing totally different from that of the people around us. It's only now, belatedly, that I can thank her for providing experiences that have enriched my understanding of the choices life offers.

As I think, generationally, of how my role as a mother must have affected my children, I'm thrown into a quandary. I tried to avoid imposing standards of behaviour on them, mostly because I was always afraid that I might damage them. I think I tried to stand as far back as possible from interfering with their development, partly because I myself had an unreasonable reaction to any kind of authority, and I swept a host of behaviours into that basket, including most kinds of discipline. I did make certain demands on them, but they were the non-threatening kinds, or so I believed. There was a rota for dishwashing; they were expected to be around for supper, and there was a stipulated bedtime. But there weren't any unstated expectations, the kind that can get under your skin and cause untold grief later on.

War Years

The year 1939 was a troubled one: the Second World War broke out. My mother decided we should move to Edinburgh. She wanted to be close to the Kingston Clinic, a well renowned naturopathic clinic that had opened there a few years previously. J.C. Thomson, who opened this clinic, had trained in America to become a naturopathic doctor. He was treating patients with many different illnesses and was having particular success in dealing with cancer. My mother realized there was a need for patients at the clinic to have less costly accommodation than the clinic offered, as most of them came from other parts of the country and needed to stay in Edinburgh for some months while treatment was in progress. She knew she would be able to supply the right kind of diet that was required, and having paying guests would bring in a modest income. My father was now fifty years old, well beyond call-up age, and there were limited work options for him. He made a connection with an engineering company that offered him a sales job on commission, travelling throughout Scotland to sell their products, but this proved to be very unsuccessful as an income provider. He just did not have the makings of a salesman!

My parents bought a house, another semi-detached stone-built house. This one was three-storeyed, with eight bedrooms, a large lounge on the second floor, a dining room, kitchen, scullery and larder; I sometimes wondered why there were lounges on the second floor. There was even a servant's room in the back, above the scullery. And there was a good-sized garden where my father could grow vegetables, some of them all year round. He drove a long way to pick up organic fertilizer from a farmer in North Berwick to enrich the soil, and he later became one of the first supporters of the Soil Association in Britain. He would also take us out in late autumn to collect peat moss from the wooded areas around Edinburgh. He loved his garden and gave it good attention. He never forgot my mother's love of flowers and grew ones that could be cut for her indoor pleasure. My mother's birthday was in late February, and I hunted out places where I could find wild snowdrops to bring her—a yearly ritual that I loved.

When produce got scarce during the war years, we found reliable sources for watercress and young nettles to supplement other shortages. My mother managed our diet well during those years. Our rations, as vegetarians, provided us with eight ounces of cheese per person per week, which was better value than a shilling's worth of meat, which was what everyone else got. Our coupon books gave us some choices that were extra to the basic rationing: beans, lentils, syrup and treacle. We always chose the beans and lentils, which were a good reinforcement for our protein needs, and my mother created dishes such as Chestnut Pie, Lentil Roast, and Cheese Cutlets.

The Kingston Clinic was happy to recommend our Guest House, as it was called, to their patients who needed accommodation, and we had some unusual and interesting guests. One was a very elderly Italian woman, Signora Macaroni. She had been an associate of Maria Montessori, who had established methods of working with young children in Italy, particularly those from poor families, finding ways of encouraging them to develop their full potential. She spoke English with difficulty, but I remember that she showed me some methods of working with wool: an unusual type of weaving without using a loom. I remember the small bag she helped me make, but unfortunately I don't recollect how we made it.

We also had two students from Thailand for a relatively short time. The Medical School at the University of Edinburgh attracted students from many parts of the world, and these two young men wanted to live where they could get vegetarian fare. However, when Japan entered the war scene, they were taken to an internment camp on the Isle of Man. My mother failed to understand the need for this. As she said, they presented no danger whatsoever; they wouldn't harm anyone and she saw no valid reason for their banishment. Fortunately, they didn't send Signora Macaroni there, even though Italy was on the wrong side, too.

We also had a German Jewish woman, Lotte, live with us for some months. She was abrasive in her manners and tended to disagree with whomever she was conversing. I know my father had a really hard time with her, although he was always polite in response to her; then again, he was never anything but polite. Lotte's English was not very good and she offered to teach me some German in exchange for a reduced guest fee, which didn't further endear her to my father, but I never knew whether it was her Germanness, her Jewishness or just her prickliness that most bothered him. I found learning German to be a bit of a pain, and I didn't do very well at it. The old German script was still being used and I had a hard time deciphering it.

The first weeks of the war were somewhat alarming. Rosyth, a major dockyard, was very close to Edinburgh, and we frequently heard sirens warning us of possible air-raid attack. We were all supplied with gas masks that, as children, we carried with us. At school we were divided into smaller classes so that we could evacuate into homes nearby the school, where each group could consecutively be given a half-day of teaching. The school itself was considered to be unsafe if bombing occurred, because it had no provision for shelters. But as time went on it appeared that no attacks were planned; the story went that Hitler didn't want to destroy Edinburgh—he wanted to preserve it so that he could live there when the war was over!

School eventually returned to normal. We no longer carried gas masks with us, and to supplement our rations, children began receiving milk daily at school. What wasn't normal, however, were the newspaper accounts of what was happening to Jews in Germany. Later we read horrific accounts of prisoner-of-war conditions in Japan. My greatest fear was that I might somehow end up in a prison camp. I remember having a vivid dream where I was trying to escape from a Japanese guard who was holding on to me. To get away from him, I bit into his arm. I dreaded the front page of the daily paper where the worst news appeared. But I pushed myself into reading it; it would have been cowardly and simply not fair to avoid knowing what was going on. I was to spend many nights haunted by these scenes.

Edinburgh offered a wide range of schooling choices, and my mother decided I should attend what was called a Merchant Company school, as this was considered to be somewhat superior to the regular Council Schools. Luckily, after taking the entry exam I was awarded a bursary, which provided the fee that all Merchant Company schools demanded. Unfortunately, it didn't pay for the school uniform that was an absolute requirement.

My brother Trevor was attending a recently opened Rudolph Steiner School, now called Waldorf, but classes there could not yet accommodate the grade I needed to be in. And although my mother would have preferred what she called a more progressive school for me, there wasn't another choice. Two years later, though, she met Eleanor Harris, who was a patient at the Kingston Clinic. They became friends, and Eleanor realized she would benefit from a longer period of treatment at the clinic and wanted to stay much longer in Edinburgh. She and her husband were the principals at St. Christopher's, a Quaker coeducational school in Letchworth, a small town just north of London. Thus she and my mother found a way of bartering boarding-school fees for extended hospitality in our Guest House, an interesting way of fulfilling both their wishes.

In some ways it was remarkable that my mother sent me there, comparatively close to one of the major bombing sites, when other parents were sending their children either to farms in the country or abroad to Canada for safety. She was really keen to take this opportunity of sending me where I could get an alternative, progressive education, and she felt secure in making this decision, war or no war. Needless to say, I was totally happy to have the adventure that a boarding school offered.

The Runaways

My new best friend, Pamela, was fourteen, just a few months younger than I was, and we dared each other to do something different, something adventurous. "We have to go to France," I said. "I really want to see Paris." She wasn't so sure about France. "How can we possibly get across the Channel?"

We were both students at this Quaker boarding school in Letchworth, a small town in Hertfordshire just thirty miles north of London, and may have been drawn to each other because we both felt like misfits of a kind. I was Scottish, with an accent that jumped out every time I opened my mouth, and she was Jewish, with a wonderful nose and a great mass of frizzy black hair that swept outwards and was likely to brush into your eyes when she turned her head unexpectedly.

"Let's run away from school," I proposed. I had read all those stories in *Girls' Crystal*, a weekly pulp magazine that my mother had tried in vain to wean me off, before I was actually sent off to boarding school. "Running away" was a constant theme in those stories and it had always intrigued me. Pam and I talked about it endlessly and conjured up visions of where we might travel. But this was 1944: the Second World War was still being waged and bombs were frequently falling on London. The Germans had just deployed a new and deadlier type of weapon. Paris, although now officially free, was probably out of the question.

So I came up with another idea. "Pam, you should come to Scotland! Come and visit my family and I'll show you around. You have to see Scotland. We can hitchhike on a lorry; there must be lots of them going up north." We certainly couldn't have hitched by car, as petrol rations had seen to that; only people with priority jobs got an allocation. Pam was happy to go along with this. We studied a map and realized our best bet was probably to get to a bigger centre first and start hitching from there. Cambridge was the closest town, so we decided to pool our resources and buy train tickets to Cambridge to give us a good start.

As the conductor at the wicket gate punched our tickets, I remember thinking that we could probably have got onto the train with platform tickets that cost only threepence each. Platform tickets allowed friends and relatives to help you onto the train with your luggage and see you off properly. Who was to know whether you boarded the train or not?

It was drizzling when we reached Cambridge. Neither of us knew the town. We had left school late in the day after classes were over, and it was already becoming dusk. We couldn't help but notice the number of American soldiers who seemed to be wandering around the town and the attention we appeared to be drawing. The soldiers were overly friendly and seemed enraptured with Pamela's amazing head of hair. Neither of us wanted to admit that this bothered us.

As we wandered around, looking for the north road out of town, we realized we hadn't thought of what we would do if we didn't get a ride before nightfall. As we left the station, I had noticed a number of houses with Bed & Breakfast signs, so I asked Pam if she thought we should try to stay somewhere and leave the next morning in daylight. But money was a problem as we had only about six shillings between us. I suggested we find out how much a bed and breakfast would cost.

We made our way back toward the station, looked at the signs and picked a modest-looking row house, with railings and stairs up to the front door. We plucked up our courage, but the woman who answered the door was brusque: "What are you two doing?" she wanted to know. We made up a story about going home from school and missing the train, but she looked suspicious and said, "Five shillings each for bed and breakfast." I asked her if we could share a bed and a breakfast. She looked even more suspicious, but after considering it for a minute or two, she said, "I'll give you a double bed to share, but no breakfast." We accepted, greatly relieved.

We didn't have any luggage with us, as we hadn't wanted to look conspicuous when we left the school, and this must have made her wonder. Now I know that Cambridge must have been a target for young women wanting to pick up American soldiers. There were a lot of perks to having an American boyfriend: nylons, cigarettes and chocolate, as well as extra food in a time of strict rationing. But that aspect of life was far outside our experience; we were still green and gullible girls.

We had a very uncomfortable night in a lumpy bed that dipped drastically in the middle, and our landlady gave us another grilling in the morning. Though relieved to get out onto the street, I was feeling less confident about my plan of hitchhiking and suggested we head straight for the station. I told Pam that we should just purchase platform tickets and simply board the train with them. In retrospect, I don't believe she had as much faith in this idea as I had.

Unfortunately, there was no direct train to Edinburgh from Cambridge. We would have to change at Peterborough, where there would be a wait of an hour or two. I had always taken an overnight train between Edinburgh and London when going to school, and I would arrive at King's Cross at 6:00 a.m., then take the underground tube to Leicester Square. I could never quite believe how much was happening in the city centre at that hour and found it quite exciting to see the night cleaners joking as they packed up their mops and pails. I'd watch the bustle of the early workers arriving to open up the Lyons Coffee House for the first customers of the day. But I was looking forward to doing this trip for the first time in daylight. I would be able to see, at last, all these places that I had passed through so many times in the night.

As I think back, I have no idea whether we had any food with us. It probably wasn't of great concern to us, as we were used to shortages of just about everything. My mother used to send me small food parcels at school, some thick homemade biscuits and a chunk of butter, both highly prized items. I would spin them out for the longest time. It must have been quite cold in the school bedrooms where I kept these goodies, because the butter always kept firm until the last scrap. Many of us treasured and often saved the dry rusks we got each night at bedtime; these were served with a small metal mug of clear soup. Perhaps we had taken some of these bread rusks with us?

I particularly remember the Peterborough station where we had to change trains. It was deserted and bare, with a very wide middle platform, several sets of railway lines on either side of it and a large clock with roman numerals dominating the central area. The station had the characteristic, curved see-through glass roof with the smoke-blackened stone-built walls that were typical of most large British railway stations. It was, alas, totally lacking in amenities. We didn't want to leave this platform; otherwise, we'd have to buy platform tickets again, and I didn't want to push our luck. After all, there was no sign of life here; whom would we have been accompanying? So we waited until the Edinburgh train arrived, and after we got on that train, we felt some relief, at least for the next few hours. The compartments were dingy and had that coarse covering on the seats that rubbed your skin bare if you came into contact with it for too long. The upholstery reeked of smoke. The train wasn't very full; it was, after all, a weekday.

I knew that an inspector would come through the train at some time on the journey, checking passengers' tickets, but I had avoided thinking about this. However, when we got close to the Scottish border, which you could only tell by already knowing where it was, as all place names had been removed because of the war and the fear of paratroop landings, I decided it was perhaps time for us to hide in the washroom to avoid any questioning. Train washrooms in those days had to be some of the most unpleasant places ever to spend time in, dirty and smelly, with a familiar notice: "Don't use when train is stopped." Pamela didn't last there very long. She was particularly fastidious, and I can see her, even now, with her face scrunched up in disgust, not saying anything but giving me a look that shamed me.

We returned to the carriage, and sure enough we heard the inspector coming. "Tickets please," he asked as he entered each compartment. I figured we could make something up, and when he opened our door I was ready. I just said that we'd lost our tickets. When he began to question us further, I got a bit unnerved, and when he asked for our names and addresses, I tried to bluff by giving him a fictitious answer. I don't think I was very good at bluffing, because I'm a hopeless liar, and I guess he knew it too. The inspector didn't say much. We wondered if we'd got away with it and tried to joke a bit, and I told Pamela how much fun we were going to have when we reached my home in Edinburgh. It was late evening by the time we arrived there, and as we got off the train the ticket inspector met us on the platform.

"Would you come this way, please." It didn't occur to us to do anything other than what we were told. He took us to the station manager's office and asked us to wait there. We were both apprehensive, and while we were waiting, a dishevelled man was brought in, bloodied and talking incoherently. A policeman followed him, and sharp words were uttered. I wasn't sure if he'd been fighting with the police, but I remember feeling scared for the first time. I suddenly knew what we had done—it was totally dishonest.

The next thing I remember was seeing my mother and father arrive to pick us up, neither of them looking delighted to see us. "We've been worried sick about you. We didn't know where you were! What do you think you're doing?" I remember thinking, what a terrible welcome for Pamela. This isn't at all what I had planned. Apparently the school had notified both sets of parents the previous evening, when they found we were not in our rooms at bedtime, and the police had been alerted nationwide. Little wonder the ticket inspector hadn't bought my story. Before we left, the station manager came in to talk to us and told us how stupid we had been to try to travel without tickets. He said we were lucky and that he would not prosecute this time; he would let our parents deal with us. My parents took us home, in silence.

It was strange, but I just hadn't thought about my parents being worried. My mother said to me the next day that she believed Pamela had influenced me, and that I would never have thought of doing this on my own. She said she didn't like Pamela very much. This hurt me quite a lot because I so wanted her to like Pamela. Since I felt that I'd been the primary instigator, she shouldn't be blaming my friend. I tried to tell her that but could not get through to her. I really did want Pamela to see Scotland. But when I told my mother that, she said we had to go straight back to school; this was not a holiday.

My parents bought us tickets to travel back the next day, and we spent the next night with Pamela's family in London. I was welcomed very coldly, since her parents rightly blamed me for the adventure. "Our daughter would never have thought of doing this on her own," they said. I knew I would never visit them again. When we returned to school our behaviour was somewhat ignored, which of course made us feel rather foolish. But in a strange way it cemented our friendship;

we had been partners in an odd sort of crime, though not one we had really intended to undertake. We had only been seeking adventure.

It's strange to look back at it from the vantage point of my age now and realize that today, just as then, youngsters are often totally unaware of the effect their behaviour may have on their parents. When the US state police called me from the Mexican border one Christmas, many years later, because my fourteen-year-old daughter was trying to travel back without enough money to pay for a bus through the States to Canada, I had to think back to my own teen years. I think my daughter asked, when she got home, "Why did you worry?" It was a sobering reminder of my own craving for adventure at much the same age.

Onich Revisited

We always went away for our summer holidays, most often renting a farmhouse or cottage in the Highlands of Scotland. But in 1945 we travelled farther, to the west coast no less, to a village called Onich, which was on one of the many convoluted inlets on the Atlantic coast. Recently, when visiting family, I had a strong desire to revisit it. But it was strange and also rather sad that I didn't recognize the cottage when I walked through the village, because I know it is still there.

Those old stone houses, small and semi-detached, with low ceilings downstairs and bedrooms with sloping eaves upstairs, hug the main street, the only street, which runs through the village. Each has a narrow flower garden either side of the front door, a side path to the kitchen entrance and a little back garden with berry bushes and a shed for tools. These cottages do not appear to have seen any changes since they were first built. The reason they looked unfamiliar to me was because new houses have been built around them. In fact, right across the street, where there used to be a low dike we climbed over to get to the beach, there are now newer and bigger houses that confuse my memories.

The only summer I spent there was a memorable one: VJ Day (Victory over Japan) was declared, my favourite aunt, Mary, died, and I fell in love for the first time. I also burned my face badly when the Primus stove exploded, and I was introduced to the nearest doctor from Fort William, who told us that he was always attending emergencies.

Usually his patients were city folk like us, but mostly they were hikers who were foolhardy enough to do the rough climb to Ben Nevis in poor weather and had injured themselves by taking dangerous shortcuts to get out of a storm. He approved of my mother's unorthodox burn treatment: my face was swathed in layers of wet cotton sheeting, moistened frequently, as they dried quickly from the heat I was generating. I can feel the pain now; it seemed as if it would never stop, but I can also hear my father's calming voice as he tended to me, "You'll be all right. It will get better."

Anyway, through this incident we developed a friendship with the doctor, the only doctor I ever remember seeing as a child. And we also got to know his son Donald, who greatly impressed me with his piano playing. I couldn't believe Donald was studying to be a doctor; it seemed such a waste that someone who could play all the Beethoven sonatas and the Brahms Rhapsodies so brilliantly would choose such a dull career. When Donald visited our cottage, he would entertain us with stories of his student days at Oxford, and one day he confessed that he'd been "sent down" for not attending properly to his medical studies. He hadn't yet dared to tell his father; it would break his heart.

I think we spent two weeks in Onich that year, which was a lot more holiday time than most people got. We had never previously afforded more than one week away from home, but it was a long, eventful summer. My mother was an avid hiker and she expected us, as kids, to join her on her expeditions. My father would prefer fishing instead, which always seemed to me a very solitary occupation. I'm not sure that we had a choice in going hiking, and I don't ever remember saying no to either of my parents. I wonder if I sulked a bit when I didn't want to do something. What I do remember, though, is that my mother tried to make hiking as pleasant as possible for us by packing especially good lunches for us to take. That was quite an accomplishment considering the shortages of rationing.

Sometimes, she would take us for a treat on the way home. Mother was always on the lookout for ice cream shops run by Italian families, as these had a high reputation in Scotland. Perhaps that was one of the reasons we always felt more indulgent toward Italians than toward Germans during the war. Anyway, the area around Onich was rich in hikers but fell short on Italian ice cream. Glens, lochs, shore walks and the highest ben in the UK; these were the offerings. We climbed Ben Nevis one scorching day, and I was terribly disappointed to find that the last long lap of the climb was over loose rubble rock. My feet hurt, I was thirsty, and there were no wee burns from which to get water, no small loch hidden up on top; just craggy stone and nothing green at all. And because I was short-sighted and never wore my glasses for walking or hiking, the view from the top did not seem in the least remarkable.

VJ Day happened that summer in Onich, in mid-August. Two of my mother's younger brothers were overseas during the war, and the other two had health problems that eliminated them from military service. Jock was posted to India and then to Burma, and David, who was barely a kid, was lucky enough to get a posting to Australia. I don't believe they were back in Scotland when their sister, my aunt Mary, died. I know it was a very hard time for my mother, as she was especially fond of Mary. As she was somewhat estranged from the rest of her family, the loss of this special younger sister really distressed her. My mother needed to attend the funeral in Dundee, so she and my father left us on our own, with Gina, our live-in house help, while we were still on holiday in Onich.

Gina, officially christened Georgina by the nuns in the orphanage where she had grown up, had been trained to be a domestic servant. It was the expected lot of abandoned girls. Had she been left on a doorstep, I wonder now? Gina was sixteen. My mother refused to use the word servant, which she thought degrading. This was one of the few times my mother had hired help. I was a year younger than Gina, but I think I was unofficially left in charge. I was, after all, the eldest of five children (though we were still only four at that time; my only sister was born later).

Being left alone was always exciting. It meant we could extend our bedtimes, eat more casually and less healthily, sleep late in the mornings and generally follow our whims and fancies. Gina got to know one of the local village lads, probably when she went down to buy cigarettes. She had taken to going out for walks with him in the evenings. He had a buddy, Jimmy Cameron, a tall, lean lad. Jimmy was the quiet one, but when he did talk, his soft western lilt quite captivated me. Left on our own, the four of us went to a dance in the village hall on the first night my parents were away. Local fiddlers were playing, and for the first time I had the fun of "swinging" to the traditional Scottish dances. I had been taught the formal steps for these in elementary school by teachers who were fussy about the precision of

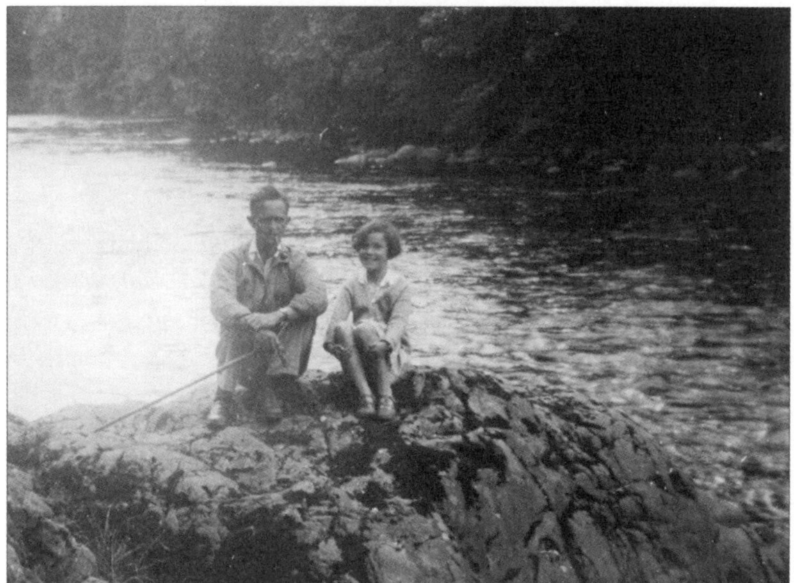

With my dad at one of his fishing spots.

the steps and the "holds," and it was sheer delight to let all this go and bring in the exuberance of the swing era. So it seemed a great idea to look for another dance the next night. But this time, it meant going into the neighbouring town of Fort William.

Jimmy had a motorbike, and I'd have liked nothing more than to ride on the back with him, but he said his father would never forgive him if he took a lass on his motorbike. We'd need a car. Jimmy's friend Ian said he could borrow one. I felt a bit bad leaving my younger brothers at home on their own, but we'd all been brought up to be pretty independent, and it never occurred to me they couldn't cope. The dance in Fort William wasn't near as much fun as the village one had been. The music was stodgy and the boys and men all stood around by the back door of the hall, talking to each other and ignoring us girls. None of them seemed to want to dance; it was really disappointing.

The drive back in the car was the most fun. The car sputtered and came to a stop about halfway home. Jimmy, being a garage hand, fiddled around and got it going again. It stopped again, but it was a grand night and the stars were up. Slowly, we inched our way home, and by then Jimmy was beginning to talk. And I liked that; we were getting to know each other. He behaved very properly, and so did I. Perhaps he didn't quite know what to make of me. I was a city girl who had spent her last two years in a boarding school just outside London, in England, no less. While other children were being evacuated to the "safety" of rural farms, or even to Canada, here I was, coming from a school located near the most heavily bombed area of the country. Our backgrounds had little in common. He'd left school early, when he was fourteen, and confessed he never made anything of it anyway. He just liked fixing things, and saw himself living in Onich, where he'd grown up, for the rest of his life.

When I went back to boarding school that September, I wrote to Jimmy and waited for a reply. But I knew deep down that I'd probably never get one. And when I went through Onich last October, some sixty years later, I thought again of Jimmy Cameron and wondered if he was still fixing cars. And I thought, he's probably too old now to take me on his motorbike, but I wish I'd had the nerve to check that out.

From My Journals

Writing about Jimmy makes me think of David. My slim book on Sibelius, published in 1947, includes an article written by David Cherniavsky, so I thought I'd look him up on the Internet. There is a reference to him, but only in the fifties, which is when I knew him; so I wonder if he succumbed to the kidney disease, nephritis, that he was getting treatment for. It was considered in those days to be life threatening.

David, who was in his early twenties, came to stay with us when my mother had the guest house on Colinton Road in Edinburgh. He came on a recommendation from the Kingston Clinic. David played the cello, and he joined me in playing in a small string group called the New Edinburgh Orchestra, where I was already part of the second violin section. I remember we played Holst's *The Planets*. Most of the music we played was unusual and contemporary. I really enjoyed going to those weekly orchestra practices with David and developed a bit of a crush on him.

One thing I remember in particular was when I was laying the table for dinner one evening, probably rather carelessly. As he watched me, he said, "Carl Jung advises that it is good to give every action your full attention, no matter how small the task is." I've never forgotten him saying that. But I have not lived by it, either. I do know that he talked somewhat sadly about his illness and did not expect to live a long life. I missed him when he returned to his home in London.

Shortly after he left, when I was looking at job postings, I replied to an advertisement from someone on the Isle of Wight who was looking for a secretary. I wrote and was offered an interview, with travel expenses paid, and thought this would be a great way of stopping over in London to see David.

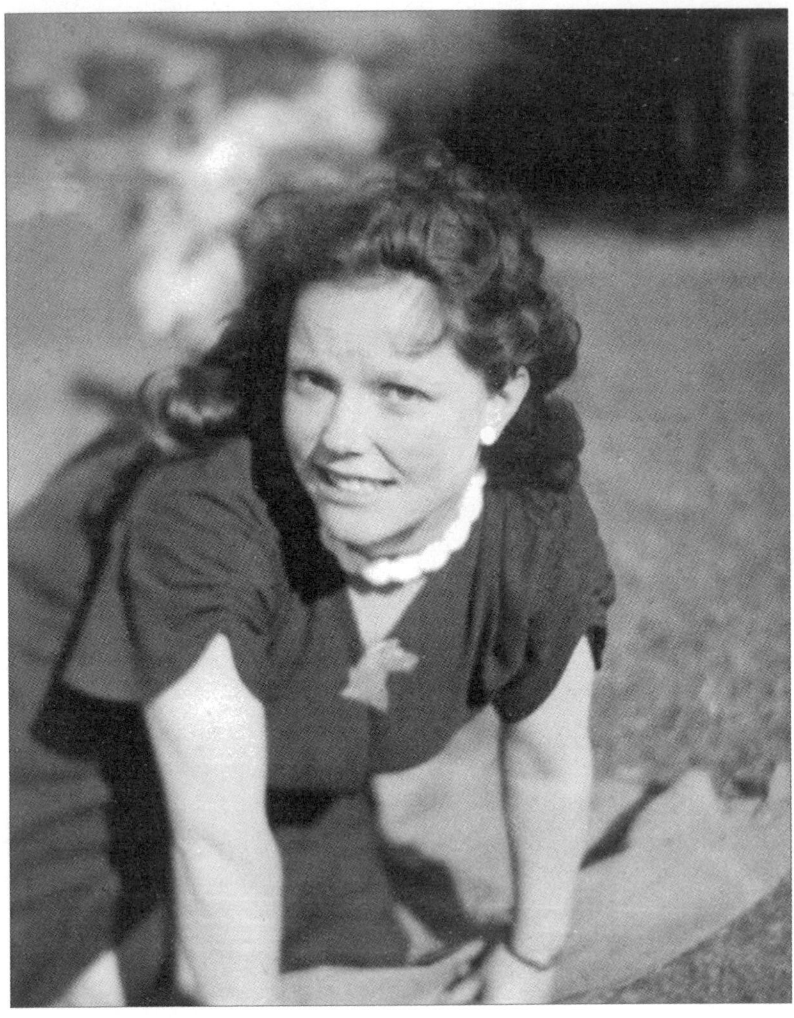

Me at twenty-one years old.

After checking out that job, I stopped in London and visited David in his apartment, and we went out for lunch. We had roast duck, which of course I'd never had before, and David talked a bit about what was happening in his life. "You are probably too young to know about love yet," he said, "but I already know something of it, and I'm having difficulty in accepting that I may not live long. You see, I am in love with someone now, and I'm not sure what to do about it…" I felt shattered—he was obviously already spoken for.

The day after writing this I woke from a very odd dream about someone else, George Thomson, whom I knew around that same time. I met George when I was seventeen years old and had my first job at Thomas Nelson, a large publishing firm in Edinburgh. George, who was the son of long-time friends of my mother's, was working in Glasgow and came over on occasional weekends to visit us. He was the assistant editor of *Forward*, a left-wing journal. I was interested in what he told me about his work, about politics and about writing, and I enjoyed talking with him; I liked the way he thought. On one occasion, I went door to door with him in Portobello, a district of Edinburgh, where there was a particularly critical by-election; we were canvassing for the Labour candidate, and I really enjoyed getting involved with George in this endeavour. However, when we hiked over the Pentland Hills together one weekend, and sat down on the grass to eat our lunch, he quietly moved closer to me, and I remember moving away to avoid his touch. And on another occasion, when we met for lunch in a restaurant, I was embarrassed to find that he was a noisy eater and decided I didn't want to eat out with him again.

George kept in touch with me by letter, as he couldn't get time off to come through to Edinburgh that often. On my birthday, he sent me an illustrated paperback on car maintenance. I don't know why this particularly annoyed me, but I know I sent him a somewhat scathing thank you, and then he just stopped communicating. I heard later that he became an MP.

Some twenty years later, when I was living in Kelowna and watching a TV news interview, I unexpectedly saw "my" George Thomson, who, as the current Commonwealth Secretary, was representing the United Kingdom (which had a Labour government at that time) in negotiating a compromise with Ian Smith and the white minority in Northern Rhodesia, now Zambia. It startled me to see he held this prominent position and was doing good and important work. I then learned that in 1973, he became the first Labour European Commissioner. George was created a life peer in 1977 and was made a Knight of the Thistle in 1981. I was totally delighted to hear how successful he had been and realized that I would really enjoy talking to him again now. It's too bad I had been such a snobby kid at seventeen to push him away.

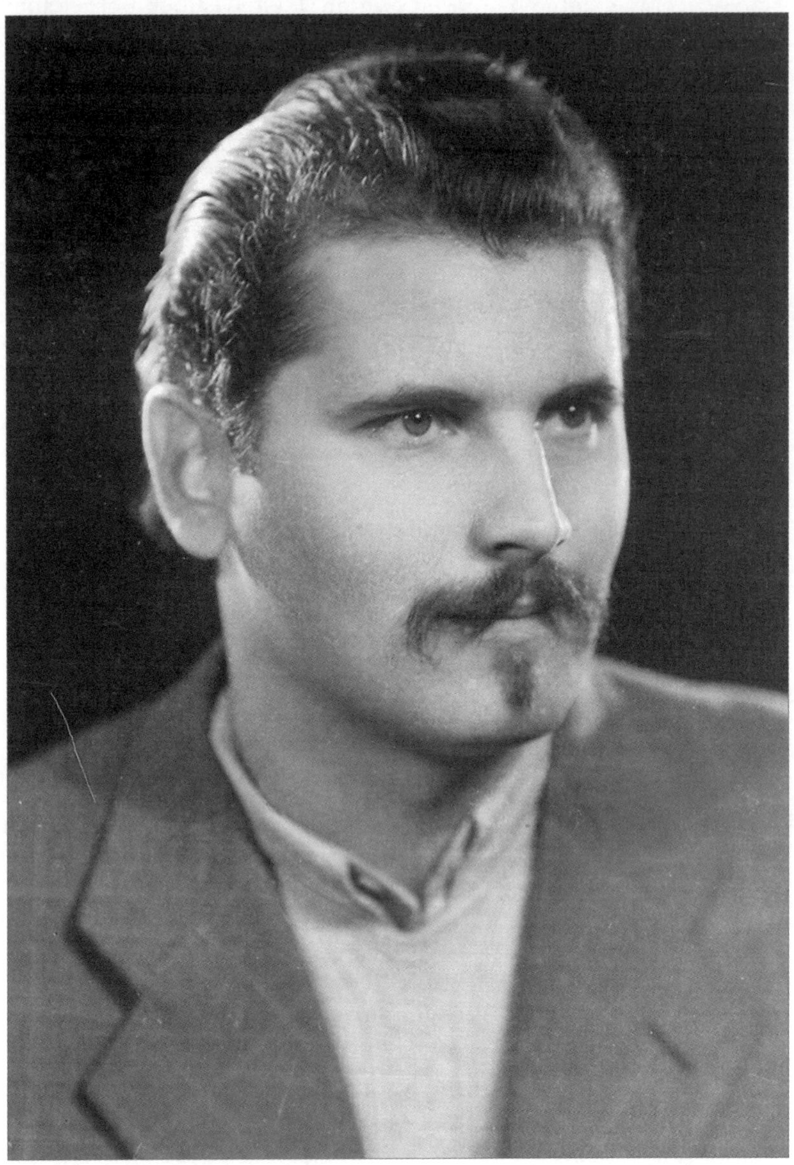

Zeljko, 1948.

ZELJKO AND I

How We Met

live to love
or love to live
let's play with words

but don't misunderstand
we knew each other
best when words were spared
–1965

Zeljko and I met in the early summer of 1948. I had just turned nineteen, had already worked for two years, but still lived at home at 157 Colinton Road, in Edinburgh. My first job on leaving secretarial college had been with a publishing firm, Thomas Nelson, which I mostly enjoyed; certainly I learned a lot about proofreading, which appears to be a forgotten art these days. It was there I met and then worked with Robin Lorimer, a Scottish writer, with whose family I still keep a warm connection. But there was a restlessness in me, and after a year with this publishing firm I began looking farther afield. I wanted to find work in the south, in London, where I believed there was so much more happening. This post–Second World War period offered many work choices to a young, reasonably well-qualified woman, even a teenaged one (though we weren't called teens in those years). I had already gained matriculation to London University through passing required exams at the boarding school in Letchworth, but university was a route I didn't want to take. I was much too eager to work and be financially independent, and the quickest way was through attending a secretarial college, which offered bookkeeping, shorthand, typing and business French. So after taking this course, I was constantly perusing the work ads section in the *New Statesman*.

When I told my parents I had been offered a job in London, my father pleaded with me not to take it. He reminded me that I'd been away at boarding school for three years and said my mother would be really upset if I left home again so soon. I couldn't resist my father's plea, but I sometimes wonder if my mother put him up to it! As I had already given my notice at the publishing house, I had to find something else locally that might be interesting.

As it happened, an Edinburgh sculptor, C. d'O Pilkington Jackson, was looking for a private secretary, and I had a rather formal interview with him. He turned out to be the Queen's sculptor in Scotland, but this title didn't impress me much, and I felt he was rather conceited about it. Anyhow, he offered me the job, and I started work the following week. It meant a longer trip to work: a tram for the first part and then a bus ride, followed by an uphill walk to his home and studio on Corstorphine Hill. However, it was a new part of the city for me, and I thought it might be interesting to work for an artist.

On my first day, C. d'O showed me his very large studio and introduced me to the four craftsmen who worked with him. I would be making up their wage packets and should get to know who they were and what kind of specialized work each was doing. Each had a different task in the production of the commissioned work C. d'O was undertaking. He made a point of telling me that the non-Scottish one—he called him Jacob—had also started work that very same morning.

He referred to him as a DP (Displaced Person), which was often used as a derogatory label. I was later to learn that C. d'O had taken Jacob from a forced agricultural camp because of his particular skill in chasing, which is the finishing of a piece after the casting has been done. DPs had to undergo two years of either mining or agricultural work once they were accepted into the UK, and they could only forgo this if they had a particular skill that could not be found elsewhere.

C. d'O had the necessary clout as the Queen's sculptor to arrange this. Jacob was a striking-looking man who immediately smiled warmly at me, but apparently he spoke little English. Without a word, and unobserved by his employer, he gently took my hand and moved it over the piece of work he was chasing so that I would feel the smoothing and get the sense of what his work was about. I have never forgotten that touch or that smile.

I realized this new job was going to be very different from my last one in terms of setting and people. This spacious workshop was a huge change from the massive, clanging printing presses I used to walk through daily in the publishing house; it was a "quiet" place, each worker individually engrossed in his particular task, whether stone carving, mould making, armature building or chasing. How lucky to have landed this.

My own work desk was in the house adjacent to the studio, and C. d'O (I never did find out what his initials stood for) made it clear that my place was to be there. My job was to answer the telephone, organize his appointments, deal with his correspondence and do his books. I was not expected to fraternize with his employees. We lived in different worlds, and his workers were not to know what went on in his. I was a little shocked to find out when I did the weekly payrolls that I was paid more than two of them were. Private secretaries were, at that time, a somewhat privileged species. The man who was to become the father of my children, and my husband for twenty years, was called Jacob when I first met him, simply because C. d'O found his given name, Zeljko (pronounced Jelko), too cumbersome to deal with.

I was instantly drawn to him. Firstly, I'd never met anyone in the least like him before, and it wasn't only his good looks. He obviously had an unusual history. I found him fascinating and, in some way, glamorous. My addiction to movies was a big thing; double features were the common practice in that era. Now I had actually met someone who could have stepped out of one of those wartime movies; he had a real living history, which intrigued me. Moreover he seemed to be interested in me. Little wonder I was somewhat dazzled.

Zeljko's lack of English didn't seem to be a problem for either of us, and over the next few weeks I somehow found excuses to go into the studio so that I could see what he was working on. It was only a short time before we found ways of spending time together outside work hours. After work we would meet outside and walk together for a while. He was presently boarding with Tom Bowie, the stonemason,

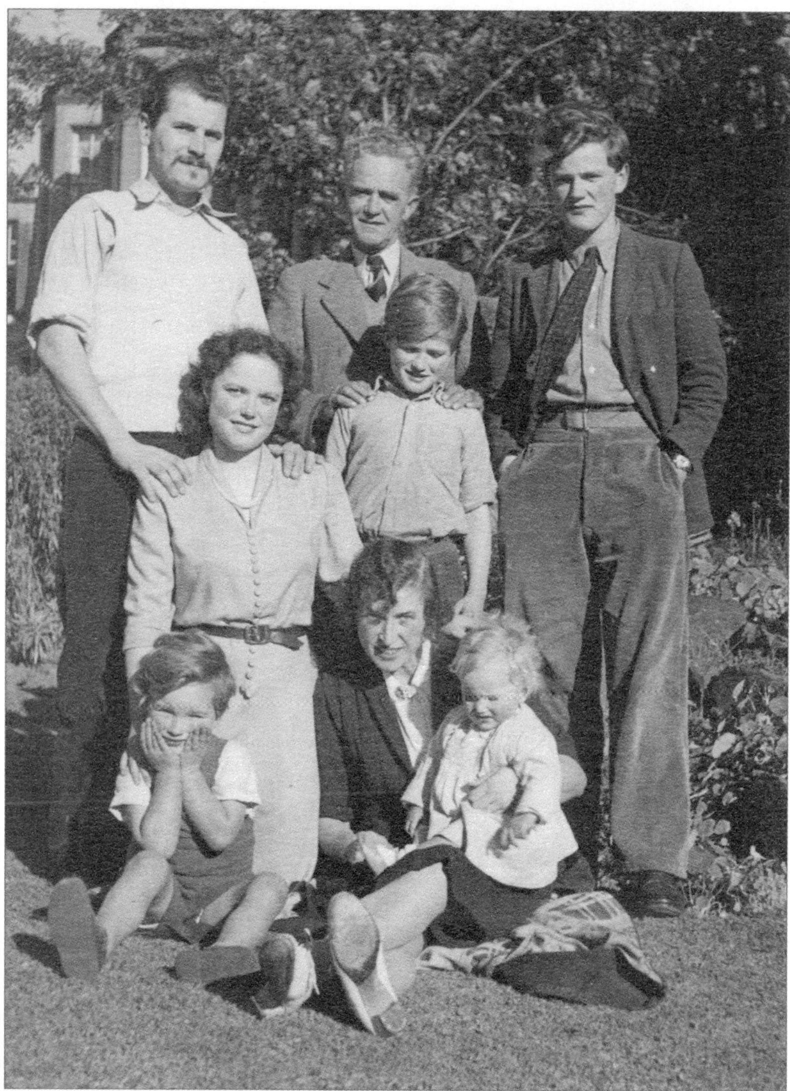

The Johnson family, including Zeljko at back left.

and Tom suggested I come and have supper with his family at their home in Portobello, which was at the other end of Edinburgh. Tom's wife had made kedgeree with smoked haddock, a rice dish I'd never eaten before, and it was delicious. I was delighted to get to know one of the other workers and his family and see where Zeljko was temporarily living.

It seemed a good idea to invite Zeljko to have supper with my family, although I felt my father was always a little worried about people I brought home. He would not have called himself a racist, but in some ways he was. His experiences as a young man during the First World War had made it difficult for him to trust other nationalities; he had encountered some hazards, particularly when he referred to being in North Africa, about which I wish he had told me more. He was a very gentle man, Welsh, soft-spoken and always courteous; his courtesy was one of the things my mother loved in him. As a member of the International Student Society in Edinburgh, I was encouraged to offer hospitality to visiting students, but my father had a hard time when I brought any non-Europeans home with me. As he never expressed his hostility openly, there was no easy way of dealing with this problem. But for some reason, he didn't seem to find Zeljko as much of a challenge as other young men I had brought home, for which I was grateful.

Because Zeljko had only temporary quarters with the Bowie family, I suggested he should stay with us; we had an empty room at

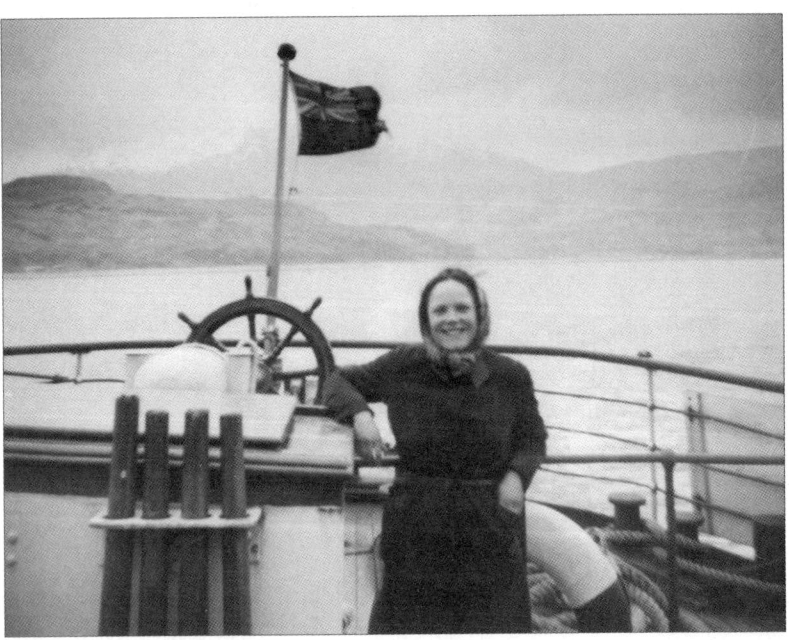

On the ferry to Skye during a trip with Zeljko.

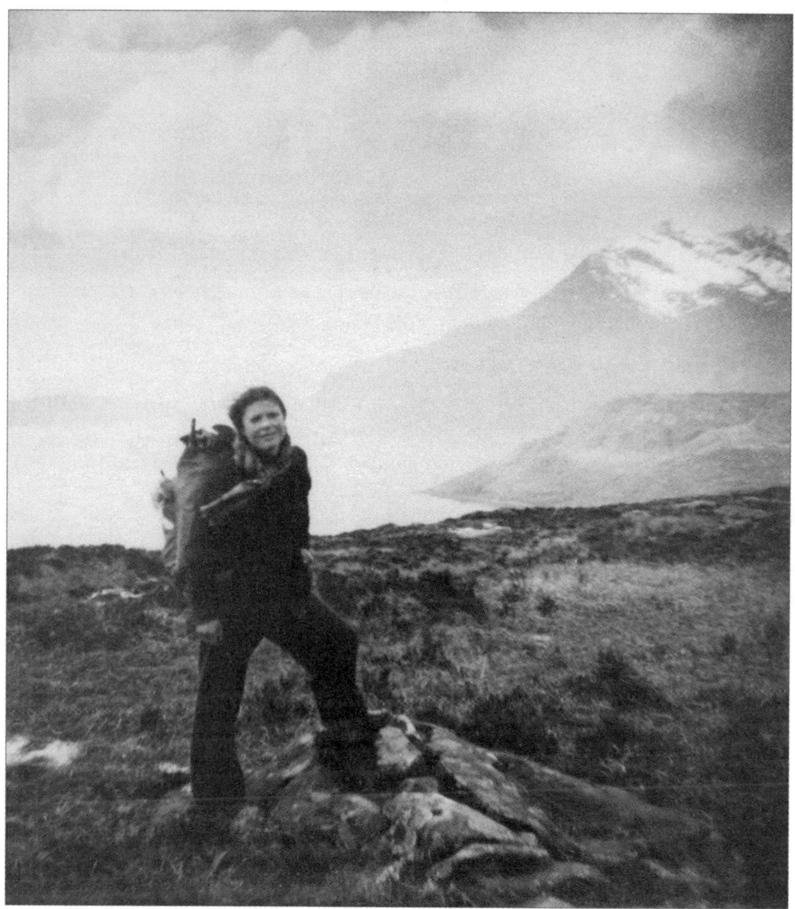

Camping on Skye while travelling with Zeljko.

the back of the house, above the scullery, called the "maid's room," though we didn't have a maid. Surely he could have that room at a price compatible with his earnings? He was an artist, making an income less than mine, and didn't we believe in fairness? My mother agreed, and I was thrilled. This meant we could spend evenings together, dawdle along the nearby canal, talk endlessly and get to know each other better. Zeljko's language skills improved quickly; he already spoke Yugoslav, Hungarian, some Italian and German. However, C. d'O noticed that Zeljko and I often left work together, and he asked me one day if my parents knew that I was spending time with a DP. When I told him he was now living with us, he was quite shocked; he said it was not appropriate that his secretary fraternize with one of his workers and that I should definitely look for another position. In other words, I was being sacked!

Meanwhile, I found Zeljko irresistible and totally fell for him. We'd sometimes walk to a fish-and-chips shop in the evening—a long walk but such fun, and I found I really liked fish! And Zeljko introduced my family to paprikash (without the chicken), which he occasionally cooked for us on a Sunday; this my mother greatly appreciated, as she loved to have a break from cooking. On our extended weekend walks we gradually became more intimate, and to his surprise Zeljko learned I was a virgin, which was something he had not expected. I wasn't in the least attached to this attribute and had often wondered why people made such a fuss about it.

His having a bedroom at the far end of the house meant that I could now quietly creep up at night to share his bed, and this I did regularly. However, one night my nine-year-old brother was canny enough to hide outside my bedroom, and he watched me leaving it. Then he told my parents. My poor father had to come up and tell me to return to my own room. Too late, the inevitable happened; I was pregnant, and Zeljko's immediate response was, "Of course we should get married." He seemed to have forgotten that he'd told me, in one of our lengthy conversations, "Artists should never get married." This comment was to haunt me often, later in life. His only concern now was that it should be in a Catholic church, because that would make his parents happy. They lived in Subotica, in northern Yugoslavia, and would want to hear this news. I really didn't care, either about being married or about the ceremony being in a Catholic church; I just wanted to be with him, wherever, whenever, however.

My parents were very distressed, my mother very angry with Zeljko. He should have controlled his lust, was how she put it, and I was completely bewildered. He wasn't at fault. If anyone was, it was probably me, and anyway what was "fault" all about? All of this didn't bring me closer to my mother. She was furious, because having a daughter pregnant before marriage would shame her in front of her family. "Everyone will know"—those were the days. When I realized her vulnerability, it was both shocking and alienating. Why should this bother her so much? (Only later did I realize that my baby sister, the last of my siblings, was barely two years old at the time—a fairly close arrangement.) We set a marriage date, and my mother decided, just a few days before it was due, to tell her family that one of her children had chicken pox and therefore they shouldn't come to the wedding. Apparently this was her only way out. It did set an awkward tone for the event. But as I hadn't been thinking to get married anyway, it didn't bother me as much as it might have.

None of us had been in a Catholic church before, and Zeljko himself was not a practicing Catholic. We were having the ceremony there to please his parents. I was the only one who knew any Latin, the language the ceremony was conducted in, and it meant little to me. All in all, it was in many ways a non-event, and my memories of it are somewhat chilling. It had little to do with the love we felt for each other and the life we wanted to share.

The Clinic

On thinking back on it I realize that in finding myself pregnant, I didn't in the least consider it to be a problem. I was totally happy with whatever this exciting new life with Zeljko would bring. I would of course need a midwife when the time came, so one thing necessary for this was to attend a prenatal clinic. Women most often gave birth at home in those days; some of the more privileged might go to a private nursing home, but only those who had problems or might need special treatment would go to a hospital.

The clinic was located in one of those handsome Georgian terraces in the West End of Edinburgh that housed all manner of prestigious services, little-known government departments and, in this instance, a prenatal medical office. The rooms had high ceilings and were often furnished with heavy chairs and desks, and the walls were mostly hung with large, heavily varnished, nondescript portraits in large, dull ornate frames. The clinic itself was a long room, with screens around a number of cubicle-sized spaces along one wall, and there were a number of women seated along the other wall, on the other side of an empty desk, waiting, some more obviously pregnant than others. I had come to this clinic in order to register, so that I would have a midwife for a home delivery. It was obvious I would have to wait for a while until someone had time to talk to me, and there didn't appear to be anyone in attendance at the moment. The only voices to be heard were coming from the cubicles.

National Health Service (NHS) had been introduced in Britain only a few months previously. It was a hugely ambitious plan to provide good health-care services free to all, financed entirely by taxation, and very much welcomed. But as I had no doctor, it was necessary for me to go through the procedures established at this prenatal clinic.

Eventually a receptionist turned up at the desk, and I approached her to tell her why I was here, giving her my national registration number (a number I have never forgotten, SBBF93-9), required by any governmental authority. She asked me a lot of other questions, including my age, which was nineteen, my husband's name and the date of my marriage. I did wonder what the latter had to do with it. I felt it was quite inappropriate to be asked this; it was irrelevant to the issue, and I was quite bothered by it. Perhaps I was still smarting from my mother's comments; they had hurt. I was then told to take a seat and wait my turn until my name was called, when I would be directed to go into one of the cubicles to see the doctor.

I felt odd and out of place. I had actually seen a doctor only once before, after the Primus stove had blown up in my face in my early teens. My mother, a health fanatic, didn't believe in the medical profession, and all five of us children managed to survive childhood and schooling without ever needing a doctor. Those were the days when a doctor would come to your house when you were sick. No doctor wanted to risk infecting a whole waiting room of patients with whatever bug you might have. And true enough, most people didn't go to a doctor unless they thought they had something serious; as likely as not, it would be something that could be passed along.

When my name was called I was directed to one of the cubicles, where I nervously moved the curtains aside and entered. The doctor, without looking up from the form he was filling in, said, "Just remove all your underclothes below the waist and get onto the table." Did he want me to take off my shoes and stockings? What about my skirt; should I just pull it up? It was a hard table, and quite high; no comfort there. I didn't know what was going to happen, had never heard of an "internal" examination and certainly didn't know what he was about to offer me. He said, turning to me, "Bend your knees up and open your legs wide." I was horrified; what on earth was he doing? His fingers were hard and cold and felt very large. I must have made some protesting noise because a nurse poked her head into the cubicle at that point and said, "What on earth are you making such a fuss about? Just wait till you deliver; then you'll have some reason to squawk."

I was horribly embarrassed and didn't want to look at the doctor. I didn't know why this was necessary; it wasn't what I had come for.

Surely it shouldn't hurt so much. "Well, that's it, get your things on now." I fumbled with my clothes and said something about a midwife. "You'll have to see her at the desk about that. Come back again in six weeks."

I told the woman at the desk that I didn't want to come back again, but could she please register me for a midwife. "You'll have to have a doctor to get a midwife. Don't you have a doctor? If you don't want to come back here, you'll have to find a doctor on your own. And you won't get your free supplements until your doctor signs up for you." I left, and reckoned I could somehow find a doctor on my own, one not likely to be any less approachable than the doctor I'd just seen. And supplements be damned.

In due course, I did find a doctor, an older, kindly general practitioner. He was a huge, ruddy man, well over six feet tall, who enjoyed working with midwives; he said they were essential to his work. He had gentle hands and minimized my discomfort as well as the need for frequent internal examinations. I had the sense that he may have found them as embarrassing as I did. Eventually he, together with the midwives, helped me deliver four babies safely at home.

Three Births

Kate, our first babe, was born, to the great delight of my mother, in the small hotel that she and my father had recently purchased in the Morningside area of Edinburgh. Zeljko and I were living with them for a while, in between other temporary lodgings. Accommodation was hard to find in those days. Kate was born in a small bedroom next to the family sitting room, and it certainly felt a safe place to be. My mother had by now fully accepted Zeljko into our family and took great pride in her new role of grandmother.

Natural childbirth was a given, and Grantly Dick-Read's book *Childbirth without Fear* had become the new standard for progressive obstetricians. My recollection is that all my births presented a long day of labour contractions that intensified through an even longer night. But one always forgets the pain, or at least I did! Kate was an easy baby to care for. I don't think I minded being woken in the night by her hungry cries, and my mother was always more than happy to look after her if I needed to rest in the afternoon. We stayed in the hotel for several months before we found another arrangement.

Zeljko had by now left C. d'O's workshop and was looking for other employment when we came across a newspaper ad: "Couple wanted, accommodation provided, for small hotel needing a housemaid and butler." Zeljko was willing to try anything and said, "I volunteered to be the barber in a prison camp in Russia, and a translator in the agricultural camp in Scotland, and I'd never done those before. I don't see why I couldn't be a butler." We asked for an interview, presented ourselves well and asked if we could bring our baby; I assured the owners she would not be a problem. We got the job and were given a room in the basement, which was pretty small and dark. We made an effort, but it didn't work for them, nor for us. Zeljko did not find it easy to serve

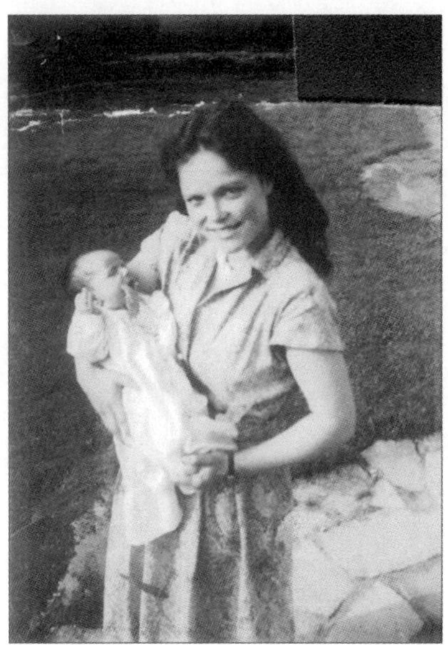

Baby Kate.

guests who constantly found something wrong, and I hated leaving Kate in a dark room in her cot.

The next accommodation we were able to find and afford provided two rooms in a top-storey tenement flat, sharing kitchen and bathroom facilities with the owner and her son and another tenant. We had differing ideas about such things as tidiness and cleanliness, and we were a somewhat incompatible lot; but there was little choice. I found a job as bookkeeper with a firm of grain merchants in Leith, and Zeljko stayed home to produce artwork and look after Kate. But I became pregnant again and knew I was at risk of being sacked; pregnant women were not welcome in the workforce.

Our luck turned. Our friends Robin and Priscilla Lorimer, who had kept in touch with me since my leaving Thomas Nelson Publishers, had bought a handsome stone-built house at the end of a small cul-de-sac, Sciennes Road, in central Edinburgh. It had more rooms than they required, and Priscilla suggested we might want to share space in it. This provided us with two rooms, a bathroom and space for an independent kitchen in the scullery. Although it was a somewhat awkward arrangement, Priscilla was confident it could work. I remember trying to avoid walking through their family kitchen at mealtimes when they were seated at their dining table, as I could only access my kitchen that way.

One day two-year-old Kate bit Priscilla's three-year-old daughter. It was a memorable event, because Kate wasn't given to biting; she was a pretty good-natured child. But I remember Priscilla was quite bothered. I had noticed that her older child tended to be rather bossy, so I wasn't totally surprised by what happened. However, Priscilla suggested that perhaps the problem lay in the fact that I was vegetarian and didn't give my youngster any meat. I could only laugh; it seemed ridiculous to me. However, we got over this and spent several years sharing their home and, in many ways, their lives.

In 2013 I had a lovely visit with Priscilla. She was living, mostly on her own, in an old renovated schoolhouse some miles west of Pitlochry, in Scotland. We kept in touch with handwritten letters. I was saddened to hear of her death recently.

We were able to move into the Lorimers' house before my second baby was born, and I hired a midwife to attend; this time she would stay with us for a week. Another girl—we were both delighted, and this one was even quieter than Kate had been. We called her Rosemary, after the beautiful shrub that bloomed in the garden right outside the room where she'd been born. This little one was very peaceful, and I did wonder about this. She was almost too good to be true.

I could breastfeed for only five months and then had to wean her. My choice was to give her milk from tuberculin-tested cows, which was an option to regular milk. Then I noticed her getting sick after her bottle-feed, and having very loose stools, and after a few days of this I called my kindly doctor. For some reason he was not available, and his replacement had a very different kind of approach; he was abrupt and quite harsh. He immediately diagnosed gastroenteritis and said that I should have been giving her vitamins. He had nothing else to offer. I felt helpless, as did my mother, who had come to assist me. The little one gradually faded away within the next day or so, without ever a cry. I couldn't believe what was happening. My parents thankfully made all the funeral arrangements, but I won't forget seeing my father weep for the first time, when the small coffin was laid in a nearby hillside cemetery on a very cold December day. I myself was too immobilized, or panic-stricken maybe, to cry. That birth haunted me for many years. I would dream of forgetting to feed her, of leaving her places and not knowing where—in other words, of neglecting her; a heavy toll.

We had been living for just over two years at Sciennes Gardens when Claire was born. She hadn't exactly been planned, but I was happy to think of another child coming. The loss of Rosemary was still with me. Claire was born in the early morning, after a particularly hard night, and I remember Priscilla staying up most of that night as well; she was somewhat worried about me. She had been a medical student at Oxford when she met and then married Robin. I knew I would be fine; both previous babies had been home births with a midwife's assistance. I had my very competent doctor, who waited for the midwife's call to come, so that he could be present at the birth. He knew she wouldn't call him until the birth was really close. At any rate, all went well and Claire duly arrived. Zeljko was, of course, present during my labour; there really wasn't anywhere else for him to go! But I remember Dr. Lamont telling him to leave the room at the actual time of delivery: "You, out!" was his normal way of putting it, but I wasn't paying much attention by then.

My mother arrived later that morning. She took such a delight in birthing and loved babies. Not an anxious mother herself, she was a good role model, and her example gave me a natural confidence. I feel very grateful to her for that. Those were the days of being told to establish a four-hour schedule for feeding the baby, and I tried my best to keep to it. Babies should be kept on this routine, crying or no crying, and the hope was that sooner or later you would get a full night's sleep and the baby would just skip the 2:00 a.m. feed. I don't think I managed to adhere to that routine very well; it didn't seem to make a lot of sense.

The first few months went well and I managed to breastfeed Claire for about five months; then she was on to the bottle. But in a few weeks I saw signs of the same symptoms that had proved deadly for our second babe: diarrhea and vomiting. I called Dr. Lamont and he came at once, advising that we send her into the Sick Children's Hospital immediately. I didn't like this, but I felt I didn't have an option, since he said that gastroenteritis was likely to be the condition, and there was no home treatment for it.

My recollection of the hospital is not good. They whisked Claire away from me and put her in the isolation ward, and they said that I couldn't go into the ward with her. Yes, I could visit, but I could only look through the glass window. I've blocked out details, but I seem to remember visiting the hospital and gazing through that window to see her standing up in the crib, looking as if she were crying. But I don't think she was standing up at six months, so I wonder if this was a dream; it was all a bit nightmarish. Those were the days when children, and babies, were not given the caring and attention in hospital that we would now consider essential. However, Claire came through it, and our doctor recommended that I give her evaporated canned milk instead of fresh milk, as gastroenteritis possibly stemmed from some problem in the milk. I did wonder what they had given her in hospital.

Sciennes to Bank Street

We shared the house in Sciennes Gardens for over three years before we got our own home, and during this time we met many of Robin and Priscilla's writer and artist friends. In particular we enjoyed meeting Josefina de Vasconcellos, a gifted sculptor, and her husband, Delmar Banner, who was a painter. Though both were well established and commanded good prices for their work, they lived modestly in the Lake District and chose carefully how and where to spend their money. Josefina was later honoured with the Order of the British Empire for her work with disadvantaged youth. I remember they both respected Zeljko's work and felt he should have studio space so that he could produce more.

Zeljko was now teaching full-time at a grammar school in Musselburgh, and he had very little workspace, although he always managed to produce work no matter how limited our living space was. His qualifications from the Royal College of Art in Budapest, as well as from his teaching position in Yugoslavia, had finally come through, and he was given accreditation to teach in Scotland by Moray House School of Education in Edinburgh. This was a big thing; teachers from Eastern Europe often had to retrain. Josefina encouraged us to look for a place where we could live and where he could have a proper studio. Aware that it was a matter of finances, she offered to loan us enough for a down payment on a mortgage. Five hundred pounds sterling was a fair amount in those days, as Zeljko's earnings were less than ten pounds a week. We were somewhat overwhelmed but were also encouraged by Priscilla to accept this offer. She told us that they delighted in helping artists; it was one of the reasons they lived a more frugal life than necessary. They really felt that Zeljko was a gifted artist

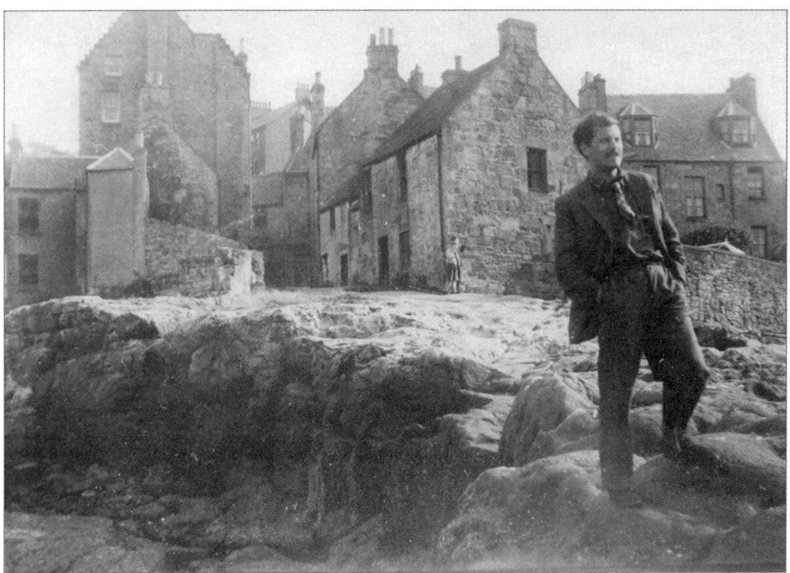

Zeljko in Musselburgh.

who required adequate studio space so that he could continue to produce more work. They were right.

So this moved us into a new stage in our lives. We began looking for possible home-cum-studio places, which was both exciting and scary. We each had our own ideas of what was needed, but we finally found a fourth-floor walk-up flat in one of the old tenement buildings in the centre of Edinburgh that offered what we needed at a price we could afford. This was 13 Bank Street, at the top of the Mound and just off the High Street, considered a slum district at that time. It had a huge room with immense windows facing north and east, with great light as well as a great view, and this would provide the perfect space for a studio—there was even room for a kiln.

There were three other rooms, a kitchen, a small bedroom and a living room. Yes, it needed a lot of work: the old coal range in the kitchen had to come out, and the coal cupboard in the kitchen had to be emptied and cleaned out so that we would have room for storing food and dishes. But we both had immense energy, and we could afford the mortgage. We could not, however, have come up with a down payment. The rooms had very high ceilings; we painted all the woodwork in

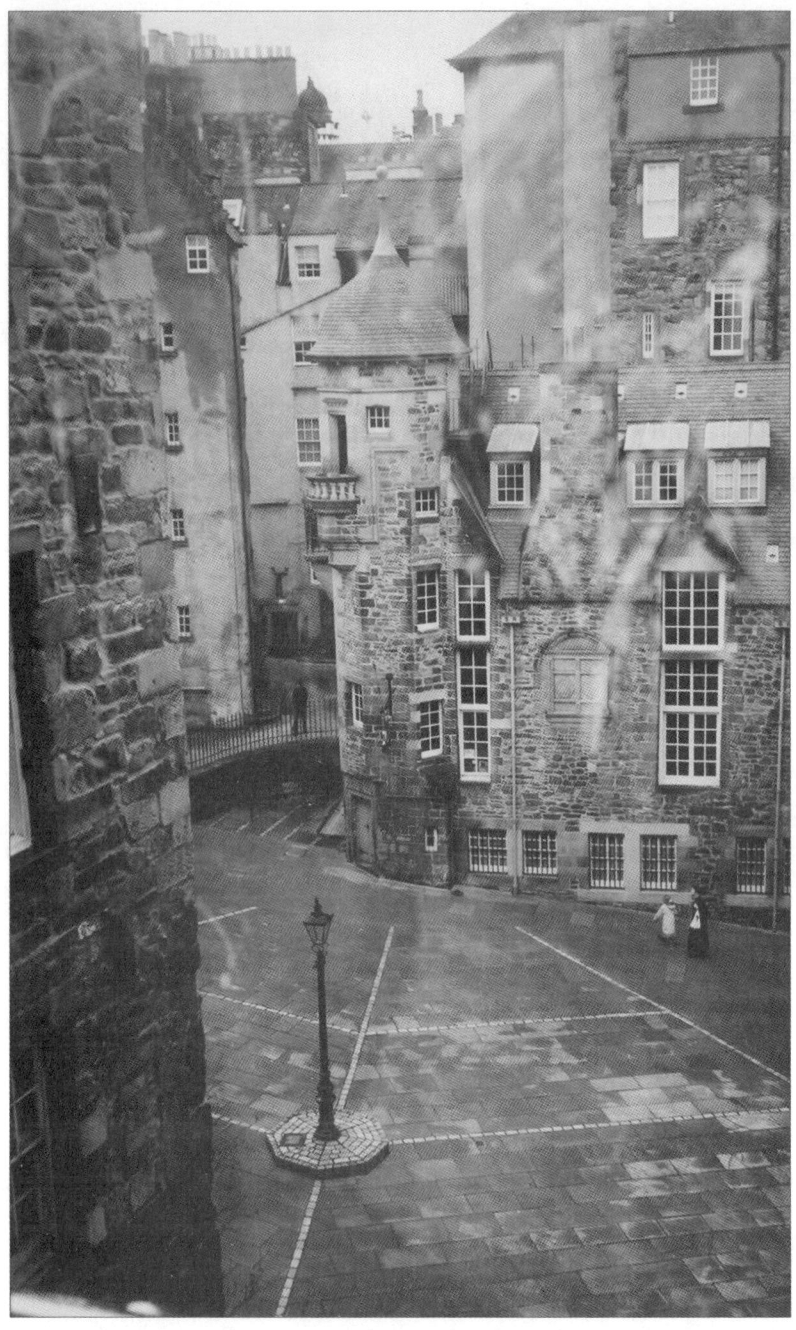

The view from the kitchen window of our Bank Street apartment in Edinburgh.

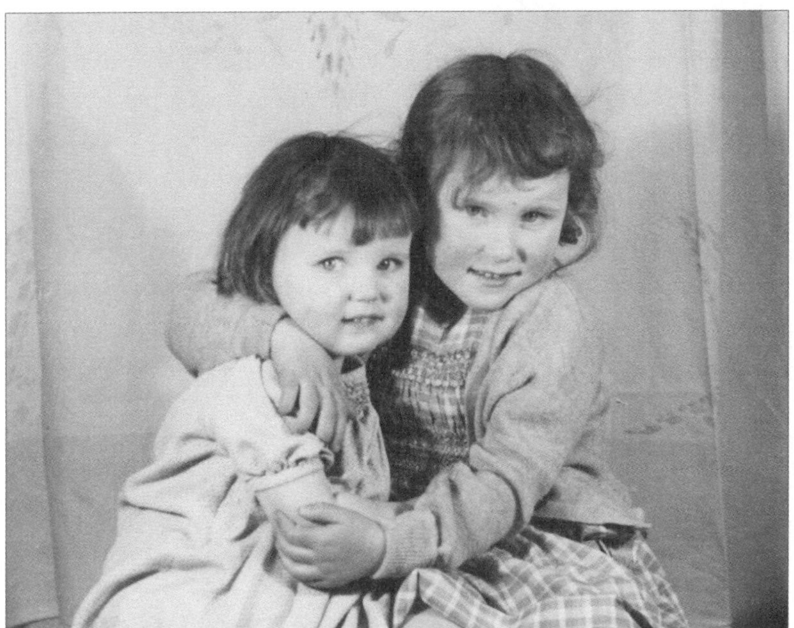

Claire and Kate.

the living room a brilliant Chinese red, found some grey-and-white-striped wallpaper for the walls, and I got some stylish material for curtains in a black and grey design on white. After all, I was good with a sewing machine; I made most of our clothes. We acquired bunk beds for Claire and Kate, as they shared the small bedroom.

I found a Montessori kindergarten for Kate, which was a long walk away, down the Mound (across Princess Street, then George Street and a few more blocks). Every morning, with Claire in the buggy, I would walk Kate to this school. Of course I had to pick her up afterward in the early afternoon. I don't remember being bothered by the ninety-two stone steps in our tenement building that I had to bump the buggy down and then back up; it was just the way it was.

My neighbour, Mary, on the same fourth floor, seldom left her home. She had several small bairns and was a good Irish Catholic. I remember her saying to me, on more than one occasion, "I'm ill again." And when I asked her what was wrong, she'd point to her tummy. I was puzzled until I realized she meant she was pregnant. She was a good neighbour and volunteered to look in and check up on our children if we wanted to go out in the evening after they were asleep, and I knew I could rely on her. Her husband, who was a gruff kind of guy, spent most of his evenings in the pub round the corner, but Mary insisted she liked being home with her kids. How lucky we were. Zeljko and I both loved going to the theatre. New plays would often be previewed in Edinburgh before going on to London, and the writings of "the angry young men" were being produced, with actors such as Laurence Olivier. We were able to enjoy these, courtesy of Mary.

A Cup of Tea

dreamt a dream and liked it not

the mask was off

my guise had gone

and in my nakedness I stood alone

–1965

Zeljko had found it particularly hard to live in shared quarters, as we had for most of our first six years of marriage. My mother, with whom we had lived for some of that time, described him as a volcano that might erupt at any given moment. But so far, this had not bothered me. I ascribed this quality to an artistic temperament and thought he was entitled to it. Our two children, Kate and Claire, shared one bedroom in our new home, and we converted the second bedroom into a living room that did double duty as a spare room for guests. Most of our living took place in the modest kitchen, where Zeljko and I slept. He built a bed to fit into the small alcove that most old kitchens had.

When I think back to that period of my life, it is always the kitchen that comes to mind. I washed plenty of diapers in that deep kitchen sink, rinsed and wrung them out by hand and then hung them to dry on the pulley that stretched lengthwise from the centre of the ceiling. It was important to wring them out tightly, as they were heavy towelling diapers; otherwise they'd drip onto the kitchen dining table where we ate. Of course it wasn't only diapers that were on the pulley; all our clothes were hung there, but I did a regular clothing wash in the sink only twice a week. The diapers I washed daily.

We often had artists, poets or other friends staying with us. On one occasion, when an exhibition of the British Portrait Sculptors Society was being held for the first time in Edinburgh, we were asked if we could host the organizer, who was coming from London, in our home. We were within walking distance of the gallery where the show was to be held, and as Zeljko had recently been initiated as a new member of this society, it seemed a reasonable request. This would be a good use for our living room. We had furnished it with a divan-style bed to accommodate visitors.

Malcolm turned out to be a rather typical Englishman, one of the congenial, outwardly friendly and personable types, but on another level a bit distant and aloof. However, he didn't ignore our children and was willing to include them in conversation, which I really appreciated. And he brought in some groceries and even helped with the dishes, so I felt quite lucky to have him as a guest. I had learned how to be a good hostess from my mother, and one basic convention I had picked up from her was the importance of delivering a morning cup of tea to English guests before they rose from bed. Although we didn't drink tea, I made sure to have a good brand in the house, and each morning I knocked on Malcolm's door, saying, "It's almost eight o'clock. Would you like a cup of tea?" He always responded with a "thank you." After delivering his tea, I'd make sure the bathroom was tidy so that he could use it while I prepared breakfast.

We had some busy and exciting days, meeting with the many exhibitors who had travelled to Edinburgh with their work. We were centrally located, and it was suggested we host a small party in our studio home so that the local sculptors, the visiting artists and the art critics could meet each other in an informal setting. I must admit I was a little intimidated at the thought, but Malcolm said he would help organize it, and Zeljko was delighted with the idea of all these people coming to his studio. He was, after all, a comparative newcomer to the elite of the art community in Scotland, and he wanted to have more connection and involvement.

I remember, vaguely, the large number of people who came; the living room, the studio and the kitchen were full. I had prepared some food, but I hadn't a clue what to do about serving drinks, never having tried anything stronger than draft cider. I remember Malcolm taking over the job of pouring Scotch for our guests and saying to me, "No, you don't put water in the glasses first!" I remember very little about this party other than my anxiety that it should be a success. I believe it was, but the haziness around it suggests I needed to forget.

What I haven't forgotten, however, is an incident that happened a day or two later. Zeljko was in a very odd mood. He first spoke disparagingly about Malcolm, and then accused me of behaviour that simply didn't make sense to me. Then I realized he thought I was flirting with Malcolm. My reaction was straightforward; I just said, "Don't be silly," treating his remarks quite dismissively. The next thing I remember is his hands, tight around my neck. We were in the kitchen, and he backed me onto our bed. Furiously, he said, "You wretched woman. You even went into his bedroom in the mornings. How can you pretend you weren't making up to him? I want to kill you." I know I didn't fight against his hands or the weight of his body on me, perhaps because he was considerably bigger than me, perhaps because I wasn't used to physical violence. I don't exactly know.

Bewilderment, anger, indignation—all of these flooded through me, but the concentrated power of his hands around my neck, choking my breath, brought next a huge flash of fear that immediately transferred to the children. I don't know how I got the words out, but I knew I had to tell him fast that he had to let me go; otherwise our children would have no mother and he, their father, would be in jail for life. What a dreadful legacy for them. Those seconds seemed to last forever, but my voice worked on him. He did let me go.

Malcolm was with us for another couple of days. Although he had not been in the house at the time of this incident, I had, without much choice as I saw it then, to be a distant and unfriendly hostess for those last two days. I turned down his habitual offer of help with the dishes, I didn't offer him morning tea, and of course I couldn't possibly tell him what had happened. I was too hurt and shaken to tell anyone. I suspect Zeljko and I were equally shaken by it, but we both set this aside and never talked about it again. I gave Zeljko the silent treatment for a while, as this was always my way of dealing with any major conflict we had. Also I became very aware of avoiding any situation that could possibly cause this kind of suspicion. I would keep a distance from men, and I told myself that this episode of violence was, in large measure, due to a cultural misunderstanding over a cup of tea.

An Edinburgh Studio

I was concerned about finding money to repay our artist friends and heard that there was a job just round the corner from where we lived. A cook was needed to provide the main meal for seminary students at the Free Church of Scotland. This would involve my being there from 9:00 a.m. until 3:00 p.m., Monday through Friday. The caretakers at the church, parents of someone my mother knew, were offering to look after Claire during those hours. It seemed too good to be true, although I think I had a lot of nerve, as a vegetarian, to take on regular meat-and-potatoes type of cooking. But Mrs. Savage, the caretaker's wife, assured me it would be straightforward, and if I brought things for Claire to play with, she would be happy to have a small two-year-old there. Claire was a delightful and intriguing child. She talked to everyone and would make them laugh with her habit of making faces; people simply loved her.

I was very nervous about cooking for around twenty-five seminary students every day, but Mrs. Savage did the ordering of the food and gave me the meal plan. It was the same every week, so it soon became a routine: roast on Tuesdays, fish always on Fridays. Soup, main course and pudding, three full courses to be provided each day—and no dishwashers in those days! It was a bit of a grind, with the cleanup afterwards always a chore. Kate was now in regular school, so I saw her off on the tram before I went to work, and I was home in time for her return; that's how it had to be. I managed to save four pounds sterling a week, which was all of my wages, until we had enough to repay Josefina for the down payment she had loaned us. By that time I was well into another pregnancy and I was able to stop working. I sent a repayment cheque to Josefina but found some weeks later that it had not been cashed. When I wrote to her about this she replied that she

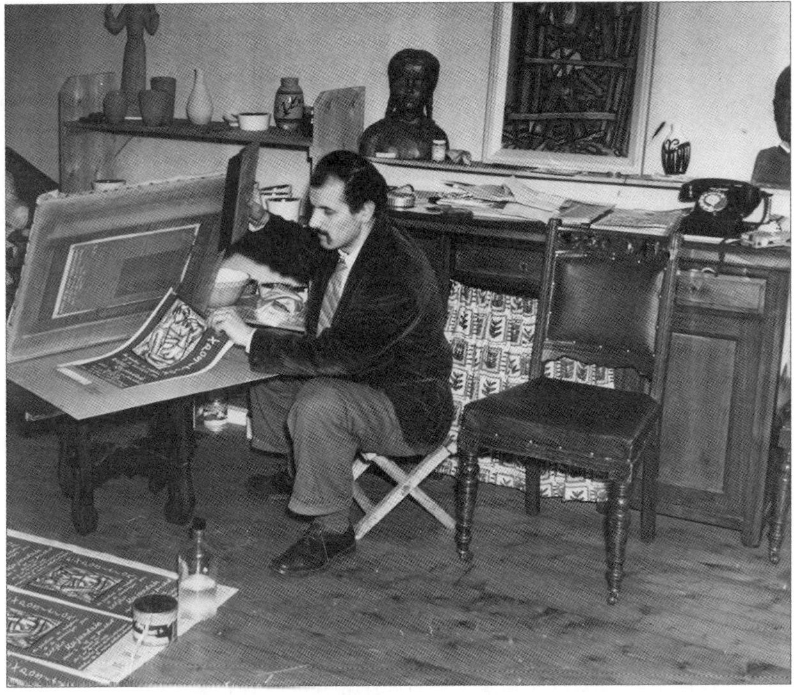

Zeljko printing posters in our living room to take to Paris.

and Delmar had not intended to have us repay them. They were glad to know it would now give us some savings. Generosity by far, and totally unexpected.

We held an exhibition in the studio, and after that we had many drop-ins who wanted to stop to talk and see what Zeljko was working on. As we lived close to both the Edinburgh University campus and the Art School, we were easily accessible to students of both those institutions. I loved living within a block of the Central Library, which was a rich resource for me. Zeljko received an excellent critique of his work in the *Scotsman*, and the art critic, Giles Robertson, purchased one of his paintings. In spite of that, he never felt himself to be part of the arts community, and this may have been in part due to his somewhat arrogant dismissal of the acknowledged leaders in that community. He simply did not have high regard for Scottish painters, perhaps a European attitude. We became close friends of the owner of a nearby art store, Miss Simms. Though we never did get to know her Christian name, we spent many an afternoon at her home in the Braids. She loved providing dress-up clothes for Kate and Claire and delighted in spending time with them. She displayed and sold many slip-work clay figures that Zeljko was now producing—everything from small animals to a very complex tartan-clad piper with bagpipes—and she gave him much encouragement. By this time we had a kiln in the studio, making it possible for him to produce steadily and have a ready market.

We became frequent visitors at a newly formed Art Centre that had found quarters in a former church, just down the way on the High Street. This place became both an informal workshop for painters as well as an exhibition place for visiting artists. Both Kate and Claire had their portraits painted there by the Miller sisters. We became close friends with one visiting artist in particular, Mary Stewart Gibson, a Scottish painter who had lived in Paris since before the Second World War. She offered to make her Paris studio available to Zeljko for an exhibition of his work, which he was delighted to accept. I remember how we printed off the posters for that exposition in our home from woodblocks Zeljko prepared. We had them laid flat in all available corners of the house while the ink dried; it was quite a procedure to get them mailed to Mary ahead of time.

That trip to Paris was exciting. We took both children with us and somehow managed to take all the paintings through customs despite whatever regulations were in force at that time. We found overnight accommodation for the two weeks of the exposition, but at some distance from Mary's studio. The Parisian authorities had granted her a studio where the rent was modest and the space well planned. These studios were designed for practicing artists. Even though Mary was not French, she had been allocated one—an interesting fact that reflects on the status accorded to artists in Paris. She had some remarkable stories about her experiences in an internment camp.

The exhibition did not garner a lot of attention, but Zeljko sold a few paintings and was particularly delighted that a young couple with very limited income and two small children made a purchase (we kept in touch with them for many years after that), as did a working-class older man who had never owned a painting. Our time in Paris was eventful, if not particularly remunerative, and we did not regret it.

When we got home we purchased our second used car, a Triumph '26, which I named Gloria. It cost all of forty pounds sterling. This was the car that it was my job to drive. Zeljko had already had his fight with our first car, a Morgan three-wheeler (which we bought for only thirty pounds), when we lived at Sciennes Gardens. He called me from the hospital after his first outing, asking me to come and bring him home. He said he'd had an argument with a tram—"The damn thing wouldn't get out of the way"—though trams really didn't have much of a choice. The Morgan didn't survive. Learning to drive Gloria, however, was a real challenge, as it needed double declutching at every gear shift, something required on older vehicles. And it seldom started without being cranked with a handle that hung off the front.

I remember when the car stalled at a traffic intersection and the bobby would have to hold up all the traffic until I could get out of the car and crank it. It often needed several cranks to start up again, and we had more bobbies at intersections than traffic lights in those days. Anyway, we now had Gloria, and once I acquired my driver's licence, I was basically in charge of her. I had failed my first exam because I didn't double declutch swiftly enough going up a steep curve near the top of the Mound, but the second attempt was successful. This car took us on holidays that were much easier than the backpacking bus trips we'd previously taken with the kids. We drove across the country several times to spend holidays with a friend who had a cottage on the island of Mull. One thing I remember about that car is that it had a hand accelerator, just below the driving wheel, which was a marvellous assist. I've never had one on any car since.

Judy's birth took longer than the previous ones. She arrived in daylight after several false alarms; Dr. Lamont was not used to being called in so often. This time I had two Queen's nurses, as they were called—midwives supplied by the National Health Service. They stayed for two days in our home until Judy was born. It was a different experience, and I remember Dr. Lamont suggesting I might like some form of anaesthetic this time. I thought not, and Judy duly arrived. She weighed a full two pounds over the others, who had all been just under a modest seven; there was a reason for her taking her time.

IAN HAMILTON FINLAY

Ian was one of the first poets to create "concrete poetry," and he became a very close friend and remained so for many years. We met him through the Lorimers. He often stayed with us when we bought our own place on the Mound. He wanted to stay when Judy was about to be born. I said, "Ian, it will not be very convenient," and he replied, "I can make you cups of tea," to which I answered, "I don't drink tea." However, he was desperate to stay with us, because as a person with agoraphobia, he needed to stay indoors, and he was running out of places to stay.

He and Zeljko collaborated on many small literary and artistic projects, such as *The Seabed and Other Stories* in 1958, but books of poetry with block-print illustrations did not bring in much income. They realized they had to find something else. Setting up a little business selling dolls' clothes, which could be advertised with Zeljko's art designs, Ian's poetic descriptions and my sewing skills, might reach a bigger audience. We spent many hours figuring this out and had a lot of fun. Zeljko produced art designs, Ian wrote poetic descriptions, and I made various dolls' dresses. But we soon realized we needed money to advertise to get it off the ground; projects like those just don't happen without start-up cash.

Over time, Ian's agoraphobia began to bother him more, and he was sure that it was largely due to his wife, Marion, who would not agree to a divorce. He felt bound to her in an unhealthy way and said she would never let him go. I remember him writing us lengthy letters about this whenever he wasn't living in Edinburgh. He pleaded with me at one point to go and talk to her about his illness and ask if she would give him a divorce so that he could recover.

I reluctantly took a bus to the remote place in the Highlands where she lived, climbing up to the cottage, which was next to a lovely small burn, and feeling totally inadequate to tackle this. Buses were infrequent in those parts, and I had to stay overnight. I don't think I've ever been quite so uncomfortable.

Marion was an intense person, and she quickly twigged why I was there. "Ian put you up to this, didn't he? I should have known he would try something like this." I couldn't deny it; it wasn't a good scene, and I regretted allowing my fondness for Ian to put me in such an awkward situation.

Ian eventually managed to get a lawyer who would take his case, and he asked if I would let him have all the letters he had sent to us, as this would furnish them with information about his history with Marion. I told him I would, on the condition that they be returned, because I valued his insights and was reluctant to part with them. Although he never returned them, I still have a folder of later letters. He wrote to us frequently after we came to Canada.

I last saw Ian when I returned to Scotland in the early seventies and met his lovely second wife, Sue. This was only a few years after they had bought a farm called Stoneypath, which was later to become Little Sparta, and it was already being filled with Ian's concrete sculptures and Sue's plantings of flowers and shrubs. I would love to have seen it later with its little "loch" and Ian's many models.

In his last letter to me, Ian wrote, "Life is not easy. I have begun to build model battleships instead of model fishing boats, and this small circumstance seems to symbolize a great change in my feelings about life, and it is a fact that we have all changed a lot, and grown, I am sure, more tolerant…and more assertive, and this is a paradox I have come to see: and there is no-one more intolerant than the modern person who thinks it broad-minded to believe in nothing (except, of course, any Cause that happens to be fashionable at that moment)."

His obituary describes him as "Scotland's greatest artist...and his sublime garden, Little Sparta, has been described as the greatest Scottish art work of all time, and one of the greatest contemporary pieces of art anywhere...combining landscape, trees, plants, sculpture and poems to make a true Gesamtkunstwerk [aesthetic]."

Bernard Leach

During this time Bernard Leach came up to Edinburgh to give some lectures. He was very much in demand and became known for his pivotal role in the establishment of British studio pottery and a new appreciation for artisanal ceramics around the world. Word spread that if you wanted to learn how to make pottery, the best thing was to go work with Bernard Leach. He came alone, without his wife. He was a man who was distant but also very present. When he first came for supper, I was concerned about what to make for someone special, so we got lamb, which we called mutton. I baked it, even though I barely knew how to cook meat at all, having been raised as a vegetarian.

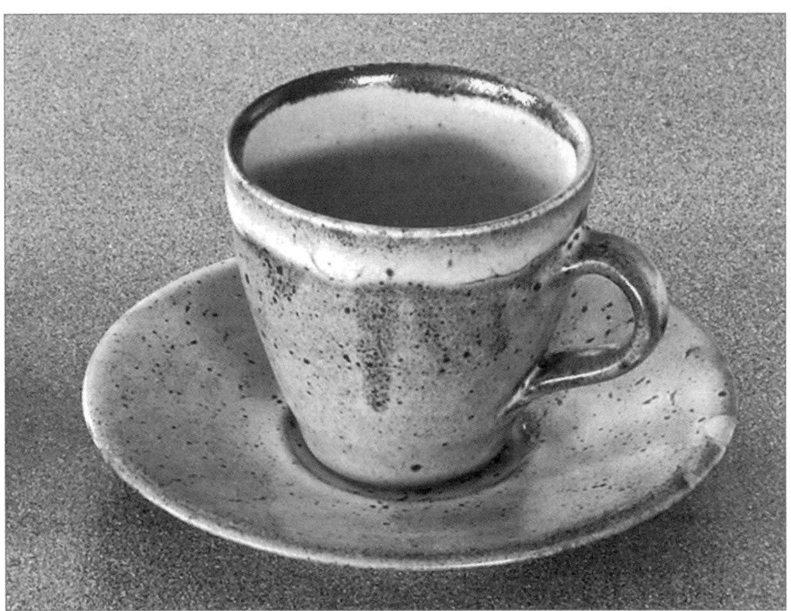

This Leach demitasse is still one of my favourite treasures.

When Bernard arrived, he interacted with our two children, in particular with Claire, in a very nice way. She was giving one of her "presentations," which were always engaging, endearing and humorous. We sat down to eat in our kitchen below a pulley of clothes. He complimented the meal, then said diplomatically, "There's something else you can do with lamb; you can put a clove of garlic under the fat—a very good thing you can do with lamb."

He talked about his son, David, who was also a very good potter and later came to stay with us. He had become a partner in the Leach potteries. Their potteries became known because Bernard had travelled to Japan, and he often talked about how much he had learned from Japanese potters such as Hamada Shoji, Yanagi Soetsu and Urano Shigekichi. He believed that they had a real feeling for clay and knew the shapes that clay should take. His own work often followed these Japanese forms. We eventually managed to get some of his bowls and small coffee cups, which we loved and I still have. I never managed to get to St. Ives, but Bernard and David stayed with us several times on their trips to Edinburgh.

Summers on Mull

We lived on a wild island open to the west
With one small harbour
that only a rowboat could find
the days were short the winters long
and we hoed a plot of ground
that held fast
to every bit of life
that struggled for existence.

and we came to cherish fish
dried, smoked, pickled
blue-silver, grey as mud
and always bones
we made a mountain out of bones
till the island took on a new shape

we asked some friends to share our solitude
don't misunderstand
our solitude had flourished
(although it had no choice)
but we felt the spoils too great for us alone

and so we harnessed four of us in toil and pleasure
sharing the generosity of the sea
but nothing more

and the friendship sadly ended
(it too, had no choice)

and the isle of women was lonely once again
except for loving us
and fish
–1965

When our girls were small, we spent several summers with a friend who had a cottage on the island of Mull. It was a wonderful place: remote, with her home above a small sheltered bay on the wild west coast. Joan was a potter, and her family had owned this cottage since she was a child. She felt good about sharing it with other artists and their families in the summer months. It was not very large, but we found ways of making it work. The only neighbour within visible distance was a fisherman, Angus, who lived with his wife close to the shore, where he could keep an eye on his fishing boat throughout the driving storms.

It was a long trek over the hills to the nearest store, where we would go twice a week to get provisions. We picked up milk daily from a farm even farther from the cottage and in the other direction. Those of us visiting would take it in turns, to go the one way or the other, to pick up what we needed.

On special occasions, and if Angus's rowboat was free for the borrowing, we would cross the water to the small island of Iona. This was always a special treat. The boat ride itself was a choppy adventure, as the water was pretty deep between the islands, and the waves would swell with foamy froth. We would laugh as sudden surges of the boat dashed us with salty sea water, which left our hair sticky and our faces moist and tasty. But there was another treat to the trip. We could look into the small general store on the island, a store that got restocked every time the large pleasure cruiser stopped by, unloading its supplies as well as the tourists who flocked for a brief visit to the famed historic abbey on the island.

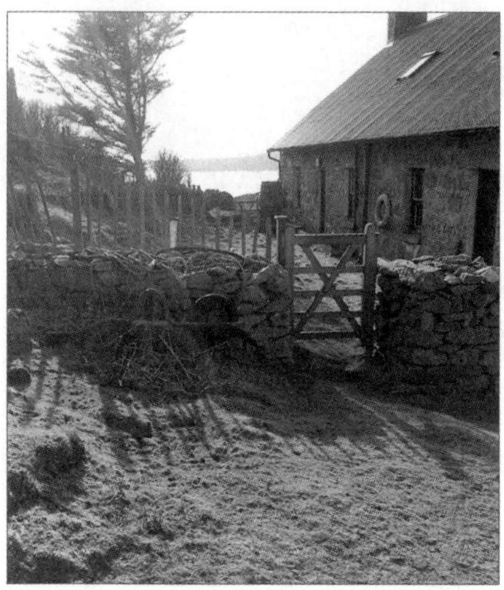

The Mull cottage, 2015; Kate Enewold photo.

Mary Jane, who ran the store, was a small, dour, elderly woman with small dark eyes crinkled into her weather-beaten face. She had never been known to smile. It seemed that she didn't like tourists, she didn't like visitors, and she didn't like hikers and campers, and who knows if she even liked her neighbours. She always looked at us suspiciously when we came into the store, and only grudgingly allowed us to purchase some of what was there. "No, you can't have any of this bread. The boat won't be in again till Saturday and I don't want to run out." We asked if we could order some for the following week, since her bread was of a heartier variety than the loaves offered in the store in Mull. "No, I can't do that either." She gave us no explanation and seemed to take great delight in wielding her power.

But the best was yet to come. As we were waiting in line to buy a chocolate bar from her one day, we heard a young man in front of us asking for shoelaces for his runners.

"No, I don't have any," she replied.

"Well, you haven't had them all summer. When will you be getting them in?"

"Oh, I'm not getting any more shoelaces for the store. It was a right nuisance the last time I had them in; they sold out right away."

I don't know how long Mary Jane ran that store. I wonder if she eventually stopped stocking bread and maybe even chocolate bars?

However, I was unexpectedly able to visit Iona some sixty years later with my daughter Kate and her family, and I was happy to find there is now a small, local bakery, as well as a regular well-stocked general store, on the island. And Kate hiked over the hill to Joan's cottage to find it unchanged, though my legs were no longer willing to tackle that endeavour!

A NEW LIFE IN BRITISH COLUMBIA

Leaving Scotland Behind

Those years living in Bank Street were full and interesting. Yet Zeljko and I, in our different ways, became increasingly restless. I was ready to leave our fourth-floor tenement flat, and each spring I experienced this terrible urge to go somewhere else. Walking up those concrete stairs, washing our section of them when it was my turn, smelling the urine at the street entrance in the mornings, was very unpleasant. There was a pub just round the corner, and those thrown out at closing hour couldn't always hold their piss.

I would often look out of our kitchen window, which faced south onto the close and square below, a somewhat bleak outlook, and wish desperately that I could be elsewhere. Dark-to-black granite stone everywhere; this was before they cleaned it up. Yet it was amazing in so many ways to live right in the centre of Edinburgh, just steps from the Royal Mile, close to wonderful second-hand music and bookstores, and close to the richly stocked Central Library. You'd have to know Edinburgh to appreciate what it meant to have a large studio on the north side of our flat overlooking the Mound and Princess Street. We were blessed with many droppers-in: writers, poets, perennial students from the university. We had a busy life and our evenings were filled with debates. But there were times, particularly when the sun shone through our grey, city-smoked windows, when I longed for greener surroundings.

Meanwhile, Zeljko was beginning to have difficulty with what he observed happening in the elitist aspect of the arts scene in Scotland. Somehow, he had never allowed himself to be part of the arts community, and he probably knew he would never become an integral part of it. He was ready for a move, and it was only a matter of where. He liked the idea of South America; Peru or Chile were his choices. But neither

Canadian Pacific

PASSENGERS BAGGAGE CONSIGNED TO CARE OF

CANADIAN PACIFIC, NORTH No. 1, GLADSTONE DOCK

LIVERPOOL

NAME OF PASSENGER ....

STEAMER ....

DATE OF SAILING ....

country was accepting immigrants with an Eastern European background. However, we were welcomed in Canada House in London when we applied there for immigration. That welcome and the offer of a job, particularly in the West, cinched our decision.

It's a long time since we came to Canada on the RMS *Empress of England*, which sailed from Liverpool in late July 1958. We came with twenty-five crates and assorted trunks, having been informed that we would be living in a remote town in western Canada. I had packed loads of books, sewing supplies and all our kitchenware. Zeljko had made sure he would have all the tools and materials he could possibly need, as well as his immense accumulation of paintings and sculpture. And we came with three young children aged eighteen months to nine years old, who had their own favourites to bring with them. It hadn't been difficult to fill those crates.

I don't remember feeling sad at leaving Scotland; I was enthralled with the adventure of it all. Yes, I was uncomfortably pregnant again, but that wasn't new to me, as I had already given birth several times. I just knew that there was always a lot to do. That never changed and it wasn't a problem. We had many good times saying our farewells to our friends and to my family. It was hard saying farewell to the lovely Danish furniture we had finally managed to buy. But I felt saddest at leaving my piano. It had been my mother's piano, handed on to me when she bought a baby grand for the small hotel they owned. I remember cashing in what money I had managed to get for selling it (which I'd put in my Post Office Savings book) and stashing it into a separate envelope to take with me so that I could purchase another piano when we reached our destination.

On the liner we were placed at a table with two Canadians, a mother and her small son. They lived in Montreal and were English-speaking. I remember being appalled at the boy's behaviour. He complained about everything, but his mother didn't seem to mind. I think she may have been equally bothered by my children's polite manners. Our youngest, Judy (not yet two years old), loved the music playing in the ballroom in the early evening and danced joyously. I envied her and would have been dancing too, had it not been for a gravelly belly!

The time eventually came to disembark at Montreal. We'd had a brief stop in Quebec, and I remember how high the dark cliffs appeared, far higher than the white cliffs of Dover. That July was the first time I experienced humidity; it came in an endless, shocking wave when we left the ship. The procedure for going through customs literally took hours. We had to line up, with all our baggage, and wait until a customs officer approached us. Because we had an immense amount of stuff, we were left until the last. I remember the children being restless and hungry, and of course, we had no arrangements for the next stage of our journey. We knew we would take the train west, but we would have to stay in Montreal until we found out about schedules and could purchase tickets. And of course we would have to send our baggage on to our destination, which was Cranbrook in British Columbia.

The first problem was that we didn't speak much French, and in 1958 Montrealers were making an intense point about their language having precedence. I thought I would be able to cope with my school French, but I found I didn't understand a word of Québécois, nor did they understand my version of Parisian French. Eventually, with the help of a rather taciturn taxi driver, we found our way to a house where we were offered a room with one double and one single bed. The landlady brought us a large drawer, which she said could accommodate the youngest. Although it wasn't ideal, we were glad to have somewhere cheap enough to put our heads until we arranged the next step.

The humidity did greatly bother me, but we stayed in Montreal for two or three days. It was just long enough to visit the mother and son we had shared our table with, who had invited us to their home. They lived in a suburban area, and we went by bus. I remember little about it, except that their home was a bungalow and she served us canned beans and canned spaghetti for lunch. That was a surprise; I'd never thought to serve canned food to guests when I invited them for a meal! But I wanted to see how people lived here, and these were regular folks, so I appreciated her having asked us.

How did my three girls find all this? I trusted that my own interest in all that was new around us might give them a way of coping by observation. I always had to find a way of coping with their father, and that was often as much as I could manage, not that I thought of it that way. It is so different from how I might do it now. The fact is that our children were added to our lives; they were not the focus of our lives. That is how it was. I had chosen to marry an artist and was never quite allowed to forget that privilege. And although he could be difficult, I always felt truly loved by him, and that carried me through.

Andy's Birth, 1959

Already pregnant on the voyage to our new home, I gave birth to Andy seven months after we arrived in Cranbrook. This birth was completely different—a quite shocking experience in the local hospital that was run by nuns. The first problem was getting through the hospital door at 2:00 a.m. on a cold March morning. I knew I was close to giving birth, but they wanted endless information before I could be admitted, and the process bogged down entirely when they asked for my religion. I didn't really want to say that I had been a short-time Catholic (necessary for the marriage ceremony), so I just said I didn't have a religion. Stony silence, then, "We have to put down a religion." I don't remember what I finally answered; the contractions were coming fast and furious, and I just wanted to get on with it. I remember walking down an endless, dark, grey corridor and being taken to a small, bare-looking room that had a sheet-covered table in it. Zeljko had not been allowed to accompany me and had to return home to look after the other children.

I was told to get onto this table and lie on my back. I could hear noises coming from other rooms, mostly crying kinds of noises, and was told that there were other women in labour. I was asked how often my contractions were coming. I knew it was frequently enough; I had delayed coming in for as long as possible. They said they were busy and left me alone for a little while. Then a nurse came in and said she would strap me down. I didn't know what that was about and asked her why. She said, "That's so you don't kick the doctor." I told her I had given birth many times already and I never considered kicking the doctor. Doctors attended home births in Edinburgh when they were called in by the midwives. I can't remember whether this changed her mind, but I don't think it did.

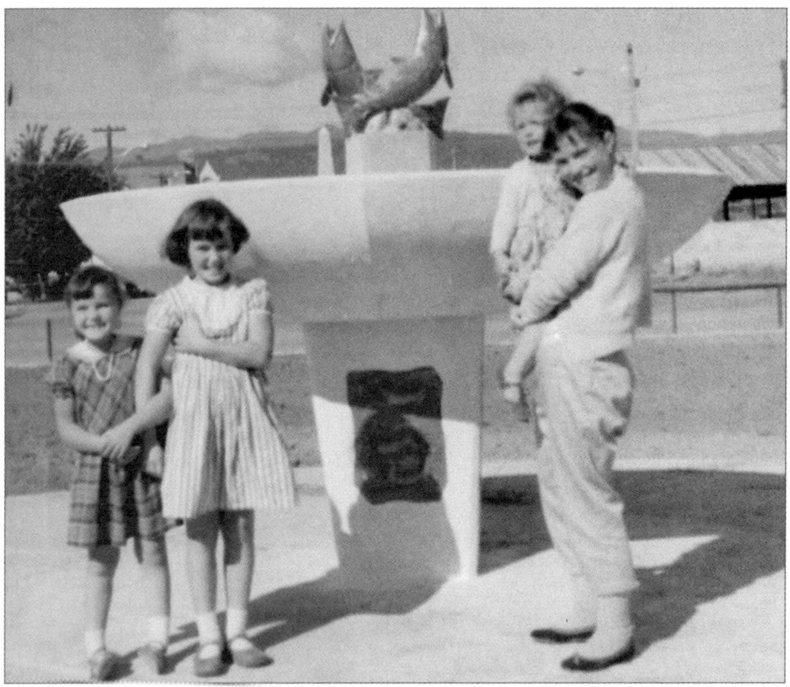

Zeljko's fountain in Cranbrook.

The next thing was that she brought one of those triangular nose covers and was about to put it on me. This time I resisted vehemently; I could smell the ether. She said it was to keep me sedated until the doctor arrived. I did win that round, though it was a long haul until I was transferred to a bed in the actual labour room. When the doctor arrived I managed to convince him that I didn't need any anaesthetic to give birth. He was used to hospital rules; perhaps he had made some of them. He certainly had no conception of the simplicity and informality of a home delivery. After all, "primitive" had been his word for home births. But he gave way, reluctantly.

So our son, Andy, took his first breath of life in a Catholic hospital. None of this unpleasant experience clouded my delight at producing a boy. The previous four births had all been girls. The next morning, I was anxious to get word to my parents; my mother had been saddened that a new grandchild was being birthed so far away. And I was happy to think the news would reach her one day after their wedding anniversary.

The Kootenay School of Art: The Untold Story

Zeljko was an artist of many talents: painter, sculptor, metalworker, ceramicist and graphic artist, often called a true Renaissance man. He was a creative man with a restless spirit who always had numerous projects in mind as well as in process. He lived to produce art, without any doubt whatsoever.

We had come to Canada in a spirit of adventure. From an early age I had wanted to travel, and Zeljko had been offered a position as an art teacher at the local high school in Cranbrook. We later thought it somewhat remarkable that this small town wanted to hire an art teacher, since there were few art teachers in those days. An exhibition of Emily Carr's work, the first to be shown in the UK, had been held at the National Art Gallery in Edinburgh a few years before, and Carr's powerful work had intrigued Zeljko. He already had a keen interest in all forms of Indigenous art, and he liked the idea of coming to western Canada, where he could connect with this living tradition. At the time, we didn't know that Zeljko's energy would be decisive in launching the Kootenay School of Art in 1960, a remarkable institution whose history has yet to be documented in a way it merits.

During our year in Cranbrook, the inspector of the Kootenay School District, Nelson Allen, who later became a close friend, visited us frequently. Allen encouraged us to consider moving to Nelson, in the West Kootenays, where a Summer School of the Arts had recently and successfully started up. He was convinced that Zeljko would be an asset to this initiative and found him a position as an art teacher at the L.V. Rogers High School in Nelson. So without much further discussion, we moved there for the 1959 fall session.

I had found that first winter in Cranbrook to be hard. Never having experienced such cold weather, I knew little about how to make any of us comfortable outdoors. Not that I understood much more about the indoors. We returned from a brief visit to the coast that first Christmas to find the main floor of our rented house had turned into a skating rink. We simply didn't think that pipes would freeze in such temperatures. After all, I had previously lived mostly in stone-built houses with thick, insulated walls. On our drive back from Vancouver through Washington State, engulfed in high snowbanks all the way, we skidded sideways, smashed the windshield and torqued the steering wheel, which prodded my pregnant belly. I was the assigned driver, as Zeljko did not yet have a driver's licence. We were told that Nelson had less severe winter temperatures than Cranbrook. This was certainly welcome news.

Zeljko was possibly the first artist to make a decisive impact on the local scene in Nelson; his work was contemporary and distinctive. His studio, located in our rented house on High Street, became a place first of curiosity and then of serious interest. His unusual dress code also drew attention. He was particularly attached to a svelte green corduroy jacket that I had made for him; it was certainly one of a kind. I made most of our clothes until we came to Canada. I enjoyed doing it and was quite proud of my dressmaking skills. Others appeared not to recognize them. On our first visit to an expensive men's clothing store in Nelson, we went to buy some shirts and pants for Zeljko, but he wasn't taken with any of them. As we were about to leave the shop without a purchase, the store owner remarked, "Anything we've got here would be better than what you're wearing, sir." It still makes me laugh!

Right away, Zeljko began broaching the idea of launching a year-round art school in Nelson and garnered support for this. After all, "Why stop with a summer school?" He proposed a model based on his own knowledge and experience of European art schools. He had attended the Budapest College of Art for four years and valued the rich curriculum that gave students not only studio practice in all the art media, but also exposure to philosophy and literature. Since I had secretarial and editorial skills, I was involved from the start to meet the constant need for press notices and letters.

Within a number of months a large provisional committee was formed, and after much discussion and work by various community groups, there was a substantial response. The school board offered to provide the salary for one art instructor, and the City of Nelson offered to house the school on Baker Street, in the former offices of the Chamber of Mines. A financial committee led a fundraising campaign for a second salary and all other material needs, which met with an excellent response. Notre Dame University College, well established at that time, collaborated by providing two of their staff for weekly philosophy and literature classes. The Nelson community certainly rallied to the call.

The Kootenay School of Art opened its doors in September 1960. It was a remarkable achievement in such a short time; it had been only a year since we had arrived in Nelson. Students came from as far afield as the Cariboo and California, partly on account of Zeljko's reputation as an artist, but also for the breadth of curriculum. The school operated for its first two years on Baker Street, in the centre of town, in a building that accommodated remarkably well the needs of

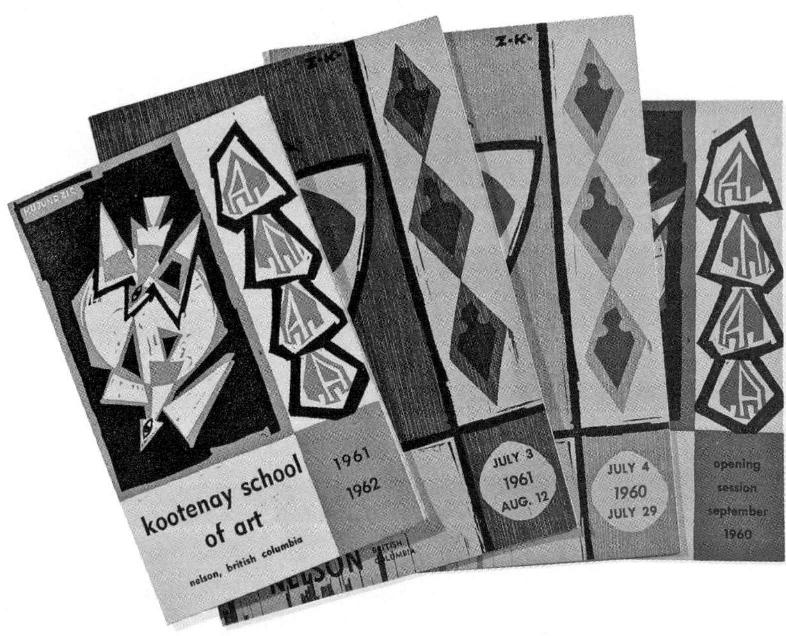

1960–1962 Kootenay School of Art calendars featuring Zeljko's block prints.

many disciplines. This venue also provided space for visiting exhibitions and guest artists, a necessary feature of art school life. Its central location made it easily accessible for the public to have an opportunity to see what students were producing, and events were open to the community. It was not an exclusive type of facility.

On one particular occasion the Haida artist Bill Reid, now best known for his powerful bronze sculptures, came to give a two-day workshop to students at the school. However, he was unable to return to the coast for almost a week due to the inaccessibility of planes landing at the nearest airport in Castlegar. There is a very narrow access between the mountains in that location, and visibility is frequently zero due to fog, a situation that still exists. This gave us an opportunity to spend more time with him in our family home. He was a thoughtful guest, and I remember him purchasing new skates for our eldest daughter, Kate, who had been unsuccessfully pleading with us for this acquisition. The hazards of living in Nelson in the winter certainly provided challenges for scheduling events, whether for music, theatre or the arts, unless road transport was to be used.

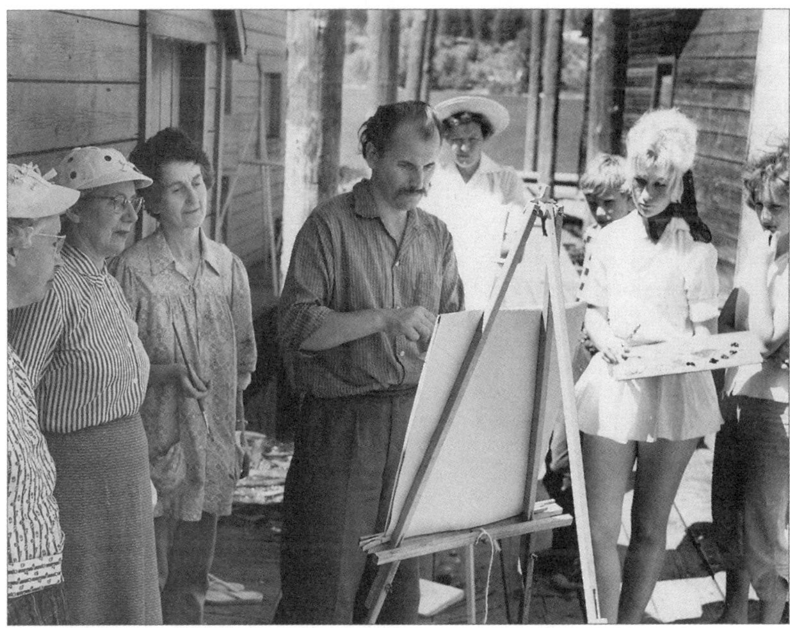

Zeljko demonstrating to a group of students.

But it also became a time of serious questioning for me. I had become aware of conflicts that Zeljko appeared to be having with the director of the summer art school, Ed Baravalle. Although they started out in a friendly fashion, these two men were now developing serious differences. Ed was chairman of the board of the Summer School of the Arts, and he assumed that the Kootenay School of Art would be incorporated within this same board. Zeljko was outraged; the two schools had different objectives. It wasn't a healthy situation. They both had strong egos: one an artist, the other a musician but primarily an administrator. Ed's wife, Mary, had become my very good friend. We enjoyed each other's company, and our fighting husbands put us into an untenable position. Our friendship suffered. I wasn't able to contact Mary again until after I heard of Ed's death some fifteen years later, by which time Zeljko and I had parted ways.

The Kootenay School of Art operated successfully for two years at the Baker Street location and was now under the administration of the provincial Department of Education. One of the objectives of the school was "to produce artists and craftsmen of versatility…for studio-based secondary industries…utilizing local materials such as minerals, clay and wood." Zeljko had steadily maintained that the rich resources of BC were invaluable for the development of local Indigenous contemporary art, and he was passionate about using local materials. He ground his own pigments for paint and used local clay for sculpture. He believed strongly that a nation's strength depends more on the resourcefulness of its people and on the vitality of its art than on the power of its armaments. I couldn't have agreed more and fully supported him.

It was now the early sixties, and there was a move by the provincial government to establish vocational institutions where one-year technical-skills programs could be established. Unemployment was becoming a major issue. Nelson was a prime candidate for this, and city officials appeared to be welcoming the move. Jack White, who represented this new educational resource, suggested incorporating the Kootenay School of Art within this new funding program. There were endless discussions with the city council, the Chamber of Commerce and Zeljko as director of the Kootenay School of Art. Eventually a proposal was made, much to Zeljko's dismay, to provide premises for the Kootenay School of Art within the new vocational institute that was being built.

These discussions took place early in 1963, and despite all arguments to the contrary, the art school was moved up to these new premises in Rosemont by the fall. All classes would now be on a one-year vocational timetable. The change lost the richness of the curriculum and sacrificed the fundamentals of an art school. There would be two art courses offered at first in this new location: Graphics and Ceramics. The building itself didn't have the atmosphere generated in the previous location; now there were simply standard corridors with classrooms attached. The two art courses would be dumped in with other vocational programs, with Hairdressing being one of them. Zeljko taught Graphics for only one year, but he began having conflicts with the administration when the art school became subject to vocational institute rules. One-year courses meant the school had lost its identity as a genuine art school, and he had no pleasure in working with this severely restricted alternative.

It took a toll on our marriage. I had decided to register as a student in the second year, which was also a way to get out of the house, but I did not enjoy the atmosphere in this new location. The building felt sterile, lacking a soul. However, I managed to produce a fair number of ceramics, both wheel-turned and hand-built, and also enjoyed creating graphics from woodblocks, a process that prepared me for a later venture we were to undertake.

I know that right to the end I was constantly typing Zeljko's forceful letters, which often took time that I thought I should be devoting to our children. But he got priority, which, though I regret, I cannot change. I was very happy in Nelson and felt it to be a healthy place to bring up children, and I was involved in many other community issues. But I also realized there was a lot of strife emerging from the continual meetings, heated discussions and arguments. These were badly affecting relationships amongst the people who supported the arts in Nelson. Idealism and fiscal reality were pitting unhealthy divisions—a situation that exists as much today as it did then. I had attended numerous board meetings in a non-voting position and had seen the antagonism develop.

I summed it up in a letter to one of our friends this way: "Zeljko has had an increasingly upward battle with provincial education authorities since their takeover of the art school in 1961. The autonomy of the school was gradually encroached, policies affecting standards of training and curriculum were imposed against Zeljko's advice, and the school became a small square peg in the vast mediocre educational system. The final blow came in July 1964, when Zeljko was called before the Board and reprimanded for his public statements, which had appeared conspicuously in the press. He was offered one last chance of graciously bowing to authority with a salary increase; this had to be weighed against several odds."

Just before the end of his second year in this situation, a few days after this offer and after volatile clashes with the administration, Zeljko handed in his resignation. Ironically, on the same day, he received a letter saying his services were no longer needed. I believe that both sides recognized the incompatibility of what an art school required and what a vocational school provided. The biggest voice held sway.

An Activist in Nelson

Shortly after our arrival in Nelson I found myself pregnant again. Birth control methods were unreliable at best in those years, and I was using an ill-fitting diaphragm that had failed once more. I went back to the old-time method of gin and hot baths, found myself bleeding profusely and ended up in Emergency at the Nelson hospital. My doctor gave me a D & C and told me very severely not to go that route ever again. Our relationship never quite recovered from that incident, and I eventually found another doctor.

I had become increasingly aware and concerned about the dangers of strontium-90 and the radiation effects that nuclear testing was having, not only on fish and wildlife, but also on mothers' milk. I discussed this with other women at one of the kaffeeklatsches held by teachers' wives. I was met with a variety of responses: "Yes, it's disturbing, but what can we do? It's all political," and "Maybe it's not as bad as they say." Most surprising of all was, "Well, I don't expect to be happy in this life. I'm just looking forward to the next one in heaven," from a fervent Catholic. However, one lively woman with whom I became great friends, Agnes Herbison, said, "Let's figure out what we can do."

Very shortly after this, we heard on the radio that a national movement was already building. It was Voice of Women (VOW), led first by Kay Macpherson and later by Muriel Duckworth. This was something we could support in Nelson, and a few of us got together. Agnes and I met frequently to consult. We began holding weekly meetings in Zeljko's studio at our home. He was always generous in providing this space; perhaps he felt it was an opportunity for exposing others to his art. We were surprised by the interest we attracted, some of which was possibly the opportunity to see his nudes.

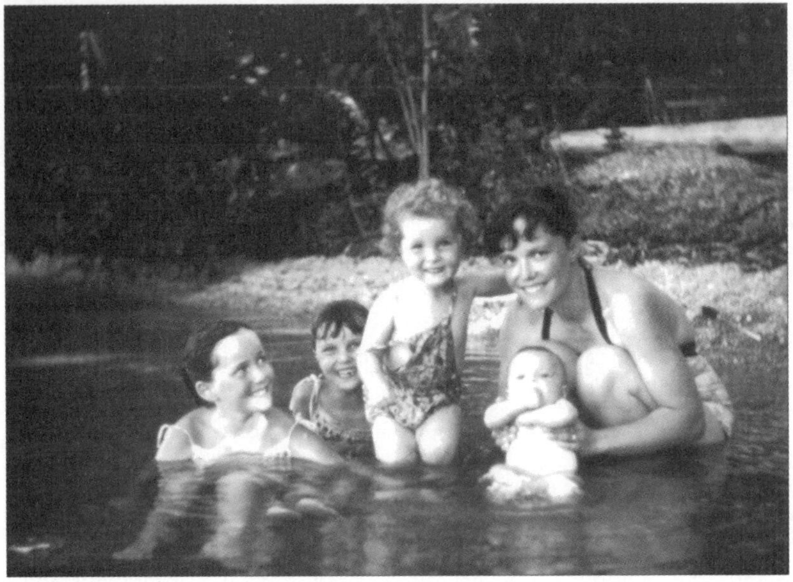

Kate, Claire, Judy, me and baby Andy.

I offered to take on the task of providing information about Voice of Women for a weekly radio show. We were generously offered a regular slot by the local station, and the *Nelson Daily News* was also helpful in providing coverage. The movement grew and women's voices were actually being heard. We were especially pleased by the response to an appeal made by the national branch of Voice of Women for funds to support the establishment of a Peace Research Institute. I spoke at PTA meetings, which scared the hell out of me, and took on providing radio and press announcements. At the last count, thirty-seven local women donated their monthly "baby bonus cheques" (called Family Allowance) to this endeavour. It was an encouraging response to our efforts and gave us hope for change.

A year later my fifth child, Natanis, was born, a month overdue. It was an extremely hot summer and I remember staying indoors as much as possible. The art school was closed during the summer holidays, and Zeljko was in Seattle at the World's Fair. I had been reading Lawrence Durrell's entire quartet, one book after another, which I found intriguing. His books were unlike anything I had read before and they provided a wonderful way of escape during the weeks of waiting for contractions to start. It was also canning season, an important time for putting away a lot of ripe produce for the winter months. I found that canning late into the evenings—once the heat had subsided—was the only way to get it done. Contractions eventually started coming but then stopped. A few days of this made me understandably impatient.

One morning at the end of August, I decided that I'd had enough. I needed to go straight to the hospital, which was a steep walk uphill. Pushing the buggy there, with Andy in it, might hasten the event. I took all the children with me and insisted on pushing the buggy myself, all the way uphill, despite Kate's concern. When we got there I was admitted immediately; my contractions were now frequent. Kate dutifully returned home and looked after the others until Zeljko returned. The nurses were extremely helpful. They couldn't reach my doctor, as he was apparently on the golf course, and they suggested giving me a spinal injection for pain relief, which for the first time I thankfully took. Natanis was born that afternoon. I'd never had such a short and relatively comfortable birth! When my doctor arrived, he was somewhat annoyed that I hadn't called him earlier. I suspect he lost the birth delivery fee he had anticipated.

I had many reasons to enjoy living in Nelson. We made good friends there. Some of us who had young children and felt the need for some connection with a non-dogmatic religion formed a Unitarian Fellowship. I had previously tried to find a place in the Bahá'í faith, but I couldn't accept their somewhat strict rules. We met in our homes to share concerns, ideas about education and morality, and a love of music. A few of us formed a film club to bring in foreign films and others not likely to be seen locally, since our one venue in Nelson provided only basic Hollywood fare, and television programming was very limited in those early days. But what I remember is that we found ways of bringing what we needed to Nelson. That is one of the good things that has not changed in that resourceful community and I trust never will.

I could walk everywhere and take the children with me wherever I needed to go, with schools and stores nearby. The view from our kitchen windows, which stretched the full length of the very large kitchen, was outstanding. Our kitchen overlooked the Kootenay River and the lower part of the steep mountain beyond, providing sparkling seasonal colours and lots of daylight. I spent a considerable amount of time there. It was a far cry from the view from the kitchen of the fifth-floor tenement building we had left behind in Edinburgh.

We became good friends with the Herbisons. Hugh was working at L.V. Rogers High School, where Zeljko also worked, and he and Agnes lived not far from us. Immediately there was a spark. They had four daughters and one son, and also, like us, had lost a second child. Agnes introduced me to the Weavers, Pete Seeger and other folk singers of the day. She also introduced me to the *Catholic Worker*, produced by Dorothy Day, the first progressive newspaper I was to find in North America. I had been feeling so bereft of newspapers when we first arrived in Canada. Back in Scotland, we used to read the *Manchester Guardian* and the *Observer* weekend editions, which I really missed.

Agnes was very musical, as were her children. Their youngest, Nancy, now known as Nancy Argenta, became a world-class singer. Hugh was very interested in Doukhobor history and we were living in an area settled by many Doukhobors. The Herbisons moved to Argenta, but we still did a lot of things together. As I mentioned, Agnes and I started a Voice of Women chapter, and we also started the Unitarian Fellowship and a film club. We were kindred spirits.

We built an A-frame very close to where the Herbisons lived in Argenta, because the government allowed us to purchase some Crown land at a reasonable price on the condition that we build on the property within a certain period of time. We enjoyed meeting with the Quakers who had settled there and established a Friends School after moving from the US to avoid their children being drafted. Argenta became a busy little hub of activity. People came from around the area to attend the Quaker meetings. The Stevensons, Wolfs, Valentines and Boyds were some of these families; all were highly educated people. There wasn't electricity at first, but eventually someone brought in generators.

Back then the road to Argenta was single lane, unpaved and without guardrails to stop you from going over the edge. That road is where I really learned how to drive in Canada. It took about three hours to get there from Nelson, and some of the drive took us perilously high above the north arm of Kootenay Lake. We did drive our

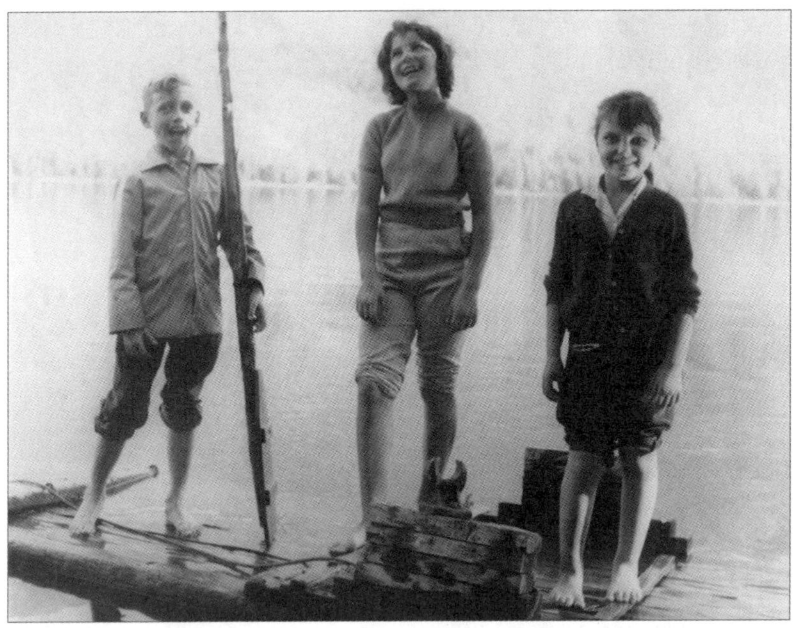

Kate and Claire rafting with Terry Hunter on Kootenay Lake.

old Dodge sedan there in the winter, but not as often as in the summer. With four children, it was a bit cramped. But it was during this time that our home in Nelson became an overnight stop for many students and visitors going to and from Argenta, which made life interesting and very busy.

We added to our family commitments by accepting immigration responsibility for Zeljko's parents, who arrived in Nelson from Hungary with those sad but nonetheless common expectations of finding the streets paved with gold. His father, a master chef, found work for a time at the Hume Hotel in Nelson, but he, like Zeljko, had European standards and told everyone in the kitchen that they didn't know anything about real cooking. "They don't even know how to make soup stock. Can you believe it?" He, too, didn't last long.

Then we started building on another front. With five children in tow we found the distance to Argenta becoming a deterrent and had begun building a workshop-cum-studio on a plot of land in Thrums. This was in Doukhobor country near Castlegar, much more accessible for getting building supplies. We spent many summer days working

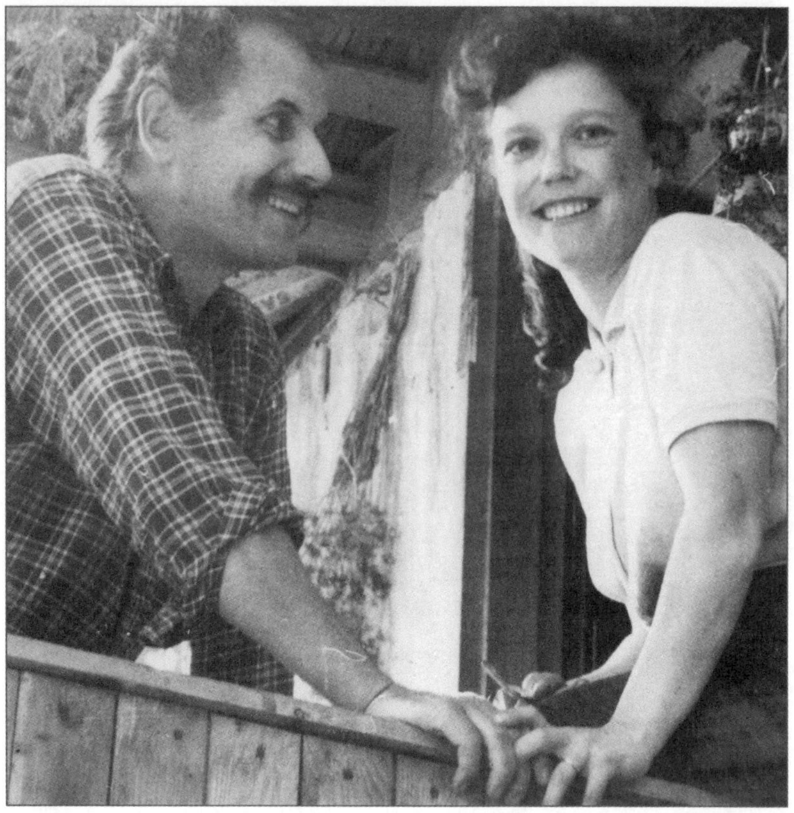

Zeljko and me in Thrums.

there and enjoying the wide Kootenay River. Zeljko, as well as the kids, loved swimming, and he was also adept at spearfishing for our dinner. He and I had made a bargain some years back that I would make an effort to be a better swimmer if he would make more of an effort on the dance floor. He was a superb swimmer and I loved dancing, but unfortunately this was a deal that neither of us managed to keep.

In spite of all this, on some level I realized that the turbulence at the Kootenay School of Art left us little choice but to make a move. Moving again meant that our children, too, had to make adjustments, such as finding new friends and new schools. It was our third move in six years. Making a move was going to be a difficult undertaking, and there were also Zeljko's parents to consider. It wasn't really what I wanted to happen.

The Art Centre in Kelowna

They looked impressed
and gazed in admiration
but then the questions came
that looks like death
it's trees in moonlight
and that like war
they're lovers

well, what's that about
a skeleton shaking hands
oh, that's the artist and his bride
they looked again
in awe
and whispered
it doesn't much look like her
but he sure has imagination
–1966

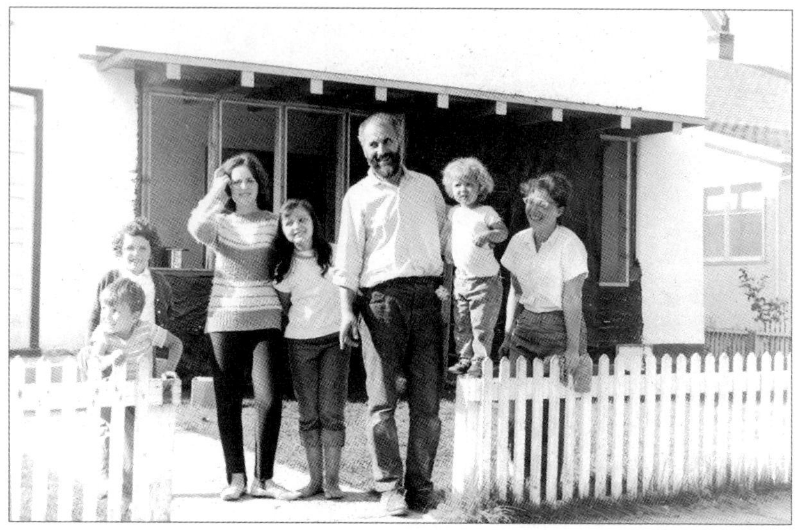

Our family at the house on Richter Street, Kelowna, 1964.

Where to go? The Okanagan Valley beckoned, and Zeljko quickly found a teaching opportunity in Rutland, an area of Kelowna. We travelled to Kelowna to look for accommodation and found that a Methodist church on Richter Street was for sale. The main church area would provide a large studio space, perfect for a full-fledged art studio, because it could house a kiln, workspace for painting and carving and a large expanse of walls for exhibiting. The family space behind was smaller than we wanted, but manageable. And the price was right: we put down a small deposit on its market value of six thousand dollars.

Moving there in the summer was an experience I won't forget. We sent our furniture and belongings ahead of us in a moving van, but we hoped to reach Kelowna around the same time as the drivers of the van. On the way, our good old Rambler had a breakdown in Grand Forks, and the replacement part needed to fix it would have to be brought in from the coast. We were stuck with finding a place to stay until the part arrived two days later. When we finally arrived in Kelowna, we found that the delivery van had deposited everything, willy-nilly, in the church. To make matters worse, the previous owners had left a massive amount of clutter and garbage everywhere and had not made any attempt to clean the premises. It was a hard beginning, certainly not a very welcoming one.

My life in the sixties has been hard to write about, and it has been helpful for me to look at letters I wrote during that time. I'm struck by the personal struggle that forced its way out during all the other struggles that faced us in running the Art Centre, as we called our studio in Kelowna. There was excitement, of course, in having a new venture—never a dull moment. Both Zeljko and I were trying to find ways of meeting our very different needs. I now realize that he needed to devote his energies completely to his art, while I primarily wanted family, friends, community and some stability. These needs were not necessarily incompatible, but we never resolved them in the four packed years we operated and lived in the Art Centre.

Excerpt from a letter to my brother Trevor, January 1965: Our first month was hard; we had only the small parsonage behind to house ourselves as well as our "stuff" in. However, we've now got the church area knocked into shape, making it a terrific studio for Zeljko, and four months of his unholy language have dispelled most of the religious ghosts. It's really quite a place: room to give classes, tackle big commissions, and we could even hold small theatrical functions or poetry readings on the dais! And eight long pews, more than enough to provide sleeping accommodation for all our visitors!

Zeljko has gone back to high school teaching this year after his fight with the vocational school, but he will hope to leave teaching next year, have some private students and get some architectural commissions. There is so much building going on in BC that there should be work. Local construction seems to be built for a twenty-year expectancy; obsolescence takes over at that point, they say, so why bother with artist-made products? Mass production caters best for this outlook. But to get serious commissions, our alternative would be to live in Vancouver or some of the big cities in the east. And we don't want city life while the children are growing up.

I still feel very new in Kelowna. It's twice the size of Nelson and is regarded as a prize spot by most British Columbians. I think, personally, that it is highly overrated. It's a tourist hot spot in summer, with lake, etc. But it's not got much character and is terribly clean and suburban looking. I do realize it's ideal for the kids, as they will be able to swim etc. and it is nice being in the fruit growing area, if not for any other reason than we can make as much wine as we can drink. And the children can eat as many apples as they want. But I'll tell you more after I've been here another five years…

Strange that I put an emphasis on winemaking, because Zeljko never drank very much and the only time I remember him getting a bit tipsy was once, after we'd been to an exhibition opening. When we got home, he became extremely morose and wouldn't take off his overcoat. He just sat and remained silent for the longest time. I had a hard time in eventually convincing him that it was quite time to go to bed. I certainly enjoyed drinking wine, but mostly I liked having it around to offer to company, and I loved the idea of making it from local fruit. Over the years I made wine from elderberries, blackberries and rosehips, and I also made mead from my own honey.

A big change I had to get used to was that we were now operating a business and would have to advertise, put out press releases, pay extra for our utilities and so on. It was a bit of a shock! Calling ourselves an Art Centre put us in that "privileged" category. It was a far cry from Paris, where our artist friend Mary Stewart Gibson prided herself on having a well-maintained studio, courtesy of the city fathers. However, Zeljko found his way to the local TV station, which was always looking for something new. They found his presence quite entertaining, and *Art with Zeljko*, a half-hour instructional program, became a weekly feature and provided adequate advertising for us. He had a lively presence, striking good looks and unconventional language and could certainly command an audience.

Excerpt from a letter to Priscilla Lorimer, March 1965:
The last year has seen many changes in us, mental as well as physical, inward and outward, individually and as a family. Job-hunting took a minimum of effort, as Zeljko applied and was accepted for a post in a senior high school within twenty-four hours of arriving in Kelowna. A relief, as procedure can often be quite deadly.

Our present home is on hallowed ground. We bought a Free Methodist Church and will be paying for it for the next ten years. We shared it for the first month with the Latter Day Saints, Mormons, and happily came out unscathed from this brief encounter. We have now, with sweat and blood, converted the church into an Art Centre, and have made the parsonage quarters attached at back into a livable, if somewhat small, home. Zeljko holds classes in some evenings and on Saturdays and has ample room to work. Potter's wheel, kiln and welding equipment for copper sculpture are installed. At the front we have set up a shop from which to sell our wares.

My own year included a course in ceramics and another in graphics at the art school, which I thoroughly enjoyed, and I learnt to produce some moderately good work. But I don't really feel as if I will ever be a producer in this milieu, as sad as this will be for Zeljko to accept. I'm afraid I am much too practical by nature, and tend to weight my imagination with too many mundane problems. I could be an adequate craftsman, but I don't persevere enough. In other words I am quite happy to remain a critic!

Perhaps my talents still lie best in house painting—or church painting, as it has now become. Seriously, I would like to get a good job, something that would make me think, before I become mentally atrophied. Whether there is anything available, or whether Zeljko could survive this "stab in the back" as he thinks of it, I don't know. The sad thing is that he should measure all my endeavours strictly as relative to his own. Thus anything I take on outside the home or outside art activities suggests to him that I find the home and Zeljko as being inadequate. This makes our lives an absurd struggle at times, and I have not been able to find an answer to it. I am increasingly restless, try hard as I do to remain stable. I realize his attitude, which is of course totally incongruous in this particular society, is tempered by his background, upbringing etc. But as he is quick to question his own traditions, particularly where his parents are concerned, this seems a trifle ironic.

Zeljko had a habit of using the phrase "stab in the back" when he thought he was being treated badly. I do wonder now whether his terrible wartime experiences accounted for this; he wrote about these in his 1957 autobiography, *Torn Canvas*, in which he describes how terrified the SS troops were in retreat with labour conscripts, of which Zeljko was one: "It occurred to me that in fact there was little chance of any of us surviving this particular situation. The Germans in defeat were behaving like raving lunatics, and if they thought they would benefit by shooting us all out of hand, the action would be no sooner performed than forgotten. Well, well, I thought, so you wanted to become an artist. What is art to you now after all you've seen? What is artistic about your dead friends, decomposing in a ditch? And Picasso; how does his symbolism stand up to this hideous, torn canvas of reality?"

Although I worked with Zeljko when he was writing this book, which he mostly dictated, I simply didn't comprehend the effect of his experiences during those war years. I realize now that he must have suffered from post-traumatic stress disorder, something that is now properly acknowledged and understood. Unfortunately, I just ignored him when he talked this way, and his response to my silence was to be somewhat disagreeable to the children, which was the only way he knew to get back at me. I just felt we would always get through these periods of disagreement if I waited them out.

This would eventually happen in bed—the one place where we never argued, and which we shared with both relief and pleasure.

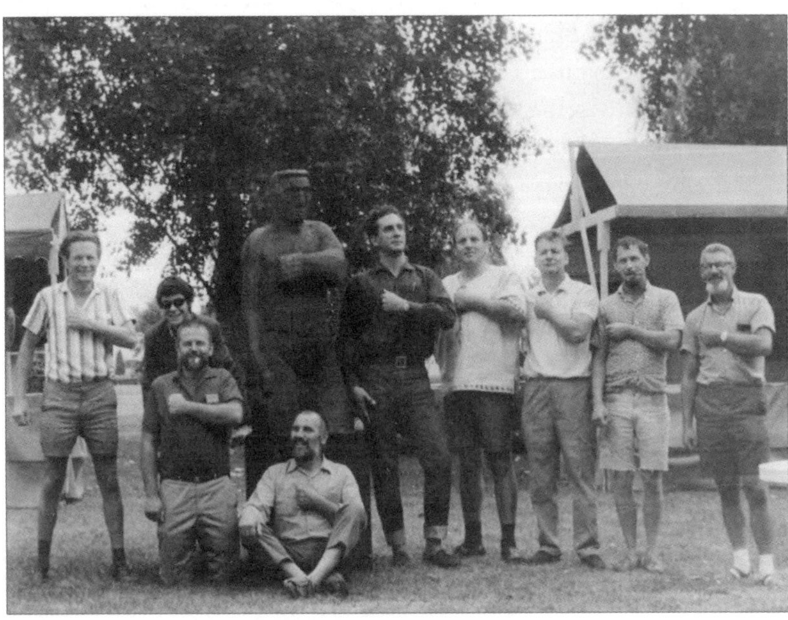

Okanagan Summer Arts Festival. Zeljko is seated in the front.

I suspect we had an unspoken agreement that we would never bring our problems there—it was almost as if this were a sacred place that we would both retreat to, hoping that it would resolve whatever issues we were facing. I find it strange to look back at that; I don't quite understand what it was, except that we had created a certain bonding that was more than just sexual. I simply cannot find the words for it; it was certainly one of the many forms of love that cannot be easily expressed in language. And I'm happily aware that despite all the struggles we had, our children were all conceived in that love.

We gradually incorporated more events into the Art Centre space, and we had weekly Unitarian Fellowship meetings on Sunday evenings. Poets and writers gave readings: George Ryga, Patrick Lane and the young Jurgen Gothe, who later became known on CBC Radio. There were Voice of Women speakers, and the Lively Arts, a women's singing group that I accompanied on our piano. All in all, the Art Centre became what was then called a "happening place" and provided a rich resource for many workshops and activities.

I met my friend Ann Macmillan in Kelowna during this period. We both participated in many art functions, as contributors as well as viewers, and we also shared a British background. Our friendship flourished, and she kindly offered to care for Natanis, our youngest at five years, during the four months of our trip to Mexico and Guatemala, which fostered a special connection. Her only child, Sean, was the same age as Natanis. Ann eventually had to return to England for work reasons, and I have visited her on almost every occasion I've been home. She writes remarkable letters and keeps me posted of her many interests, and I have immense respect for her enquiring mind. She constantly inspires me.

Travels South

A woman, young
skin taut—a Mayan breadth of face
eyes blind
diseased from childhood
sits with outstretched arms
silent—
a piece of supplicating sculpture
waiting for the coins to fall
–1968

Zeljko was able to resign from teaching after one year in Rutland, and in the following year he was offered a three-month position at the Instituto Allende art school in San Miguel, Mexico. We decided to take advantage of this by first making an extended trip through the southwestern US, visiting many Indigenous reserves and seeing the rich art of the Zuni, Hopi and Navajo nations, and also viewing many archaeological sites along the way. Zeljko built a wooden sleeping cabin to fit on top of our Rambler station wagon, and we took two of our children—Judy, who was nine, and Andy, who was seven—for an educational journey south. Kate had by now left home to find work in Vancouver, while Claire lived in Summerland and Natanis stayed in Kelowna. While the trip was rich in new sights and sounds, it wasn't always smooth sailing.

We had a particularly harrowing experience in New Mexico, just before we reached the border crossing. Zeljko had had a nightmare some days earlier in which he was going to be killed on a certain date. He was alarmed and treated it as a serious premonition. Nothing I said managed to calm him. However, since I knew that he didn't really pay attention to dates as a rule, I thought that I might be able to fool him by bringing the date ahead by a day. So on the evening before that fateful day, I told him, "Hey, you've survived it; you've passed the day—it was yesterday!" He believed me and looked relieved.

We were at that time in a fairly isolated area, looking for a place to camp for the night. I noticed we were coming to a small township and was horrified to discover its name: Truth or Consequences. I didn't say a word, but this did not appear to be a good omen, since today was the day that Zeljko had dreamt would bring his death. We found an off-road spot just a bit farther on, with a small pond, which would be pleasant for the kids to paddle in. I was trying to decide whether I should push for going ahead to reach the border crossing into Mexico, but it was getting dark and I was outvoted. So we pulled up for the night. We waded into the pond for a treat, only to be attacked by leeches. It was very unpleasant; I'd never experienced them before. Then we had a picnic supper and put the kids to bed; they slept in the back of the car, and we slept in the wooden bunk on top. I remember deciding to lock the doors of the car. Zeljko, as usual, brought his trusty scabbard knife up top with him. He slept with it under his pillow, a habit from the war that lasted many years.

We were settling down for our nightly reading when we heard sounds of motorbikes, lots of them, slowing down and coming with whoops of shouts and laughter into our space. And then we realized they were circling around us, round and round, probably wondering what we were doing there. Zeljko's response was to go for his knife, saying that he would open our upstairs cabin door and tell them to clear off, get lost. I didn't think that was a good idea. There were a lot of them, at least ten. I convinced him just to keep quiet. The car doors were locked and the kids were safe; I suggested we just wait it out and pretend we didn't hear them. I heard a few bottles smashing, suspected they were drinking, and hoped that they wouldn't do any harm if we just ignored them and pretended to be asleep. It was a while before the noise dropped down and we heard the bikes slowly moving away.

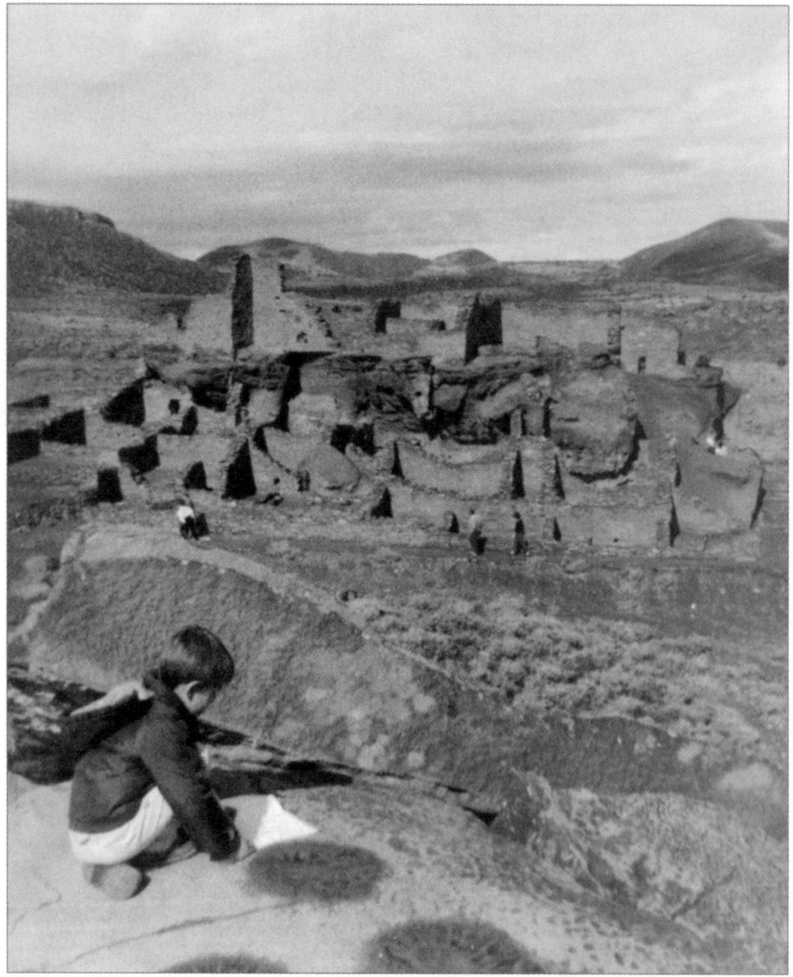

Andy working on his daily "journal" while we were in New Mexico.

I admit to being terrified, but I was firm in the face of an unexpected and unnerving experience.

Our time in San Miguel was rewarding. Both children still have vivid memories of it and produced great travel journals to bring back to their schools. Judy decided she'd like to try going to school in San Miguel. She liked it so much she would have happily stayed there. She was quickly learning the language. I took an intensive course in batik at the art institute, which I enjoyed immensely and continued to practice for many years. Vats of dyes became a constant in our household.

And later I made wall hangings and clothing items out of batik fabric, which sold well in the Art Centre boutique. We continued to travel after Zeljko's term at the art institute was completed; we went south to Guatemala for a month, where we spent some days in Sololá, which has a rich tradition in weaving. The remarkable clothing to be found there was unique, both in colour and design, to that specific area of Guatemala. We also visited Quetzaltenango, which at that time was reached by a very narrow, winding and rocky road, and it became obvious that the people there, who practiced an interesting mix of Indigenous and Catholic religions, did not welcome visitors taking photographs. Undeterred, Zeljko took pictures of what he chose, and I remember an Indigenous woman coming up to him, outraged, shaking her fist at his camera. The strange thing is that when we got home, Zeljko found that the particular roll of film containing shots of people in Quetzaltenango couldn't be processed. Nothing came out—it was completely blank. Her curse had been effective, and it was no doubt justly deserved.

On our way home in early January 1967, we stopped north of Phoenix, Arizona, to visit Paolo Soleri, whose vision as an architect was to become best known through his imaginative urban development, resulting in the building of Arcosanti. He was a delightful host, and he talked to us about his concept of "arcology." This is architecture integrated with ecology, which advocates cities being designed to maximize the interaction and accessibility with an urban environment, and to minimize the use of energy, raw materials and land, thus reducing waste and environmental pollution. We brought back from him exciting new ideas, as well as some handsome bronze bells with wonderful sounds, which he produced and sold to fund Arcosanti's construction.

Today, Arcosanti is a thriving community that teaches and welcomes thousands of visitors. It continually evolves and "seeks to embody a 'Lean Alternative' to hyper consumption through a smartly efficient and elegant city design. Leanness is inherent to the sustainable health of any living system. The city needs to be such a system." We were fortunate to know the founder of this visionary city and to be there when it was in its infancy.

Excerpt from a letter to my brother Trevor, May 1967:
I've just started a large tapestry, three by five feet—a commission, actually. The theme is Indigenous masks and it's going to look good, but a lot of work time-wise. The tapestries sell well, but it's very hard to relate prices to income needs. I've been working out that we need a basic four hundred dollars per month to keep a roof over our heads and food on the table—and this is really basic, allowing for no frills such as clothing. It would take a lot of tapestry work to earn four hundred dollars. The regular artist has it tough, for it's only the fluke artist that gets into the hundreds for his work. Most people imagine one does it for fun! No one really believes that you'd take it seriously enough to make a living by it.

We've both been doing our community service (so-called), and I'm getting experience again in public speaking. Zeljko addressed the Canadian Club at their annual meeting last week, and the same evening I addressed the University Women's Club at their annual dinner. Zeljko enjoys speaking and never prepares notes, but relies on audience reaction to stimulate him, and always gives a highly entertaining talk. I sweat for weeks beforehand, and in this case wrote four or five completely different talks, before finally coming up with one that was called "erudite" in our local press. Hmm. Between us we cover some strange ground...

That year was a busy one. Zeljko decided to organize an Okanagan Summer Arts Festival and was given good space in the Kelowna City Park to hold this open-air event. It included an exhibition of paintings, sculpture and ceramics, with demonstrations in each of these; live theatre with John Juliani; poetry readings; mime; folk singing and a festival of documentaries and shorts from the National Film Board.

Zeljko had made a good connection some years back with an artist in Spokane, Wirth McCoy. Wirth had high regard for Zeljko's work, and he and his wife invited us to stay with them in Spokane on several occasions; they always welcomed us bringing all our kids with us. Wirth was now head of the Department of Art at Pennsylvania State University, and he wrote asking Zeljko to consider being artist-in-residence at Penn State. Zeljko was more than happy to do this, and

PAGE 8A KELOWNA DAILY COURIER, FRI., OCT. 22, 1965

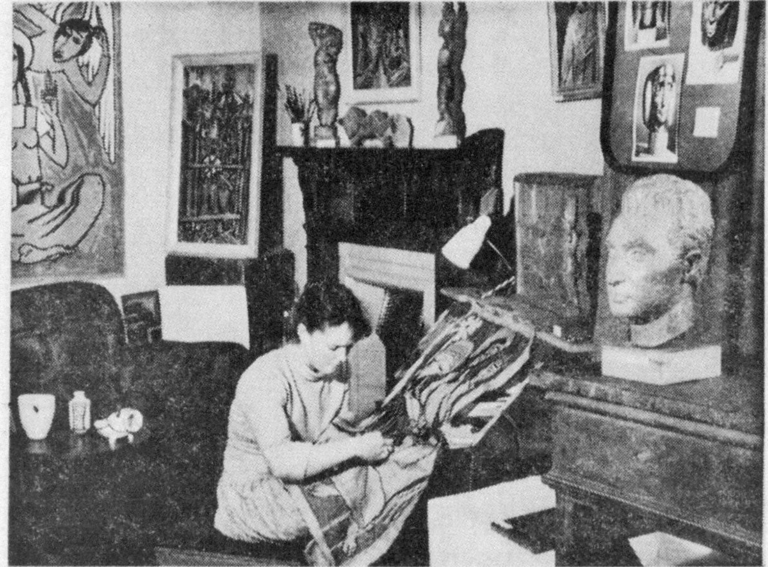

ANN KUJUNDBIC WORKS ON TAPESTRY IN THE STUDIO

Artist In Her Own Right Is The Mother Of Five

By FLORA EVANS

In a unique studio in Kelowna called the Art Centre, Ann Kujundzic, wife of internationally known artist Zeljko Kujundzic, teaches and creates fascinating tapestries in conjunction with her husband as well as raising a lively family of five, baking, dressmaking and housekeeping.

Using mainly burlap and wool backgrounds to give warmth

the pattern is excluded is tied rather than waxed as in Batik. She also teaches children's classes in forms of picture making such as string outlines, pasted cutouts, mobiles, collage, simple forms of graphic art and modelling in ceramics, and one of her latest projects is an adult class in the designing and making of tapestries which commenced on Wednesday, Oct. 20 and will continue on Wednesday evenings at the studio. At these

This month Mrs. Kujundzic and her work were featured under "What's New" in Chatelaine magazine. Why not visit the Art Centre and discover her work for yourselves? Both Ann and her husband would be happy to show you around. They don't expect you to be an art critic, they probably would not agree with you if you were, but they would welcome you warmly if you care to visit them and look at their work.

we spent the winter semester there. I remember an incredible drive across the States in late December, facing the worst snowstorms I'd ever driven in just north of Buffalo, with the three kids and luggage in a rather old station wagon.

We rented an apartment for three months in State College and found out what living in a college town was like—very pleasurable in many ways, though I sensed it had a bit of an ivory tower feel about it. We were to get a very different feel from a visit to Uniontown, in

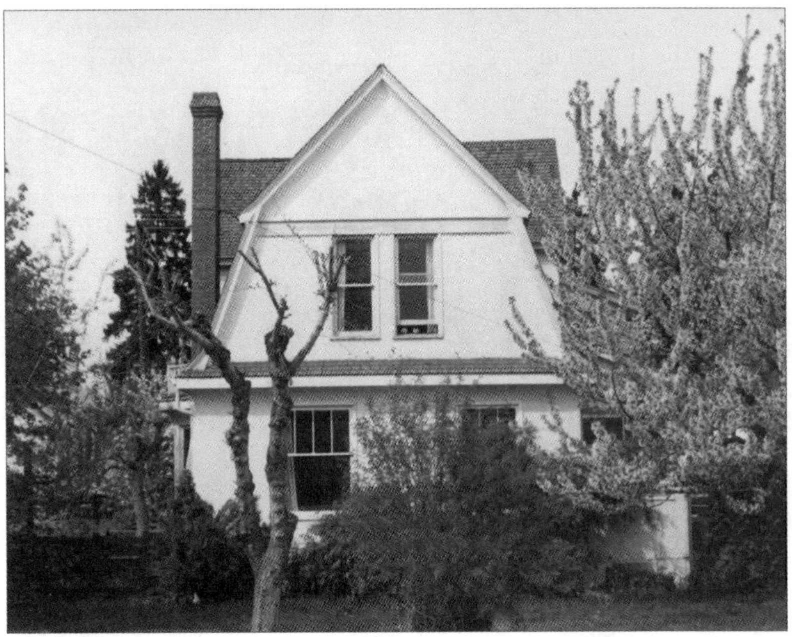

Our second Kelowna house.

southern Pennsylvania, where the Fayette Campus was located. We went there because they offered Zeljko a position to open an art department at this campus, starting in the fall session. My first reaction was that I simply didn't want to live in the States. It didn't fit us, either socially or politically. But I could see how this offer might finally give Zeljko the opportunity he needed. He would have more freedom to pursue his own work and enjoy the stability, as well as prestige, that would flow from this position. He had enjoyed teaching adults who wanted to be taught; he just didn't enjoy the grind of high school teaching. So we returned to Kelowna with this new prospect facing us. Zeljko was determined to accept the offer of a professorship—I was equally determined not to live in the States.

We realized that the Art Centre no longer had a future with Zeljko moving into this new position, so we decided to sell it and buy a house nearby instead. I have happy memories of that house; it was rather unusual looking. From the street it looked a bit like a Dutch barn. Inside it had an interesting layout, and we finally had a room for each child. There was even a partial basement, something we hadn't had before, as well as an unfinished attic. And I liked the garden: cherry trees in the front and space enough in the back to grow vegetables! Best of all, a big porch ran the full length of the house at the back; the children all loved it and so did I. But I know we really avoided talking about how this would affect our marriage.

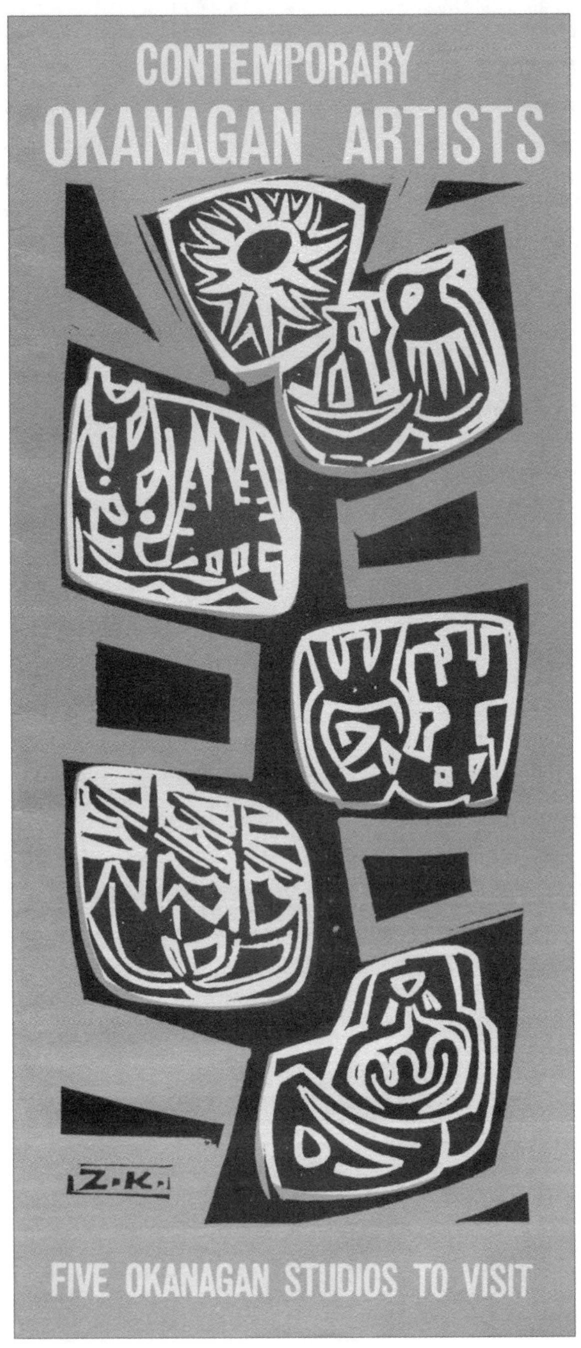

Promotional material designed by Zeljko for the Okanagan Five.

Gallery

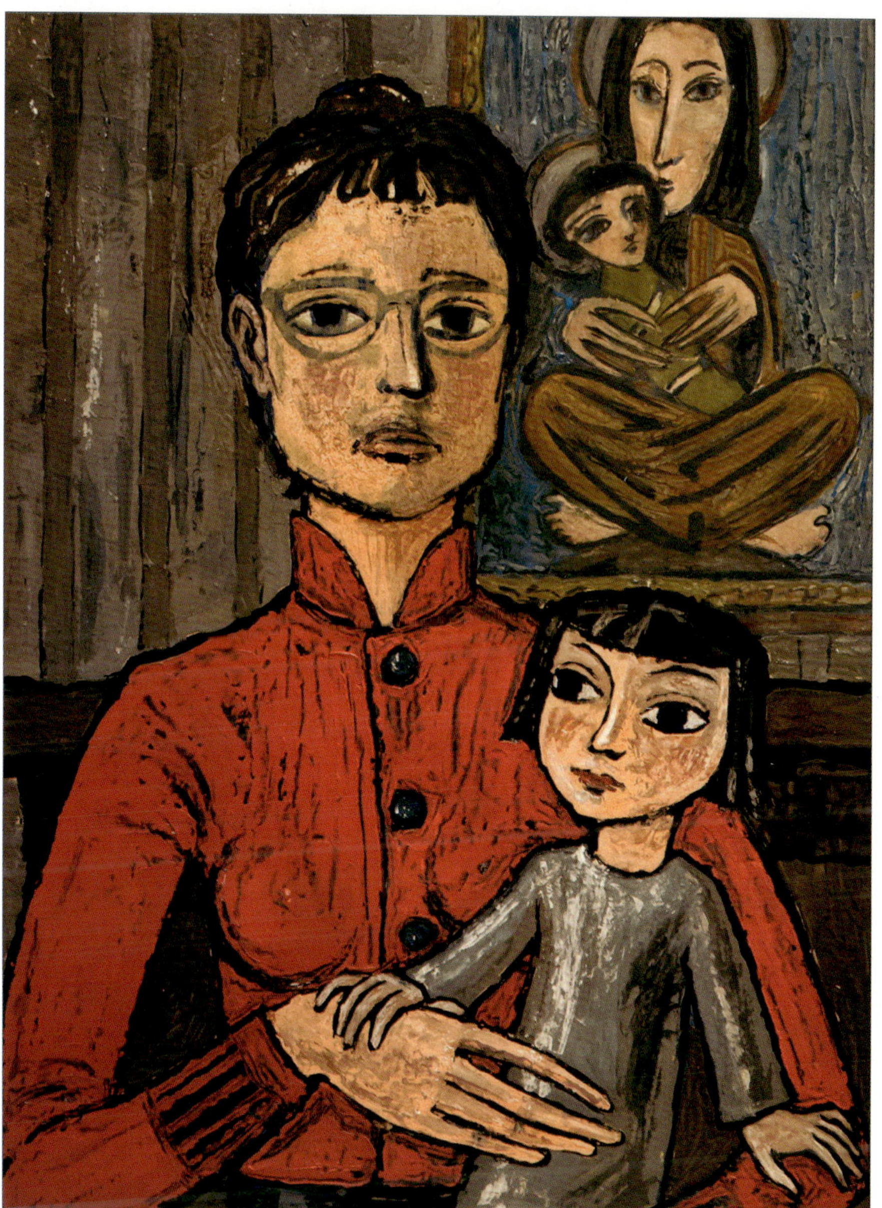

Zeljko's portrait of Claire and me, painted in tempera.

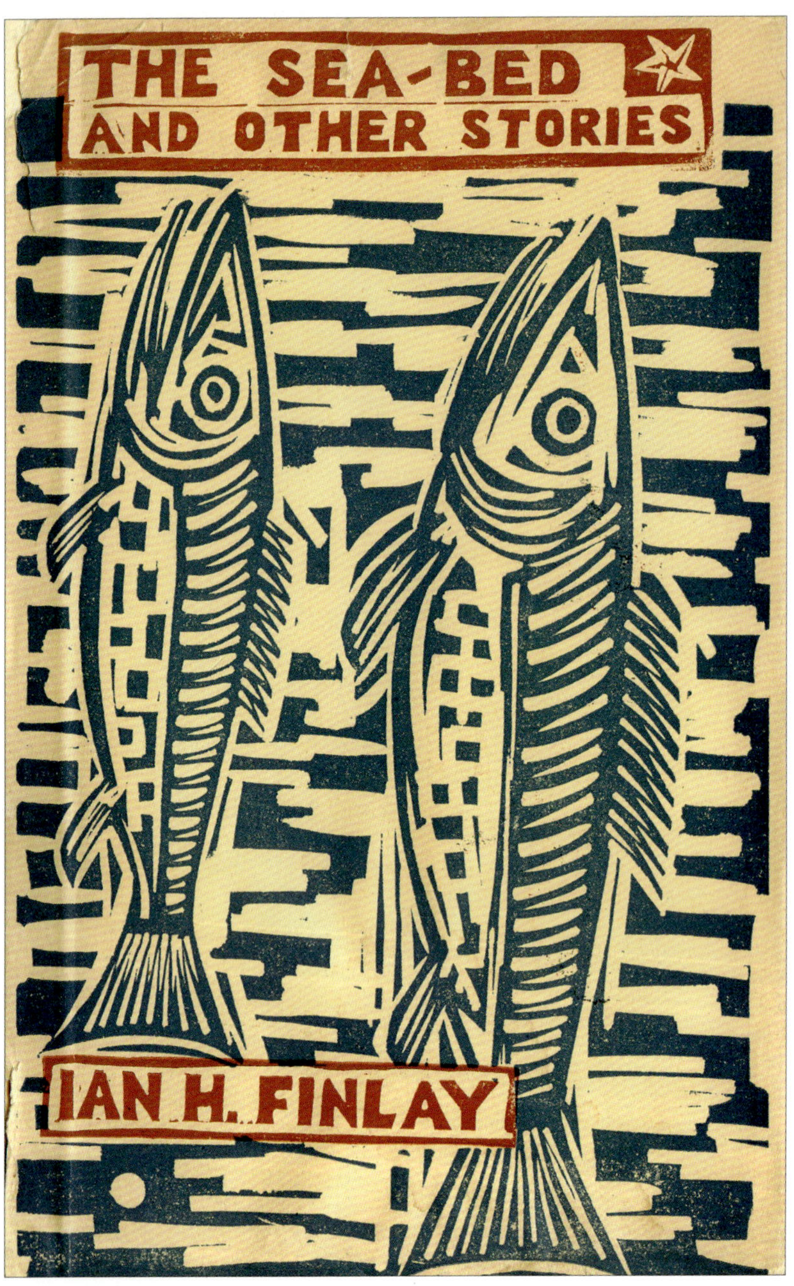

The Sea-Bed and Other Stories by Ian Hamilton Finlay, illustrated by Zeljko.

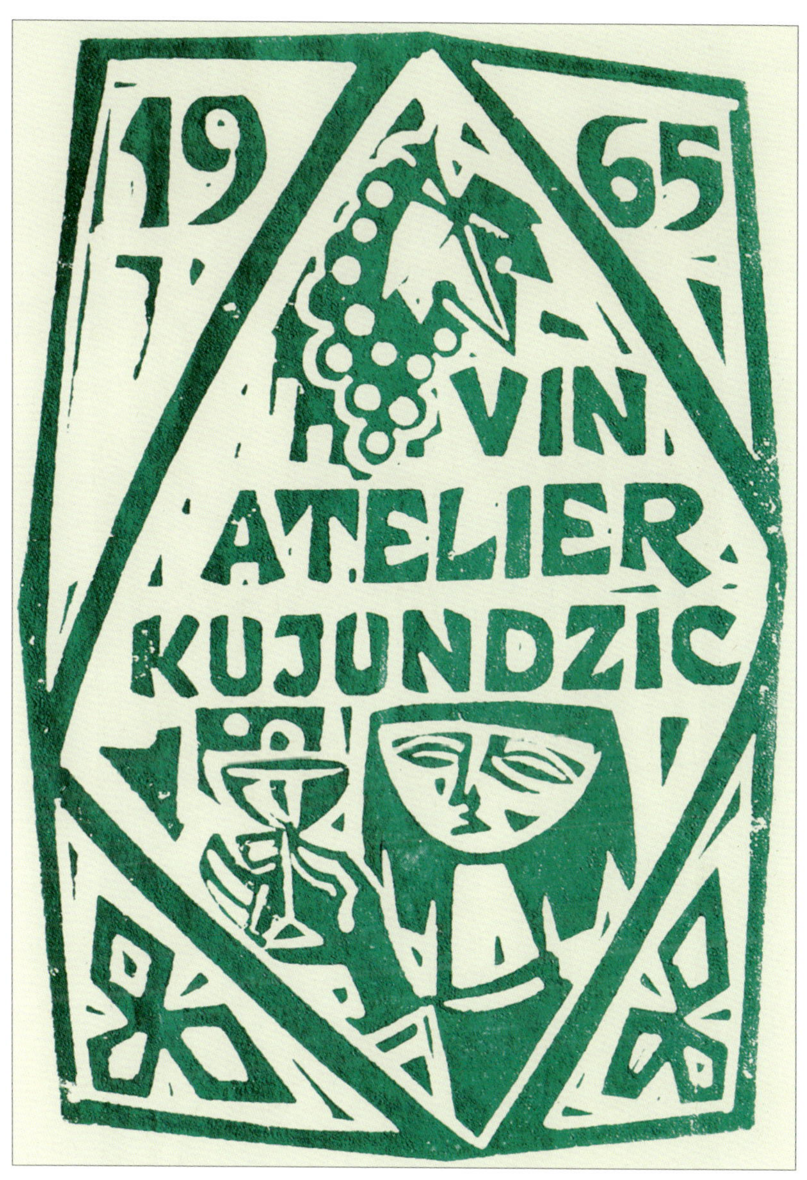

Cheers! Our homemade wine label.

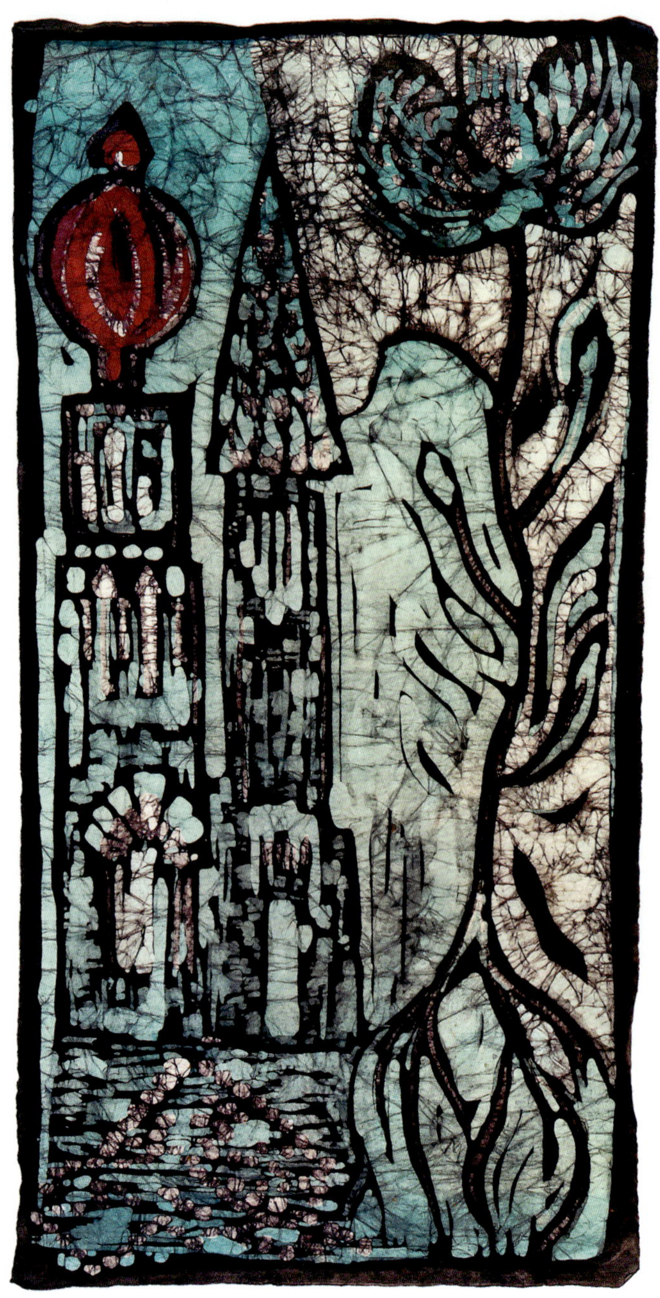

One of my batiks, Vaki dyes on cotton, 1967.

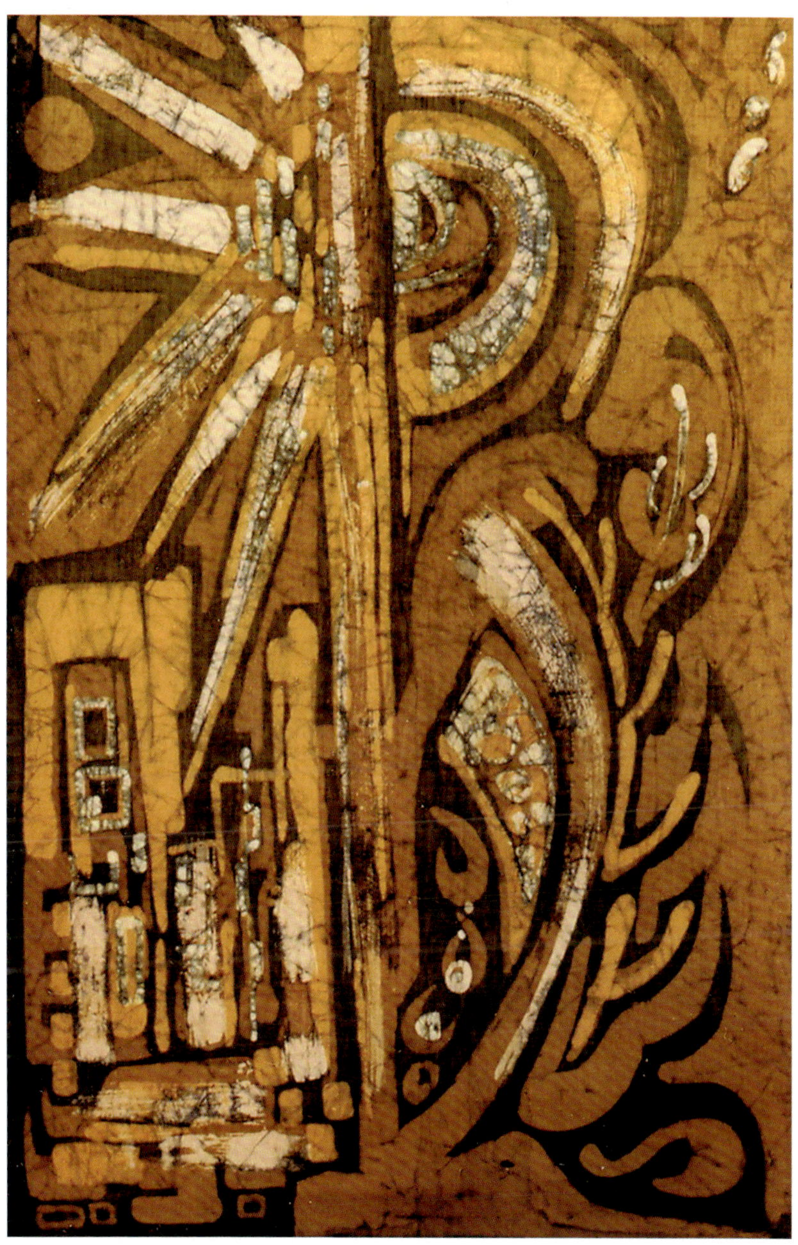

Another one of my batiks, Vaki dyes on cotton, 1972.

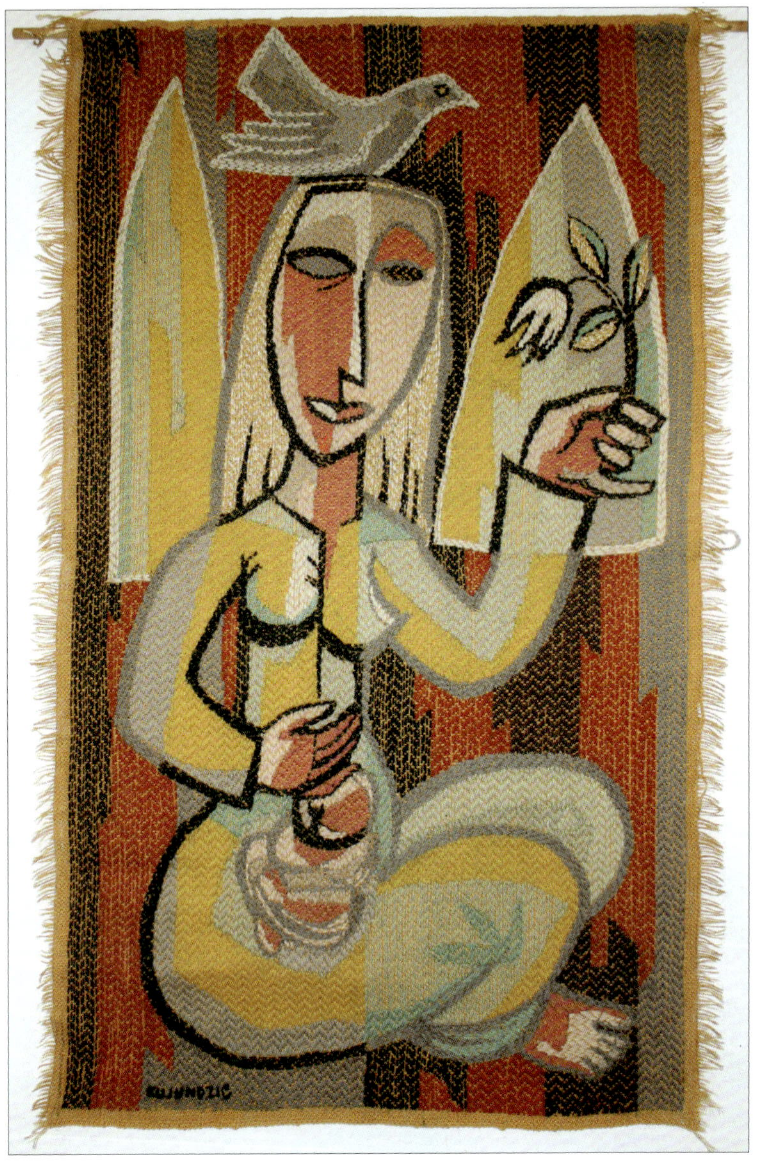

Nativity (1966), a tapestry I stitched by hand.

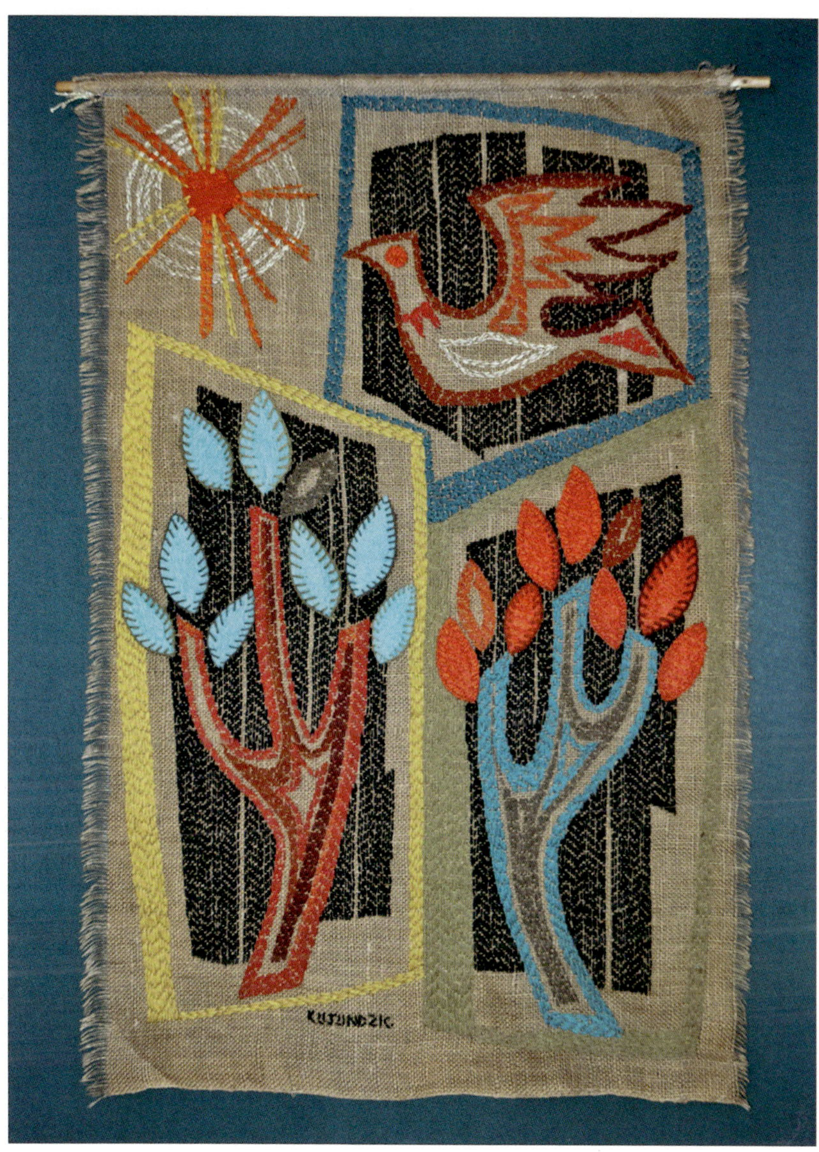

Joyful (1968), another one of my hand-stitched tapestries.

SUMMERLAND

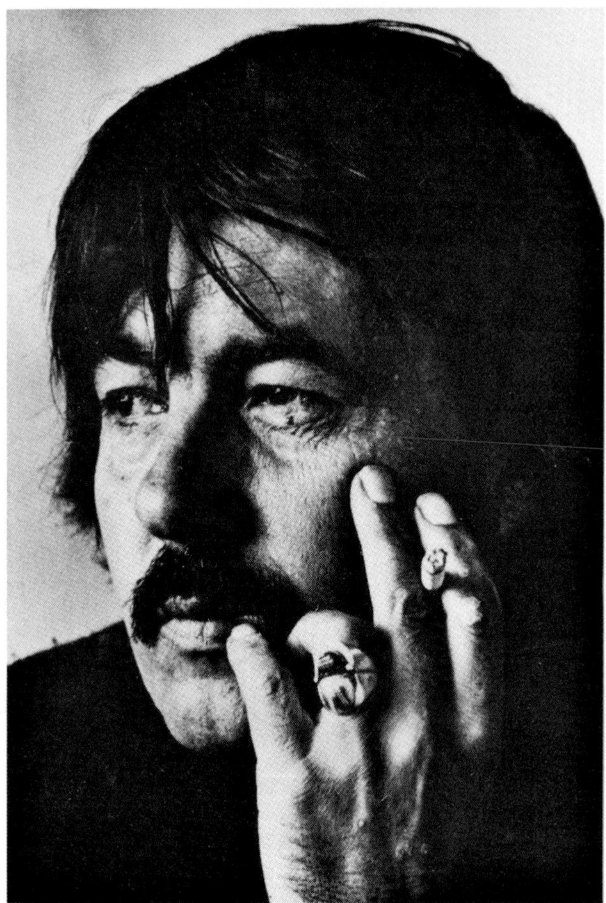

George Ryga

Edited by Ann Kujundzic

I edited George Ryga's ***Summerland***, published by Talonbooks in 1992, five years after George's death.

The Rygas

We first met Norma and George Ryga in 1964 when they came to visit our Art Centre in Kelowna. They, too, had only recently arrived in the Okanagan; the small community of Summerland appealed to them as an alternative to an increasingly costly life in Edmonton. Older properties were readily available for a reasonable price and gave them the prospect of growing their own food. Norma and I had a lot in common. We each had several children. Both of our husbands were of Eastern European descent. George had Ukrainian parents who had settled in Athabasca, while Zeljko was of Yugoslav-Turkish origin. Both of our husbands were artists: George a writer and Zeljko a visual artist. Norma was of Scottish descent and had grown up in Nova Scotia; I grew up in Scotland. Struggling with the philosophy and economics of raising young families on precarious incomes, we had found kindred spirits. However, I also remember Norma saying,

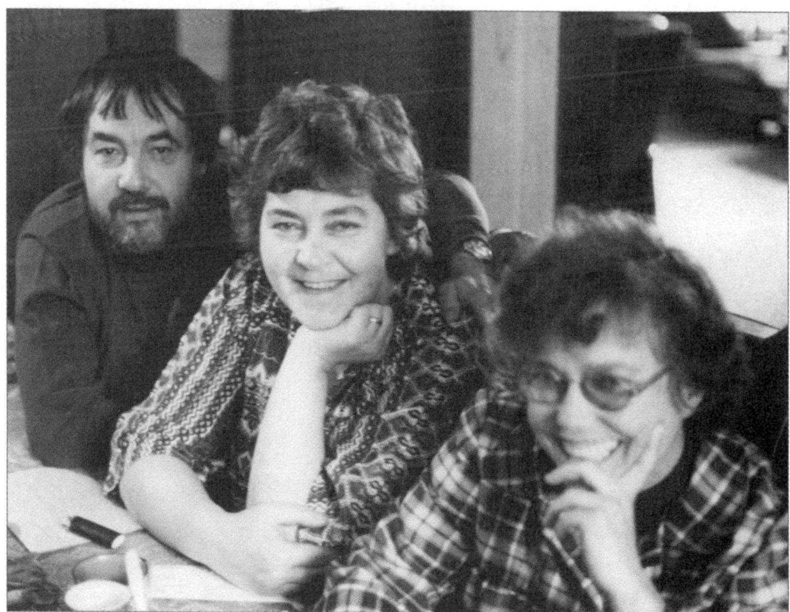

George, Norma and me.

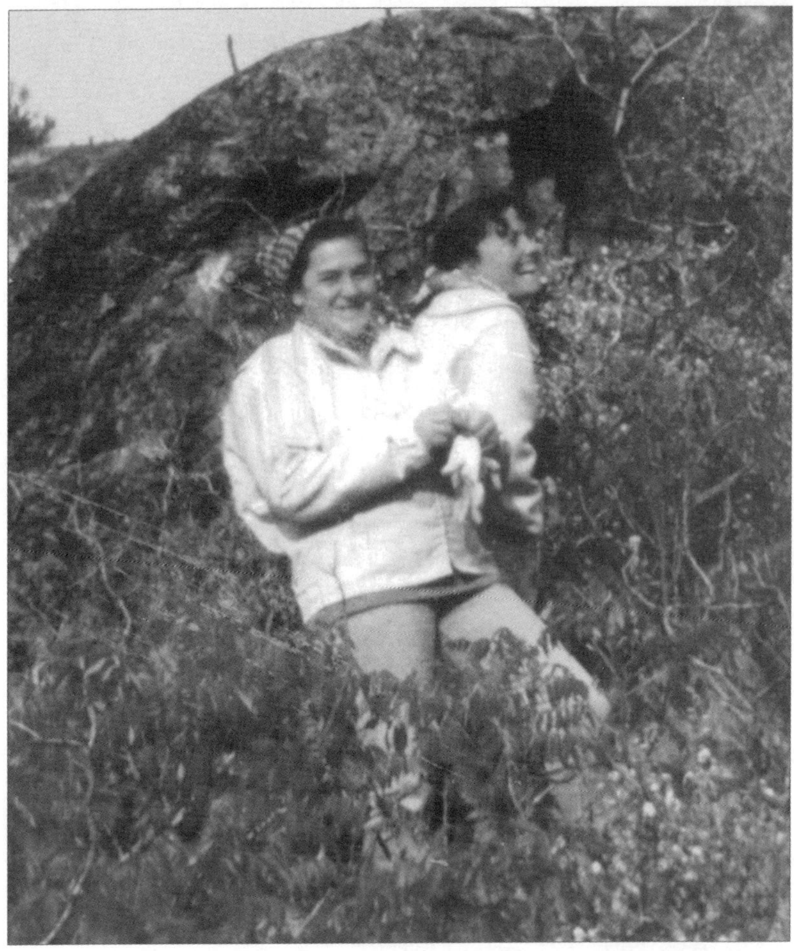

Norma and me.

"We've always thought that artists are privileged people, doing work they choose to do. And for us, being at home with our kids more than compensates for the poverty."

In an early conversation I had with George, I was questioning the relevance of art to people's lives, and I felt confused over my responsibility to "art" through my alliance with Zeljko. George's answer was that a writer or artist's work isn't due greater elevation than the work of any other; that all honest work is equally worthy. He said a good plumber deserves acknowledgement, just as a good writer does—that credit is due to the integrity with which the work is undertaken.

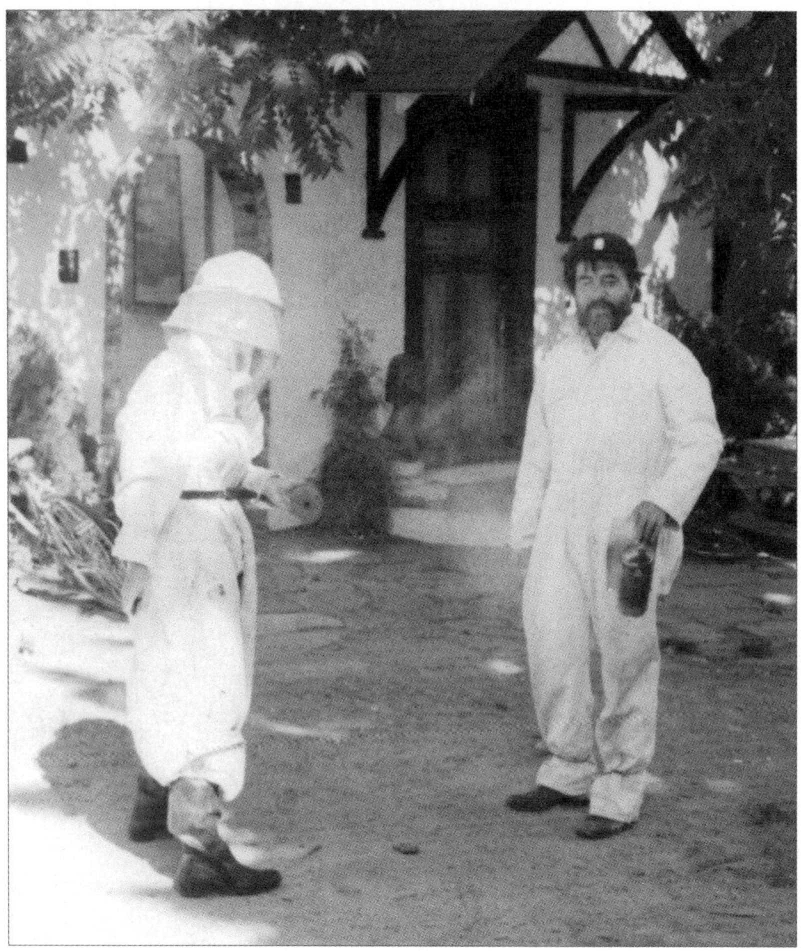

George and me in our beekeeping suits.

That remark about valuing honest work is something I notice we lack in our present society, when work is often given a somewhat demeaning role. We tend to value the latest gadget, machine or technological advance more than the physical work of the farmer, the shoe repairer or the hospital cleaner. Finding the quickest method of doing things has taken over the handmade skills we were once proud of.

Norma and I played very different roles in our relationships with our spouses; both of us were supportive, but in very different ways. Norma was an obsessive reader of both political and literary magazines and books who would pass on distilled versions of all this material to

George. I would spend hours at my typewriter, writing press notices, letters and manifestos, with editing as needed, to keep Zeljko's work "in view."

George's comment, though, has often made me wonder how he would have expressed himself if he hadn't decided to write. He said more than once that it was the partial loss of his right hand, in a work accident in his teens, that had catapulted him into writing as a livelihood. Norma, who had a particular ability to create stories out of the most ordinary events, persistently egged him on, because she, too, had the soul of a storyteller.

His disfigurement didn't stop George from building. The swimming pool they inherited with the house they'd bought in Summerland turned out to have a leak. He transformed it into a place for hootenannies, a space for extra friends and guests, a workshop for three potters with a kiln, and eventually a complete "casita." He ignored many regulations. The anarchist in him won out, and what he did with plumbing and wiring was remarkable. When I said I wanted to build a dining table that could easily be dismantled for moving around (I'd drawn up what I wanted), George immediately said he'd show me how to build it, using his tools. It turned out well and was a great project!

The Rygas brought and sent many of their friends to our Art Centre over the years. Many collaborative meetings were also held there, some for the Okanagan Five, a group of artists, painters, potters and sculptors, with George as their writer. They organized festivals, as well as many evening readings. I remember on one occasion Patrick Lane arrived with his young wife and three small children, and I fed them fish soup, a standby in our home. Zeljko used to catch carp in Okanagan Lake. It was a delicacy in Eastern Europe, though I soon found it wasn't considered that here! Norma knew that it was just fine to send people on to us; they could be fed at our house just as easily as at theirs. I always had homemade bread and soup; they always had a bottomless coffee pot. The Ryga house rang with music; ours displayed interesting artwork.

Right from the beginning, the Rygas' home in Summerland became a haven for artists, musicians, young people and their friends and, later on, media people, aspiring writers and political refugees. Their door was always open. Their kitchen table welcomed an endless stream of callers, and they always found sleeping space. In those first years George took on a contract with the CBC to provide scripts for television dramas. These provided his basic income. However, the contract required that he provide three scheduled drafts for each drama, and as a consistent two-draft writer he found this tedious. I was there one time when, with a production deadline to meet and with the third and final script overdue, a neighbouring farmer called George for help with the apple harvest. George didn't hesitate; he dropped his writing and hurried out the door, saying, "The apples won't wait!"

Their home became a haven for me on many occasions, and Norma became my closest friend. I loved her fearless challenging of situations, whether it was around health conditions, such as her diminishing eyesight, or making her famous war cake or ice-cream meringue without having a recipe or the necessary basic ingredients. She would just say, "It will work," and barrel on ahead, throwing ingredients in a bowl. This was combined with a remarkable empathy. "I just have to send Beth something at Christmas. She needs it," she would say while wrapping up a piece of pottery for the mail. This consideration for the emotional needs of a mutual friend who had worked with her in the health lab in Edmonton showed a discernment I came to appreciate many years later.

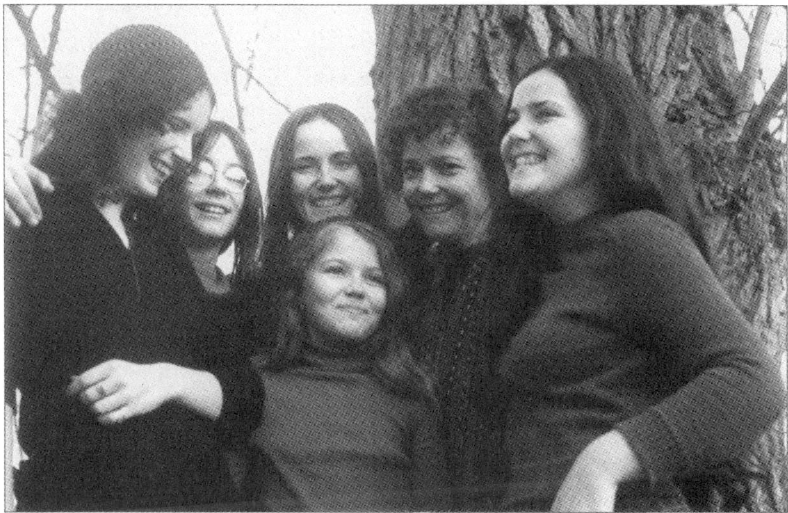

At the Ryga house while they were in Mexico: Judy, Andy, Kate, me and Claire, with Natanis in front.

In the meantime some of George's frustration with what he considered the arbitrary rigours of contract writing spurred him to explore the field of stage work. In 1967 the first production of *The Ecstasy of Rita Joe* at the Vancouver Playhouse catapulted him to national attention. *Grass and Wild Strawberries* followed the next year.

His spectacular public acclaim affected their household very little. George spent hours fixing and extending the house, landscaping the garden and planting new, exotic greenery. Building a goat house was one of his projects at the time; goats would provide milk and he could make cheese. But the goats inevitably became more trouble than he'd expected. They'd get loose, eat everything and climb up onto the steepest part of the house. As his son, Campbell, later wrote to me, "If you don't have enough problems, buy a goat."

Over those years Norma and I took many road trips together, and that was one area where I held my own. I was a fearless driver and never hesitated to take roads that were off the beaten track. In fact I loved them and would choose them unless Norma downright refused. We agreed to differ on that; sometimes I won, sometimes I lost. On one occasion I had to turn back quite some distance on our way home from Vancouver. We were on a dirt and gravel road, which I thought would be much more interesting than the highway, but I had to accept that Norma's apprehension was very serious. She feared we might not make it home by nightfall and was quite panicked. In hindsight, and because I too now deal with limited vision, I realize that her fear may well have been on account of her diminishing vision, which I tended to ignore, just as she mostly did. Another issue was that when we took the Ryga car, Norma had a habit of never filling it more than half full of gas. Her reasoning was that the weight of a full tank used up more gas. Thrifty as I was, as a Scot, I couldn't go that far. But we had great trips together.

We also found a way of "sharing" teenagers, although I suspect I got the better deal. When Claire was adamant that she did not want to join the family trip to San Miguel de Allende, Norma offered to take her into their home. Upon our return to Kelowna, we learned that Norma was having a hard time with her eldest daughter, Leslie, so I suggested that she could live with us for the balance of the school year. So Leslie joined our home, and Claire remained at theirs.

It worked well for all of us: the kids were delighted and so were we. I have recommended this solution to many other parents since then. Claire was so happy at the Rygas', that Judy, the next in line, also wanted this opportunity. Unfortunately there wasn't a trade available, as both the Ryga boys were totally occupied with excellent music programs in their Summerland school. Still, Norma and George happily accepted Judy into their midst, and later it was to be my youngest, Natanis, who joined them for a while.

One friend described the Ryga house as a social work station where people were rescued and given attention and validation before they moved on. Part of the reality of their household was that George was always there for the many people who relied on him to write letters of reference or introduction, to read over a manuscript, to fix a vehicle or give a driving lesson, to pick someone up at a bus depot or airport, or to run to the store to pick up groceries. These were the numerous demands he quietly absorbed in a day's schedule, refusing no one. I marvel at the numbers fed at their supper table. Suppertime became a ritual in their household. It was always preceded by the sharing of a pot of coffee, and the table would be set so as to expand easily for unexpected guests. Yet they never considered going on welfare in some of the lean years they faced.

The Playhouse Theatre commissioned George again, a third play, for their 1970–71 season. The script he produced for them was *Captives of the Faceless Drummer*. He described it as a morality play based on the then-current October Crisis, when political kidnappings in Quebec resulted in the War Measures Act and jails in Quebec were crowded with activists and cultural personalities. The Playhouse Theatre Board was upset by the politics of the script and refused to produce it. Within a few short years George's reputation had shifted from the famous to the infamous. When he hit the front page of the *Weekly Sun Review*, Norma remembers him saying, "It's something to walk along a street on a rainy day in Vancouver and see your face lying on the sidewalk, and people stepping on it."

In the meantime Norma's eyes continued to deteriorate. She was eventually diagnosed with Behcet's syndrome, a rare autoimmune and systemic disease that can affect the eyes. They travelled to Europe in the hope of finding a cure, while I lived in their home to look after their children, as well as my own, which I greatly enjoyed. Visitors still came; it was not a house that could be closed! I was working in Penticton at that time on a project called Imagine Penticton, and this made my job more accessible.

Despite not finding the cure they hoped for, Norma didn't give up. Work was coming in fast for George. They took a family trip to Mexico, where they rented a little adobe house in San Antonio, a community of farming people, and soon acquired six chickens and a cat. Norma wrote me frequently from there, although her handwriting was becoming harder to decipher: "Time is taking on a new dimension. George's *Paracelsus* is a beauty—just pouring out. It seems to come very smoothly—probably because he's so relaxed…I think he'll have very little to rewrite. He figures he'll have another two plays done by the end of March." They returned to Summerland some six months later.

Shortly after this I sold my house in Kelowna and was now living mostly in Vancouver. Work requirements had taken their toll. I missed Norma and George greatly. I missed their hootenannies, the discussions around their table, their company, and I had to rely more on their visits to Vancouver. However, for several months, I worked as George's assistant when he took on the job of setting up Arts Access, a project initiated during the NDP government's brief three years in power in the seventies. He rented office space for this from Talonbooks, and he and Norma came to live for some time in Burnaby. We enjoyed what the city had to offer. Norma and I explored the jazz scene together. She took ceramics classes and produced some remarkable stoneware sculptures, while I attended Women's Studies programs at UBC and began creating large batik hangings. We lived full and interesting lives and shared many theatre, music and film events.

Throughout the seventies Norma's eyes deteriorated further, until she lost her sight altogether. George accompanied her on several trips to see specialists and to get treatment in the United States, but there were no effective answers forthcoming. Her illness was costing them money. Norma underwent further surgery at UBC and for a brief time regained vision. The euphoria was short-lived; within a few weeks she returned to living in total darkness. After this she and

George again spent some months in Vancouver, with the purpose of enabling her to access skills through CNIB services. George took a break from writing so as to take on the role of caregiver. I remember Norma's frustration with using a white stick. She'd say, "Just give me your arm. I don't like this thing!"

I found myself travelling up to Summerland whenever I could. Norma enjoyed swimming—it was her favourite way of getting exercise, so she and I would always spend time in the pool. She was often critical of the music they played. She found ways of putting on a brave face, and in retrospect I marvel at her amazing spirit. We later began communicating by tape and sent each other music, stories of what was happening with our kids and anything of interest that we'd come across. Norma had become a fervent radio user and found some amazing pieces that she would then relate to me. I still think of those tapes; nothing as good has ever replaced them. "Progress" has replaced them with a digital format that lacks the human element. I still have some of those lovely tapes that Norma made.

George took on a teaching assignment at the University of Ottawa in the early eighties. He thought that by living in the central hub of Canadian political life he could be more effective in presenting policy changes on issues of Canadian publishing, copyright law and other matters he saw as crucial to the survival of writers in this country. From his home out west he had not received answers, or even attention, to his written appeals. However, he was shaken to find that when he knocked on doors in Ottawa, the doors simply wouldn't open. Being there in person didn't get him any better a response than his letters had.

Ill health began to plague George. He had always taken bouts of ill health in his stride, with a conviction that his strong constitution would surmount any temporary inconvenience. That's how he always treated his own symptoms, as inconveniences. There was simply no room for them to get in the way of his writing and other commitments. Before I left for a trip to Australia and New Zealand to visit my sister, I went up to Summerland to see them both. George had tried every possible alternative cure for the cancer that had taken hold, but none were working. I remember him saying to me, "It's not so bad," but also remarking, when I put my hand on his shoulder, "That feels like a two-by-four." He made a particular point of being available to his friends and family, many of whom he recognized to have a fear of cancer.

I had just arrived in New Zealand when Claire sent me news of George's death. How strange that, on the same day, I was attending a ceremony prior to the scuttling of the *Rainbow Warrior* after the French had bombed it, with local Maoris exorcising bad spirits, church dignitaries digging up biblical passages to deify it, and the New Zealand minister of tourism giving a speech to justify its fitting end as a fish sanctuary. This all happened in a tiny fishing village on the north island of New Zealand, at 5:30 a.m., before the replacement Greenpeace vessel towed the *Rainbow Warrior* outside the harbour to its watery grave, with a flotilla of assorted boats following it. George would have appreciated hearing about this.

I've been unable to part with the large collection of letters I have from Norma from 1966 to 1979, despite having moved many times since then and always attempting to downsize. It has given me joy as well as sadness to read them and remind myself of the journeys we each took. We both had rich lives, and it's been hard, as well as rewarding, to revisit those. I've been fortunate to extend my life so much longer than Norma's, and certainly much longer than George's. I wish I had understood and enquired about the various medications Norma was taking for both pain and vision problems for those many years, for they were affecting not only her memory, but also her moods. As I was living and working in Vancouver, it was not easy to visit her often, and I was upset by her increasing anger and insistent denial of facts, such as telling me she'd never ever drunk coffee, only tea, and that George used a computer when in fact he'd actually never even owned one.

I heard later that she'd apparently suffered a series of mini-strokes. She lost her ability to read Braille. Norma was already leaving me and I didn't recognize it. Geographic distance was one factor, but the other was memory distance. I was upset, and I didn't know how to handle this "different" Norma. I've never been particularly good at handling anger. Some years later, when I heard she was seriously ill, I remember talking to her son, Campbell, and telling him I wanted to see her. His comment was, "Don't go; it will be upsetting for you, and Mum isn't remembering people." But I should have gone. There is some irony in that it was her daughter Leslie, the one who gave her a hard time as a teenager, who not only cared for her (always making sure to have her favourite beer available), but also shared her home with her in those last months in Armstrong.

Here is part of an obituary, written for Norma's wake by Patrick Lane, which honours her well:

Above your house the scree
fell from the mountain and one night George
and I climbed it and came back down to your
smile, the food warm on the table. You
lifted me out of the dark at the end of a life
and gave me a place to hide for long enough
to remember who I was. So long ago.
your eyes were blind, but you still
could smile, George fierce in his love
for you. That's what I remember most,
his love, yours, the boys pushing at being men,
the girls gone off to be women.
I wonder sometimes at the truth in me.
I know you and George helped put it there…

I was a managing director for George Ryga & Associates for many years after George's death, and I edited *Summerland*, a collection of George's previously unpublished writings, which was published by Talonbooks in 1992. Norma and George played an incredibly important role in my life and I owe them both a huge debt of gratitude.

MILLIE

During the early years of knowing Norma and George, when I was planning to travel back home to the UK with my teenaged daughter Claire, Norma gave me her sister Millie's phone number in London. Millie was living there so her three children could continue schooling while her geologist husband worked in the Middle East.

Upon our arrival in London, we found a cheap, scruffy room in the Kings Cross area, as we would be leaving from there to travel up to Scotland. We dragged our bags up the three flights of stairs, then went out in search of a telephone booth to call Millie. She asked where we were, then immediately said, "Ray's at home for a few days. He'll be happy to pick you up and bring you over for supper. I'd love to meet you both. Just stay where you are; he'll find you."

Within an hour there was a knock on our door. Ray took one look at our room and said, "Pack your bags and come with me. You're staying with us." I looked at him, a bit shocked, and said, "But we've already paid for three nights." He looked at me and said, in a deliberate sort of way, "Wasn't that punishment enough?"

Within a few months of that visit, Ray died suddenly. I visited Millie in Montreal when she moved back to Canada; I was going to massage college in Toronto at the time. We reconnected and in the early eighties we spent four months together travelling through Europe, the UK and Ireland. We started with three weeks in Paris, where we each took a crash course in French at the Sorbonne. We stayed with my friend Sonia, whom I had met at a contemporary dance class in Vancouver in the late seventies, and with whom I had immediately bonded. Sonia worked with immigrant women in Paris, many of them from Algeria. We have visited many times since then, and she feels like family.

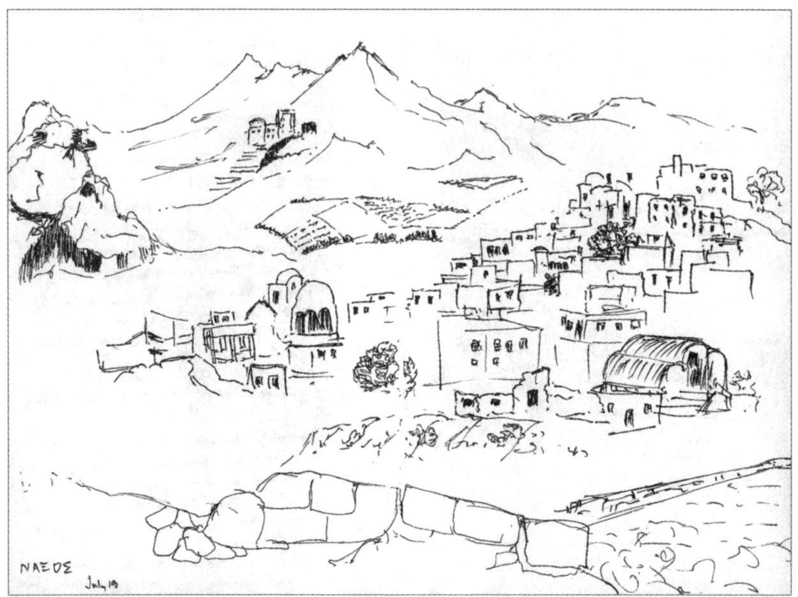

One of my sketches on the Greek island of Naxos.

After Paris we spent a few days at Antibes in the South of France, lolling on the newly tolerated topless beaches before moving on to Italy. We were travelling on the cheap, looking for youth hostels wherever we went. No doubt this caused some surprise—two women in their late middle age travelling as students. In Greece we discovered that knowledge of German would have been a lot more useful than the French we had spruced up on. We were both equally frustrated at not being able to figure out what all the graffiti was telling us; political issues were besieging the country, and we both wanted to know what was going on.

From the island of Samos we took a small boat to get to Kusadasi on the Turkish coast. Millie often reminds me of our stopover in the old capital of Bursa, where we heard laughter coming from a public spa on the way to our hostel. We peeked in and saw women of all ages, shapes and sizes filling the place, with welcoming arms encouraging us to join them; lack of language just wasn't a problem. We were obviously foreigners, and thus to be feted—no swimsuit required! At the amphitheatre in Ephesus we checked out the acoustics; it seated an audience of twenty-five thousand without amplification.

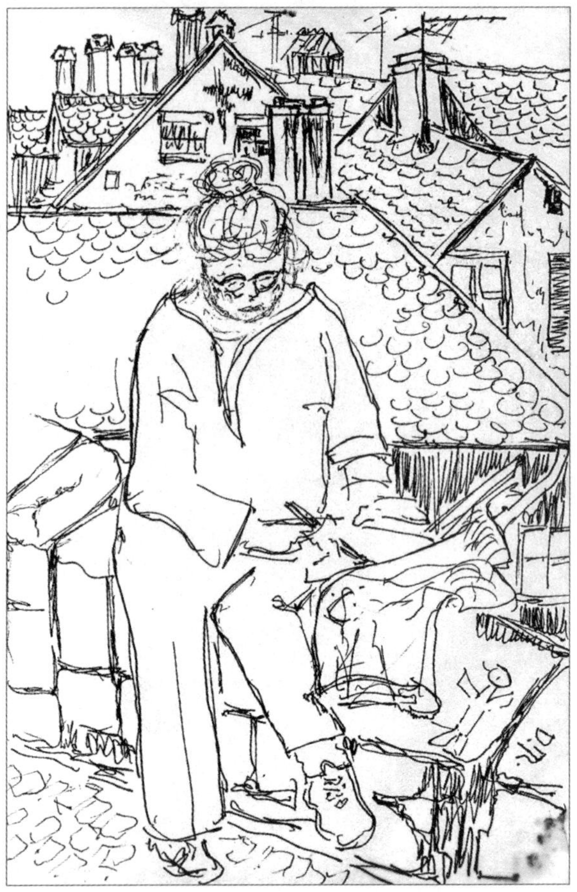

One of my sketches of Millie.

Later on during this trip, she met all three of my brothers. One was a Scottish Nationalist, another was seeking our father's homeland in Wales, and the third was living and working in England. I noticed she was much more perceptive of their emotional disturbances than I had ever been. Only later did I fully recognize that all three suffered from serious manic depression.

Our journeying together gave us shared experiences, as well as insights, and cemented a friendship that has endured and grown with the years. Millie is now in her ninety-fifth year and lives in Qualicum with her partner, Jim.

NEW DIRECTIONS

Ambivalent in Pennsylvania

we have shared much
you and I
laughter, tears
and new beginnings

we have done much
you and I
crossed many bridges
travelled many miles
and laid our heads in strange places

we have talked much
you and I
in bitterness and anguish
and then sweet silence
more eloquent
than all our words

we have been builders too
you and I
of earthy homes
and castles in the air
seen some stand, others fall—
too delicate
for human feet to trample through

we have seen much
we have been spared much
you and I
reached depths and heights
stood still, held fast
and left our mark
–1968

Fall came quickly that year. We had just moved into our new home, and Zeljko was preparing to start work in Pennsylvania. He was just assuming that we would all travel there, rent a place in Uniontown and live with him in his new position. I kept saying, "No! I don't want to go there; I want to stay in Canada." Until the last possible minute he kept thinking I'd change my mind; it was not an easy time. However, he packed up our car and took off. He phoned me two days later from the Midwest to ask if I had changed my mind. I hadn't. What became even more troubling, though, was that I found myself pregnant again a few weeks later.

I went to my doctor and pleaded with him to find a way of giving me a legal abortion. No hope for that, he said; the only way was if a psychiatrist could find grounds. As I had previously seen our local psychiatrist when I was feeling extremely depressed about my inability to communicate my needs to Zeljko, I hoped he would be helpful. However, he told me that the only way he could authorize an abortion would be by stating that I was incapable of raising another child, and he would also need to have my husband's permission. I felt stuck; another child was not going to solve anything. But I didn't want to have to ask Zeljko for his permission—how absurd. In the meantime, Zeljko was writing from Uniontown, telling us that he wasn't well; he had some stomach disorder that appeared to be ulcerous and was causing him grief. I sent him a package of supplements recommended by Adelle Davis, a health guru of the day, and advised him on diet.

A few weeks later he was taken into the hospital and it became clear that I needed to see him, find out what was happening and also get his written permission for an abortion. I don't remember which of my children was looking after the others in my absence, but it must have been Kate again. And so I flew to Uniontown. When I arrived, Zeljko was still in the hospital, with an unclear diagnosis. Relieved to see me, he told me he'd found an apartment that was big enough for all of us—it was ready and waiting for us to move in. Yes, he would give me written permission for Dr. McNair to proceed with an abortion. I should go back, get the abortion and join him with the children in time for Christmas. He convinced me that I should at least try the rest of the year at the Fayette Campus before condemning it. But his immediate recovery after my arrival had given me concern; was it basically a psychosomatic illness he had been suffering from?

I returned home, but I was well into the fourth month before I finally got into the hospital, and I became very ill after the operation. I was told I had an internal infection; there was a large abdominal incision and a lumpy, messy scar. One of the nurses looked at my chart and said, "Well, you've been through major surgery. You had a Caesarean, a tubal ligation and your appendix was removed. The doctor said he might as well take your appendix out; he was in there anyway." No doubt he got a substantial fee for all those services.

I was much troubled by Zeljko's expectation of my joining him, but I felt I had to honour it. So I prepared for this. Claire decided she'd rather stay in Canada and was welcomed back at the Rygas' home. Judy said she definitely didn't want to come, and the two youngest didn't seem concerned. Andy had already experienced time off school without any apparent difficulty, and the youngest, Natanis, had only just started school in September. So off we went.

Letter to Norma, March 1969:
I've been told that every married person ought to see *Faces*, so I'm curious. We're poorly off for films here, so we only see things if we cadge a ride to Pittsburgh with someone. Went there for some art shows last week. A very bad major exhibition on environmental art, but an excellent craft show, and a very good painter. One of the

first painters I've seen for many years that really excited me. So we were lucky.

It's really been interesting meeting people around here. We've had some very funny evenings, with Yugoslav-Americans one night, with Catholic-Italians another, and sometimes even with American-Americans. How this country ever became one is surely one of the most incredible happenings. I have never come across so many diametrically opposed viewpoints, attitudes and behaviour, and I just can't sort it all out. At a moment of extreme confusion the other evening I found myself saying to someone, "Do I really hear what you are saying?" and of course he thought I was drunk. I had heard, but I didn't believe I could have heard another "unprejudiced" statement about "niggers." But a few things are emerging slowly from the chaos. Without exception I've found that the rooted American is liberally minded and genuinely concerned about his country, whether it's the race problem or pollution or soil conservation. The second- and third-generation American, usually of European origin, is to be feared. I suppose this is the person who has a sentimental attachment to the old country—based on exactly nothing now—and who has no real concern for the new, other than what can be got out of it. The most recent immigrants, on the other hand, seem to have some fire still. But that middle lot is certainly the biggest in number, and the wealthiest, so it has the most to lose, I suppose. It's unfair to categorize, but the categories are very clear and people move in very defined circles, so it's hard to avoid.

By the way, I've found someone with a sense of humour, the Lebanese girl who taught the English course I took. I can enjoy her company now that the course is over. She's going to spend the summer touring Britain, so she'll be able to visit my family and tell me about them, which is great. I found we could laugh about the same things.

It's a bit shocking to realize how little things have changed in regard to race relations, and sad that I am no longer as surprised as I was back then.

During that first visit one of the staff at the campus made a point of seeking me out. He asked me if I'd give a talk to some of his students, and I asked him what he was looking for. He looked at me and said, "You are a 'real' person." This teacher was a black man, quite intense. I was a bit puzzled, but his word "real" stuck with me. He said I could talk about anything I wanted to, perhaps about Canada and about my own experiences as an immigrant there, which I did, without writing a speech. He thanked me and said he didn't know many "real" people. I wish I had asked him what "unreal" people were like; it might have been enlightening.

I registered for four classes at the campus and found it good to have to attend classes regularly and pay attention to assignments. I preferred this to meeting up with other campus wives who had lives filled largely with social calendars. We returned to Kelowna in June, and I began enjoying our new home there.

LETTER TO MY BROTHER TREVOR, SEPTEMBER 1969:
Yes, we're back on the shift system again: I'm staying here in Kelowna for a while with the kids and will probably join Zeljko again after Christmas with Andy and Natanis. It's a compromise at best—not very easy to manage, but somehow we do! I was tempted to return and get further along with my university course—but golly, it would take four years to get a degree, and I don't see that we would stay that long in Uniontown. Two years isn't going to do anything in the way of giving me qualifications, unfortunately. I started work as a secretary to one of the managers at BC Fruits, a large company in Kelowna. The work is dull so far, but they say it gets hectic in the busy season that is now only a week away. Actually I enjoy working; it's better to be out of the house, as I'm not the kind of housekeeper who enjoys dusting or cleaning.

Anyhow, it gives me some small satisfaction to be family supporter for a while. Reckon I can keep the home going, modestly, on what I earn. As long as all the girls don't need glasses this year or something. It will give Zeljko a chance to catch up on some of his debts (he forgot to pay income tax last year, so has a whole year to catch up on, and they've decided to give us no allowance for all our travelling, which is ghastly—we spent a fortune on air fares). Our one extravagance this year was a 1966 VW Bus—greatly needed, as we are always bulging at the seams when we move. I travelled with seventeen pieces of baggage on my way back here in June. As we take a fair amount of household stuff when we travel, it is quite a problem. Z's fixed a double bed in the bus, so that will be quite a help; we can pile stuff under it and on it.

We took Claire and Kate for a week's holiday down the Oregon coast during the summer and on to San Francisco for a couple of days. One of the reasons we wanted to take Kate was because we felt she really needed a break badly. San Francisco was pretty lively while we were there, although we didn't go through the trouble spots in Berkeley. I guess it's the only place on this continent that has really accepted the hippies. Whether they've actually accepted them or not is another matter; they are certainly there in droves. Hairstyles and clothes are so wild that Zeljko actually looked a square. Actually, it's really a very exciting place to go to. I like it much the best of any place I know in North America—cities, that is. If you saw *Bullitt*, then you would see something of the city, for it was shot in San Francisco, even though it didn't show the spots that I like best. It's built on several hills, making driving quite an experience.

As always, when we go there, our car took exception to the undue stress—this time the accelerator kept getting unhinged from its pedal, so I spent a large part of my time on the car floor, holding it in position while Zeljko drove! But a sad part of things there is the bad feeling that keeps increasing: tension between blacks and whites, tension between students and police, tension between hippies and squares. It's bound to burst out in more incidents like the Berkeley Park, which was a terrible thing. California has a tough administration—Reagan as governor is a disaster. Young people are in revolt. And the bloody administrations give them every good reason to revolt, almost as if they wanted confrontation. Have been reading Eldridge Cleaver's latest writings from Algiers, which makes pretty grim reading. And he is moderate—moderate on the black/white issue. He is sound, too. The black/white problem is really only an outcome of all the others: of the inequality of the economic system, of the crippling type of education (mentally restrictive), of the narrowness of vision that the system imposes on youth. Everything geared to money, acquisition and whatever power (or emptiness) these breed.

And of all sad things, Canada is leaning the same way. We just had an election in BC—very disillusioning. Our same wretched, highly corrupt government has been returned. They really killed the NDP socialist party by a fear campaign. So we can continue on the great golden wing of prosperity, soaring on US investments—immediate dollars in trade for future resources. So our water power is sold down the river, our forests cut and shipped across the border, our minerals and raw ore ferried over to Japan. And our farmland is bit by bit being covered with concrete foundations, and the air smells of industrial waste. But this way people can have their second or third car, a private swimming pool and recreation rooms. They'll need those private swimming pools, because the lake is contaminated, and they'll need those indoor recreation rooms since the air is polluted. Oh, it's crazy. And where is there left to go?

I've come to love Canada. But it seems impossible to escape the trends. Somehow one must come to terms with it and keep pressuring or hoping for some kind of enlightened public attitude. But will they have ruined this magnificent country before they decide to call a halt...Surely they must see what has happened to those industrial parts of the States. It's ironic: Pennsylvania now has government grants for training experts in pollution control and they are busy reclaiming all the land they ruined early this century. We are now busy ruining ours here...

We're fighting again right now to keep farm acreage in the land reserve, something the NDP brought in during their short term of office in the seventies. And as for our resources, we're busy selling them off with enticements of up to twenty-five years of tax-free investment to the exploiters.

In March 1970 I was enticed back to Uniontown by the offer of a full-time job to promote and administer the arts festival that Zeljko was organizing for May. Andy and Natanis came with me again; they were getting quite used to this situation.

Return to Uniontown

It surprises me that I could find any humour in writing letters while I was working for the arts festival, but I suspect it was what kept me going. It took a lot of work to get it organized.

Letter to Norma, April 1970:
I finally feel relocated—after a week of being non-existent, so to speak. It doesn't really get better each time. The shock is still as bad; in fact, it seems worse, which is rather depressing, and this is all to do with being an alien (in case you wondered what it was all about). But I feel very much myself again after having consumed a more than fair amount of wine and also after having had a first-class outraged discussion about the terribleness of the American scene. I've been offered a permanent soapbox and told that I ought to remain here, if for no other reason than to put things right (which really got my latent missionary zeal going). But in fact I ended up wishing that I'd kept my mouth shut, except that I feel a whole lot better and I wouldn't want to change that right now.

I feel badly that I've been given such a good welcome and didn't expect it. I really wanted to remain an outsider and maybe I'm not going to be able to stay on the outside. And that's where the conflict comes in, I guess. For every phony American around, there's another genuinely constructive one. No, the proportions are probably wrong there. Anyhow it makes it hard not to get involved. The incredible thing is that I see so many of both kinds all the time. I can't crawl into a hole somewhere and pick my companions and pretend the rest don't exist. And so I get caught up in crazy arguments like the one about the liberation movement, earlier tonight. I guess it's getting pretty strong here. After all, it must be more than a fad to reach the pages of the *Atlantic*, but boy, it's the women who are really bothered by it! I should have known of course. After all, "Who wants to be liberated?" Who wants to lose a magnificent home and on top of that be expected to think? After all, liberated, their affluent-slave husbands might decide to make a break for it and these decorative dolls might even be left without alimony. And let's face it: life is so much simpler if someone else deals with the problems. Yes, that really was part of our pre-dinner conversation. I kept thinking, I can't be hearing this. However, as I got going on my soapbox it seemed to change, or maybe it was an illusion that it changed, or maybe it was just the wine…

Anyhow, thinking back, today was good in other ways. I went shopping in the east end. It says something, having an east end in a place smaller than Kelowna. I go there when fish comes in fresh from the coast. There's a black family that brings in a van of iced seafood from Baltimore once a week. The wife cleans it all in the store, and they have a beautiful assortment of strange-looking kinds. I usually end up buying the same thing (because all I really know how to cook is fillet), but it's fun to look at it all and think it over, then buy the same anyway. They're an interesting family. I was particularly surprised that they remembered me from last year.

They wanted to know why it had taken me so long to return, and then the next question: how long am I going to stay? It's difficult to answer this so many times a day, especially as I haven't thought up a concise, definitive answer (although I'm working on it). So we ended up in a philosophic discussion, which sounded much better in a fish shop than in someone's plush drawing room. They've got eight kids, this family, and I reckon it takes a lot of fish to clean to educate that many. The kids look a lot more prosperous than their parents, so I suppose they educated them well. As Tracy, their pa, said, "Well, you know how it is, a man and his woman—they can only just make it, and then their kid comes along, and they still make it. And then another kid. They end up with a whole lot, and they still make it. We thought we stopped at two. Well, you know how it is." I told him I knew.

Had a disappointment last week, as I'd planned to go into the Carnegie Institute in Pittsburgh to hear Lawrence Durrell give a poetry reading, but because the weather was incredibly bad—gale-force winds, torrential rains and lightning storms—our car wouldn't hold the road. But we had another good day in Washington (long drive), where we saw an exhibition of Paolo Soleri, the architect we visited in Arizona. An incredible exhibit. He's designing vast Arcologies, which are super-sized cities for overpopulation. By building vertically (sometimes up to a mile high) he reckons that man and nature can both survive. In fact he says this is the only way they'll survive. Given the present population forecasts, he's no doubt right. I'm sending on a box of his poster designs (the form his catalogue took) for you to look at. His language is sort of complex, but I guess it's necessary for the things he's saying, which are also complex technically. In some respects his concepts are quite frightening, but what's most frightening is probably the thought of all those people. His models were magnificent—beautiful pieces of sculpture.

What else—my job? I'm located in the Chamber of Commerce office as a sort of buffer between the Chamber's executive director and a professor of art, both of whom have quite decided ideas about how a festival should be run and both completely unaware that the other guy doesn't know it... Whatever results from this should be interesting. Unfortunately, it's only one of them that has the money. The mayor has already made vocal statements about how it cannot be allowed to become "one of those hippie things." His statement got interesting results: the hippie youth from far and near has been roused by his call.

Now I really have to work. Press releases are my first job and then an appeal for funds. I didn't know I'd be doing the latter; it serves me right for being paid!

Letter to my brother Trevor, May 1970:

It has taken a hell of a lot of work to get this festival going. And it's been nerve-wracking too—the usual negative attitudes to combat: temperamental artists, hardheaded businessmen and a bloody awful newspaper that has sat on all my press releases. The activity is all taking place this weekend: four days of it, with artists demonstrating, concerts, dance ensembles, poetry reading, folk singing, a theatre group and various bits of local talent that we couldn't avoid.

Clouding everything is the turmoil amongst the students—that very bad episode at Kent University last week when four students were shot and numerous others seriously injured when the National Guard let loose. The political scene is very bad. Feelings are strong, and getting stronger. Extreme right-wing elements of reactionary groups are stirring up trouble in opposition to the pacifist element. This particular campus has the right-wing problem; it is only the faculty here that is opposed to the Cambodian entry.

And our own ironic situation—art and politics both become secondary to the social scene of dinner parties, which the elite here excel in. The opulence of some of these beats all description; one could be in Victorian England with the measure of elegance which that age no doubt offered. When the Americans do things well, I challenge anyone to beat them. It's just a pity so few of them do things well. And in our shabby rented apartment, where the four of us are sharing two rooms, my constant anxiety is to be called upon by some of these socialites. Or maybe it wouldn't be a bad idea; it might shame them into seeing that their professors were paid more! Zeljko gets paid less than the minimum rate for skilled labour. Certainly he has many other advantages, such as a very easy teaching schedule. And of course the status, because Penn State is very highly regarded. The only trouble is that we always seem to rub shoulders with the affluent, who seek us out for the status of having an artist at their dinner party!

My own state of mind during this time was in turmoil. I felt completely "wrong" in the States and knew I couldn't live there. I realized that Zeljko had found a place where he had all the facilities he needed and also enough status as well as income to feel secure; it was probably the right place for him to be. Surely it was a time when I could leave him and not feel bad about it. My efforts to talk to him had not worked well. I tried writing to him each time we were parted and had reams of correspondence from him declaring his devotion to me, as well as his critical questioning of my love for him. I hadn't been able to explain that the problem wasn't that I didn't love him, but that I

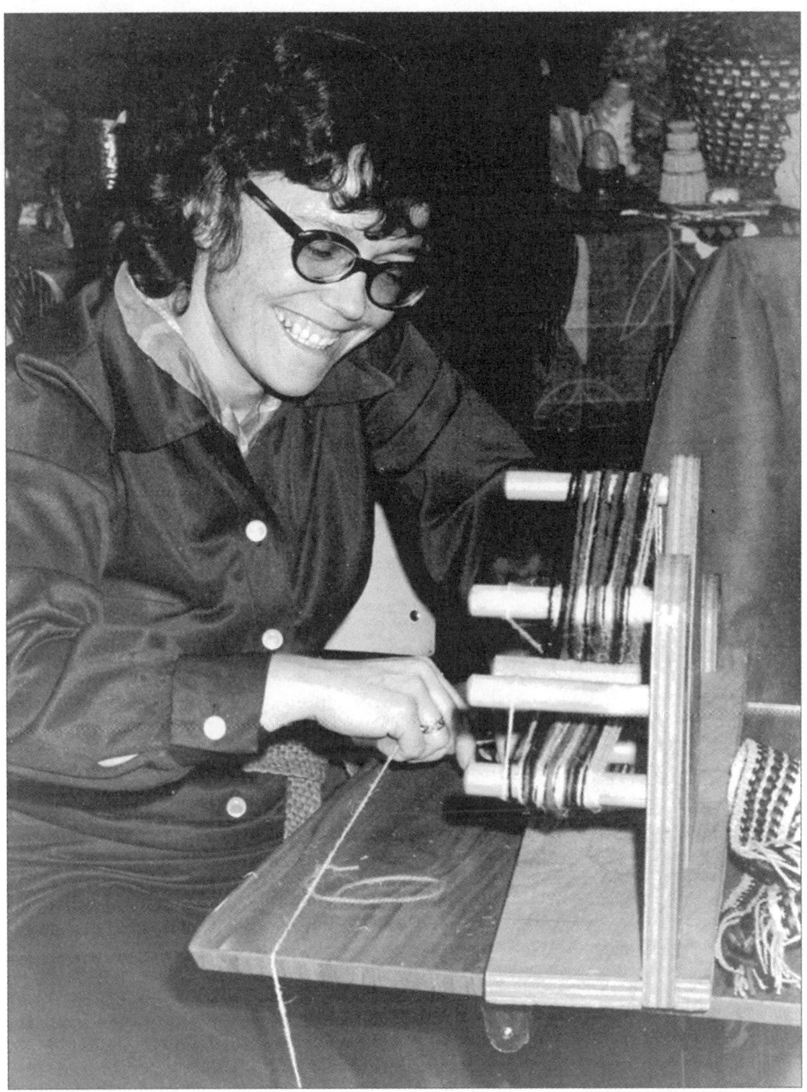

Demonstrating a loom at a Kelowna Arts Council event, November 1970.

needed a situation totally different from his. We were at a place in our lives where it was necessary for me to establish my own priorities. But I couldn't get through to him and felt hopeless.

I was suffering from severe depression those last months in Uniontown. Although my body was performing whatever had to be done, I felt I was dying inside; it was quite frightening. I knew I had to

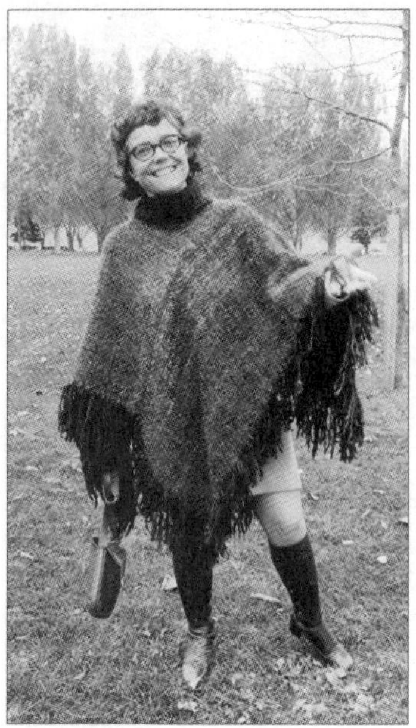

On a lunch break while working for the National Film Board in Kelowna, 1971.

leave and not come back again; I just wasn't ready to die. And I couldn't talk or write about that; there was no one there I could confide in about my state of mind, but I did write to Norma. It helped that I was flying to the UK at the end of the semester to visit my family in Scotland with my daughter Claire. I badly needed something to look forward to. Zeljko would take the younger kids back to Kelowna, where we would join them for the rest of the summer.

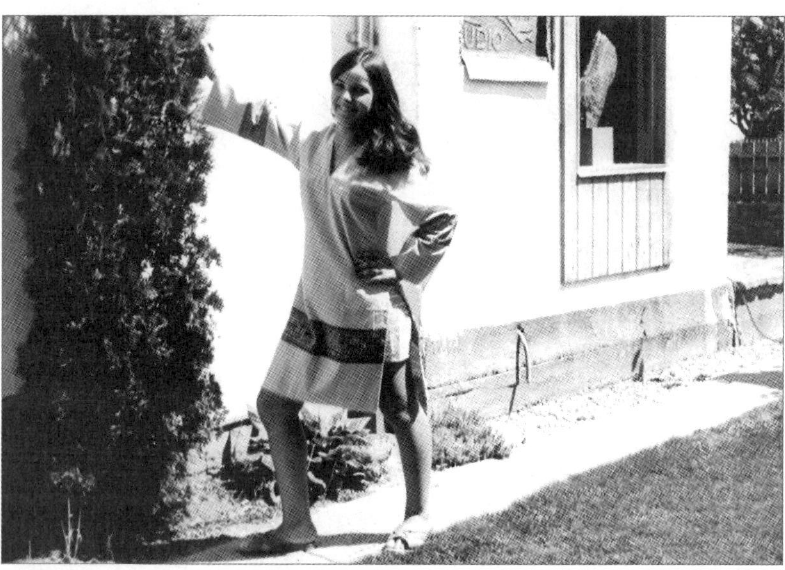

Claire models a dress that I designed, block printed and sewed.

Rethinking My Life

When I returned to the UK in the summer of 1971 I found that my three brothers, all younger than myself, had established themselves quite separately. Trevor had decided to find his Welsh roots and was living in a caravan near Snowdonia. My brother Jervis was a fervent Scottish Nationalist candidate, living in Edinburgh. The youngest, Roland, had married an English girl and was happily working just outside London. My sister, who was eighteen years younger than me, had not long since immigrated to Australia with her Scottish husband. Much as I loved my time going back, it became clear to me that there was now no longer a specific family location that provided what I wanted. I needed to accept Canada as my home; my children certainly experienced it as such. So I returned to Kelowna with a determination to forgo my financial dependency on Zeljko and find my own way.

At first I looked for work, but job-hunting in Kelowna proved to be harder than I expected. I started off with two part-time jobs, a boring one with IBM and another as a piano player for ballet classes, which exceeded my competency. Following my full-time job at BC Tree Fruits, I found a much more interesting one at the National Film Board office. I managed to earn enough to keep things together.

One thing I enjoyed was that our household became a place for many young people to stay. My kids were very friendly and visitors were always welcome. Moreover it was a time of movement, of disillusionment with the American dream, and many who came from south of the border hoped that Canada would offer an alternative. Ironically there were three of these who turned out to be from Pennsylvania, all arriving separately, out of the blue, and those ones in particular added interesting accomplishments to the house.

Tom, the first one, made me a simple cabinet for my hi-fi and also got us started on an organic garden. Ivan, the next, helped build a playground at Andy and Natanis's school and also washed dishes and helped clean the house. And the other, Len, played the drums and taped a magnificent reel of jazz music for me. He was of Italian origin and cooked like an angel. These three had all done their national service, so they had no fears of the authorities catching up with them and hijacking them back. But we had others stay with us briefly who had those fears; they were the draft dodgers, who could have either been turned back at the border or actually been taken back across the border. Most Canadians disapproved of such actions. It was rumoured that the RCMP were offered bounties for the return of draft evaders, but I don't know if that often happened. Mostly they were welcomed.

Zeljko was still insisting that I join him in Uniontown, and his letters came daily and more disturbingly. To make it clear that I had decided to make my life in Canada, I finally asked him for a divorce. I told him I did not want alimony or custody of the children; they should be free to make a choice of where and with whom to live. I only wished to have a small allowance for anyone under fifteen years of age who stayed with me. It took some months for the divorce to come through. Zeljko wanted to file for it (his choice), and I accepted his grounds of mental cruelty on my part. I didn't really care about grounds; I only cared about ending the misery it was causing us both. I hoped that we could keep in reasonable communication after this was arranged, but unfortunately that didn't prove to be the case. My hope for some real conciliation was never to happen.

Later that year, when Claire became interested in pursuing art, Zeljko invited her to join him in Uniontown, where she could take courses at Fayette Campus. She had been living in Vancouver after being fired from her job dunking donuts at a Kelowna supermarket. Natanis also went east. She had decided she should spend alternate years with us. Being fair to both parents was something she took seriously.

The Violinist

My first introduction to Alan was when he popped his head round my open front door late one afternoon and said, "I pass this way nearly every day and your house looks really interesting. I've always wanted to stop." True enough, you could probably see a lot of the artwork that was in our front room, though I'd never thought about it: stylized figure paintings, batik and woven fabric hangings, clay sculptures, unusual window drapes that we'd brought with us when we emigrated from Scotland. And an assortment of well-used bicycles stacked outside the front door. "Do you think I could come in?"

His youthful frankness disarmed me. I'd recently left my marriage of twenty years and was struggling with two very boring part-time jobs. Four of my children were still at home and I'd taken in a couple of friendly boarders to supplement my wages. One more? I welcomed him in. He soon became a familiar face in our home. He would drop in, violin tucked under his arm, after he had given music lessons to groups of primary students at the end of their school day; our house was on his way home. He would bring armloads of music, often classical, and the strains of Mozart and Beethoven trios and sonatas came wafting through the house as I made supper—highly inspirational. He and Claire really hit it off well. It was such a change to have a larger male household, good for Andy's sake and good for mine too.

Alan brought a new record one day, Laura Nyro's first album, and I'd never heard music quite like it. "Come on, you should be dancing too! It's great music, isn't it?" He was right; this was music that had to be danced to. He wore boots of soft royal-purple leather, with high velvet cuffs adorned with small shiny bells and thonging. When Alan danced in them he looked like an overgrown elf or leprechaun. His enthusiasm for this music was something I needed, something to take me into a world where larger boundaries existed, where my day-to-day struggles to plan, look after and cook for a household of seven while running between jobs, had a reward more stimulating than a late-night movie on TV. This was music that spoke compellingly with a voice that grabbed my insides and flung me into movement that had no care for propriety. It pulled me into an inner world of rhythm and sent me back out with energy that spilled over in abandonment. I loved Alan for bringing this into my life and for his treating me as a peer even though I was more than twice his age. He was only nineteen, and his idea of dancing was not confined to that stilted world of "partners." It was a great freedom we shared, each moving with our own independent response to the life of the music.

Our living room became alive. The new Heathkit record player that I had just recently and tediously finished putting together was serving us all magnificently, as Alan brought yet more records for us to listen and dance to. Life in the house certainly changed. Our boarders, Finn and Brian, decided that we should share this fun and host some parties. It was summer and we could easily expand to the outdoors if the house got full. We had some marvellous musical evenings.

This was an old house with a big back garden, well shaded, as were most of the gardens on our street, but I had already managed to enrage our closest neighbour, a rather sullen woman who would shout across the fence at me from her back door in the mornings, using obscene language directed at my awful behaviour in having "all these men" in my house. It wasn't the parties that seemed to bother her; the parties were never too late anyway. I never knew quite how to respond to her. She didn't want to talk to me, didn't welcome company. Other neighbours said she was just a little crazy and not to be bothered by her. But I was bothered. She didn't know that "all these men" were gay, and I certainly wasn't about to tell her. There's no knowing what kind of reaction that information might have provoked.

In any case, the fun didn't last forever. Alan left the Okanagan within the year. He found it hard to face so many unenthusiastic children every day; children who didn't want to stay in for music lessons after regular school hours were over. He said it was the parents who really wanted to play an instrument and they should be coming to take lessons instead of sending their children who didn't want to. So he decided to leave home and seek his fortune at the coast. I would hear snippets about him occasionally from people who had come across him in Vancouver and described him as an intriguing, wild-looking young musician. When the spirit moved him he apparently played his violin on the streets, gathering crowds around him and making enough money to get by. I later heard he busked in Victoria as well. He was a good musician and I was always delighted to get news about him. Then, for the longest time I heard nothing; he just disappeared from the scene.

Some twenty-five years later I unexpectedly heard of his whereabouts and sent him a letter. He sent back a tape of music and said that he and his partner had recently released this hauntingly beautiful composition for harp and violin. He also enclosed a photograph of them both playing their instruments. In his letter, he had written, "I miss my partner greatly; he died of AIDS two months ago. I miss him for our music and for the loving that we shared. Please let me know if you ever come this way."

The following year I wrote to him from San Diego, where my daughter Judy and I were attending a two-week cleansing retreat. I told him we could make a stopover in San Francisco on the way home if he'd let us know where to find him. He wrote back with information on where he could be found playing. That is how we came to be sitting in the spacious and formal lounge of one of San Francisco's older, majestic downtown hotels, feeling somewhat out of place. I had been so delighted to hear news of Alan again after so many years, but this venue seemed a bit strange.

I was thinking of that letter as we found a corner table in this overpowering lounge, where frilly-aproned waitresses were serving afternoon tea on silver platters to well-groomed, expensively dressed women who were passing the time of day in chatter. It was a luxurious but stifling setting. Alan, wearing a professional musician's formal, nondescript black suit, was playing his violin, standing beside a grand piano. He and the pianist looked equally uninvolved with the music and the audience. They were playing music that didn't speak of anything, the dead background music that no one really listens to. It was, after all, what they were being paid to play.

In the intermission, Alan came over quietly to join us. He told me he was now living with a nice woman who had two children. They would probably get married sometime in the future. Then, with the first sign of animation, he said, "Perhaps you have time to come and visit us?" I thanked him but explained that we were just making this short stop on our way home after a long trip, and unfortunately we had to leave early the next morning. He looked at me, somewhat indirectly. "That's too bad; perhaps the next time you come through."

Tears began to roll down my cheeks. They fell increasingly; they were coming in floods, as were my memories. I stumbled out, choked by them, feeling so blinded that it was hard to find the washroom. Why did I so desperately want to wash those tears away? There was such a feeling of loss. Was it mine, or was it Alan's? It was so very sad. I wondered if he had felt a need to change, to be straight, and whether he loved this woman who was now in his life. One thing I really sensed: he was not enjoying this way of making a living. Where had his own music gone?

Why Not?

I never really knew Bill. I saw him only when I visited Norma and George in Summerland. I would often find him sitting alone in their living room. He would be on the couch in the bay window that overlooked the driveway, close to the front door, as though waiting for others to join him. He looked to be my age, an ordinary sort of bloke with a crewcut at a time when many middle-aged men were experimenting with more unusual styles. He rarely initiated conversation, though I noticed that he liked to be heard when he did say something. I never saw him in the kitchen, where everyone else seemed to congregate around the crowded family table with its ever-filled coffee pot. But Bill was obviously a bit of a loner and may not have liked the familiarity the kitchen offered. Or maybe he just didn't drink coffee.

This was orchard country, and he lived in a nearby cabin that was used mostly by fruit pickers, who were always needed in the summer. Fruit picking may have been what brought him to Summerland in the first place; I never did know where he came from. This was a house where you could always find artists, writers, creative folks of all ilk, and though Bill didn't fit any of these categories, he was a neighbour; one of the many who dropped in. The doors were never locked; there were no keys.

Though Bill wasn't much of a talker, he had a fair knowledge of classical music and sometimes brought this up in an offhand sort of way. This was a house where music abounded and hootenannies took place regularly. George loved folk music and strummed a mean banjo, even though his two-fingered hand had been mangled in a mill injury when he was a teenager. Norma had a passion for jazz and had some remarkable recordings of early notables, her favourite being Bechet.

And they both loved Phil Ochs. The house would ring of an evening with both live and recorded gems. And Bill would often be there.

One weekend I found Bill sitting in his usual place, but when I came in from the kitchen he unexpectedly spoke to me from across the living room.

"I'm moving on," he said.

"You're leaving Summerland?"

"Yes."

"Where are you going?"

"Don't know for sure. But I have to sell my reel-to-reel. It's a good one, a Sony. Want to buy it? It's worth at least four hundred dollars." This was one of the few times I'd had any communication with him. It was certainly true that I'd love to have a good reel-to-reel. I could put so much more music on all those large tapes. It was tempting.

"I'll have to think about it. Are you sure you want to give it up?" I never got an answer to that, but he just said I could have a bit of time. And I thought, or maybe supposed, that he probably needed the money if he was leaving.

He phoned me a few days later to ask if I wanted it. I had already decided. I couldn't refuse the opportunity; it was too good to miss. I'd never get around to buying one otherwise. He said he had already packed everything up and was ready to leave. He'd bring the reel-to-reel to my house in Kelowna, as he was planning to come through that way, and he would come the next day, Monday. That meant I'd have to get some cash out of the bank (there were no ATMs in those days), so I told him to come a bit after five, when I'd be home from work.

He was waiting there when I came home. He must have joined my kids and our boarders for supper; visitors always did. I do remember that he still didn't seem clear about where he was going, which seemed a bit strange. Not to mention that it was a bit late in the day for anyone to embark on a journey. I know I offered him the couch in the living room for the night, which was the only place I could put a visitor. Later in the evening, when the kids were in bed and the boarders probably out somewhere, I got round to preparing the couch for him. I remember that couch. It was a very popular Danish style, with smooth charcoal-grey fabric, and the back could be removed to give it a slightly wider sleeping space. It was one of the best pieces of furniture I ever had.

Bill said abruptly, "I want to sleep with you."

I was totally taken aback. There was nothing in our fairly limited communication that led me to expect this. I answered something like, "I don't think so, not really."

He just said again, "I want to sleep with you," with some kind of insistence that flummoxed me.

Those were the seventies, when a wave of sexual freedom was sweeping the culture. "Sleeping freely" was becoming an accepted practice to an increasing section of society, and I wasn't a total outsider to it. After twenty years of monogamous marriage, I was now divorced and cautiously exploring this new territory. There were the obvious reasons: the pill now finally provided a needed safety from pregnancy, the hippie movement was in its prime, and the "make love, not war" slogan emerged during the Vietnam conflict. But confusing times nonetheless. I certainly made some mistakes.

I didn't have any desire to sleep with Bill, but in some way I felt sorry for him, something I'm ashamed to admit to now. His loneliness seemed to be taking up a lot of space. And if physical closeness might bring some temporary comfort and help him on his way, then why not? And that's how it ended up that I slept with him that night on the couch in our living room. Why there? Maybe because I didn't want to share my own bed. Maybe because I didn't want my kids to know. Maybe because the bedrooms were all upstairs. Maybe, maybe.

It was a pretty uncomfortable night for me, and I did wonder if he had ever slept with a woman before. But he was much the same age as me. Surely he must have? But we didn't talk about it and I didn't ask. I wasn't able to. I was too shy as well as too embarrassed.

The next morning I expected him to get up and leave, but he didn't want to. He said he'd like to stay on and again became quite insistent. I was in the habit of being hospitable, but not this time. I knew I couldn't take him on; my life was already complicated enough. I explained that we didn't have room and that he must carry on with his plans. I must have given a clear enough "No," because he did in fact leave before I went to work that morning. And his leaving certainly was a relief to me, though I did still wonder, a bit uncomfortably, where his next stop would be.

It didn't take long to find out. The following day at the office there was talk about a horrifying incident in a nearby camping site in the Kettle Valley. That was the direction Bill said he might be taking. I listened to the radio as soon as I got home. A newcomer who arrived at the site that day had killed a family of five who were already camped there. The police reported that it seemed to be a random shooting and they had the killer in custody. And I do remember, as clearly as if it were yesterday, that I felt an awful kind of visceral recognition in the pit of my stomach, before the killer's name was released. It was Bill.

In Summerland, the unexpectedness of this caught everyone by surprise; they all knew he'd stopped at my house the night before it happened. But it was only Norma that I could confide in. Did I have to take some responsibility for his action? It's something I have questioned many times since. We heard not long afterwards that he was incarcerated in Riverview, a mental institution outside Vancouver.

A couple of years later, on one of my visits, George said to me, "I had the oddest letter this week from Bill what's-his-name in Riverview. He's asked me to send him some dried apricots. He says he remembers us drying those from our trees here. Do you think I should send him some?" I don't remember what my answer was, but I have a hunch that it may well have been, "Why not?"

Co-operative Effort

In Kelowna the job scene wasn't getting any better, and I was wondering what to do. At this time, the Pierre Trudeau government introduced the Local Initiates Programs (LIP), modestly funded and targeted at youth participation, and to me one of Trudeau's best accomplishments. Taking advantage of this, a small group of us got together and decided to operate a project that tackled food economy issues, as well as home maintenance and repairs. We offered daily demonstrations on bread baking and soup making, and this spurred the setting up of the first food co-operative in the Okanagan. Many of us in the seventies were questioning how to proceed, how to live differently, how to consume less and share more.

I also attended and shared ideas at ecological forums, work initiative programs and land resource meetings. Through these I met people who wanted to create a constructive, socially responsible, self-sustaining and environmentally sound way of life. Eight of us began looking for land. Some of us had shared work experience, some were escaping the city, some barely knew each other—we were an assorted bunch. Making a reality of our commitment to the preservation of agricultural land, we were convinced we should, and could, make it work.

We eventually found a quarter section for sale in the Salmon Valley area that included an older farmhouse and a small cottage. It was located near a creek and already had three acres of arable land in use. Areas higher up were just asking to be planted with fruit trees. Could we manage to buy it and live our ideals? We would each start with an equal number of shares and see whether that would be enough for a down payment. Holding a mortgage did present some problems; banks weren't too keen on co-operatives. Then we realized we had to form a co-operative farm, and banks weren't too keen on farms either.

Somehow we managed to get one. None of us approved of the capitalist way of buying properties with the intent of selling them later to gain from the rise in market value.

There were now ten of us: a nuclear family of four, two couples and two singles. We lived on that farm for nearly three years and for most of that time we shared living space in the old and rather small farmhouse. I was one of the singles. My daughter Claire joined her partner, Ian, on the farm.

We grew and harvested a wonderful crop of wheat, which we milled for Uprising Breads Bakery in Vancouver. Its flour had a cinnamon fragrance. Of course we made mistakes, too. That first year we planted two acres of sweet corn for our major crop, because corn always brought good money. But we hadn't formulated a proper marketing strategy and we couldn't even give it away at the height of the season. We ended up trying to dry what we had left, but a bonus point was that it meant our pigs were exceptionally well fed that year.

We also had over an acre of vegetable garden and we took a bountiful assortment of varied and colourful vegetables to the farmers' market in Armstrong every Saturday. But we hadn't banked on the season

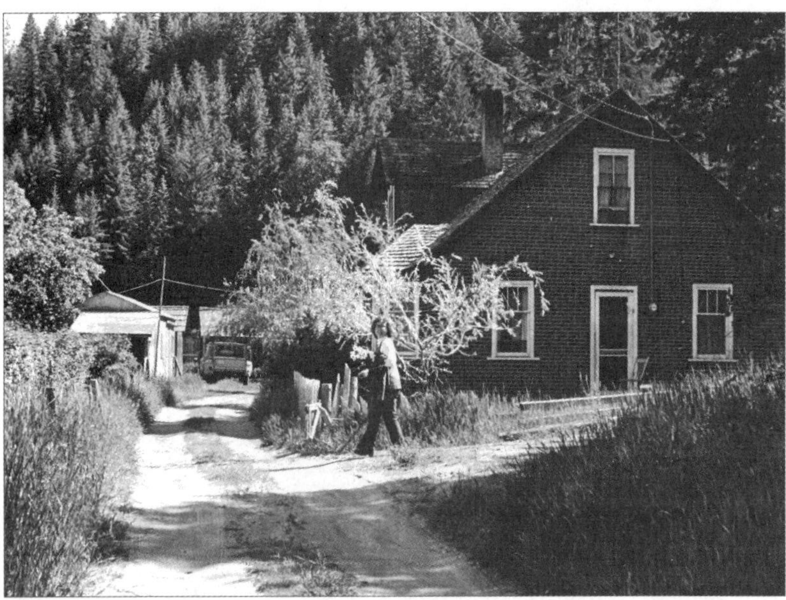

At the co-op farm.

being so short. In early September we had our first frost and lost a large part of our lovely crop of peppers and tomatoes.

That winter we noticed that potatoes were bringing an unexpectedly high price. We'd planted only a small crop for ourselves, thinking to grow higher-priced and more unusual vegetables. How were we to know that we'd regret not having grown the modest potato? Of course we would put that right the following year. We decided to make potatoes our major crop the next spring, as they would be easier to store and we wouldn't have to sell them all at once, like the corn. But every other farmer had the same bright idea, and the glut of potatoes on the market meant that the price dropped drastically that summer. In our zeal we planted them too close together to harvest mechanically. After our laborious harvest, we had to rent storage from a neighbouring farmer and sack our potatoes for transport to his cellar. That was the season I wrecked my back. I was determined to be capable of physical work equal to any of the men on the farm and thought I could carry sacks of potatoes round like the best of them.

Making an income on the farm wasn't coming easily. We all took on outside work; one available short-term job was with a neighbouring chicken farm. They needed workers to unload a shipment of young hens. We had to unload them from the crates they came in, hold them feet up—two in each hand—and then carry them and cram them, four apiece, into the small crates they were to be kept in until ready for slaughter. I'd never seen this procedure before and was appalled. I vowed I'd never allow myself to be paid for doing this job ever again. We had chickens too, but they ran around outside and seemed content. It became clear that if I was not prepared to be part of our own killing procedure, then I should also be prepared never to eat chicken again. It was a traumatic experience.

The same applied to milking; I felt I needed to learn to milk. We had only one cow, but I found it was much harder work than I expected. Fortunately Annie, the other mother in our co-op, was more than happy to take it on as one of her regular chores. The only success I had with animals was with bees. I enjoyed learning about them and eventually had four hives that produced lovely honey. No one else particularly wanted to work with them. This gave me an extra appreciation for honey that I might otherwise not have had.

One especially exciting time on the farm was the birth of a calf. Annie had arranged to have our cow impregnated, and when the birth was imminent most of us were present. I'll never forget watching the wobbly young calf trying to stagger up immediately after birthing, then falling and struggling to get up again, this time successfully. It was wondrous. Knowing how long it takes for a human baby to find its feet, I'm now more aware than ever how vulnerable we humans are.

One day one of our members said that what he liked best about being on the farm was that there was always something to do. I was puzzled by that at the time, partly because I was looking forward to a period in my life when there would not be so much to do. I'd never remembered a time when there wasn't more than enough to be done and not nearly enough time in which to do it. It's only now, many years later, when I'm struggling to get back to a place where I can again feel the joy of intense involvement in a project, that I can appreciate what he was saying then.

I converted the loft above the barn into my own living space, but I couldn't conceive of not having electricity for my radio and reel-to-reel music system. So I learned how to wire it, which gave me great pleasure.

It was a struggle to put a floor into the loft with tongue-and-groove wood that I'd give my eye teeth to be able to buy now. And I still don't know how Claire and I managed to build a set of stairs with an extra notch on one side of the stringers! But Annie and I managed to put up great lengths of metal sheeting onto the barn roof to weatherproof it. One of us would hold the sheeting in place while the other hammered in the rubber-ringed nails.

I decided to insulate the inside of the loft in an effort to keep the flies at bay, as they continued to breed ferociously in the barn below me, even though the horses had long gone. Then I covered the insulation with light plywood sheets, which helped retain heat but still provoked the flies. They loved the warmth, and insulation wasn't going to stop them from finding a way in.

Annie and I did share other chores, especially when it came to canning; this was one good way in which we connected. We were both Scottish and had immigrated to Canada at around the same age, in our twenties. But we came from very different backgrounds and

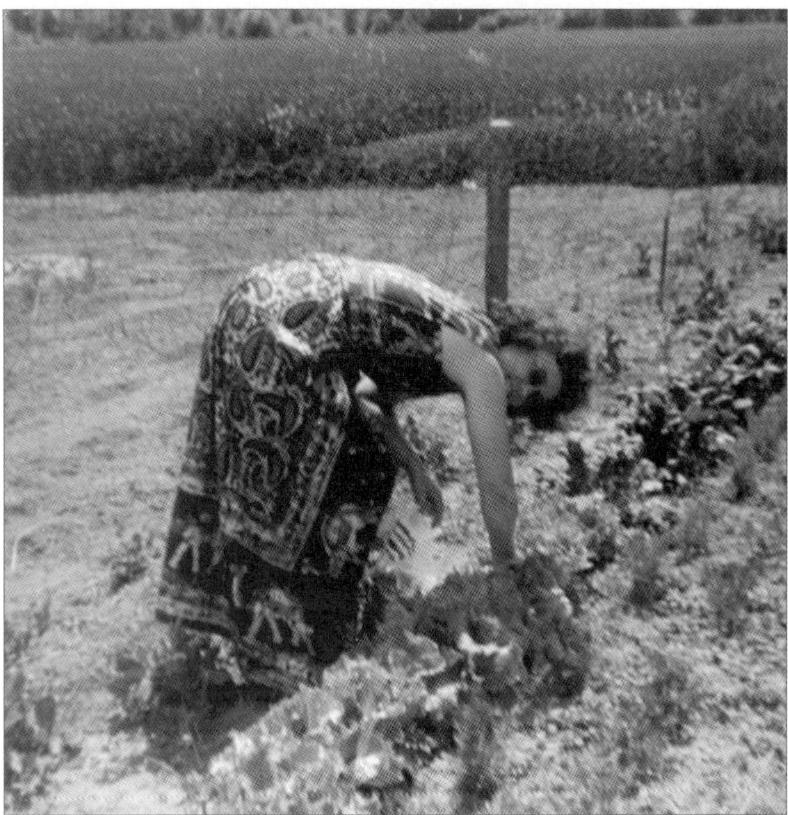

Picking lettuce on the co-op farm.

saw life through very different lenses. Annie came from a more formal and conservative family, and because of that she seemed quite able to criticize other ways of being. She would sometimes say to me, "I don't know how you can do that; I couldn't think of doing it," and I was never quite sure whether she was offering me a criticism or a compliment. It might have to do with having a certain kind of "nerve" to do whatever it was, like driving over the back roads on my own or trying to get a women's centre going in a conservative town. Although it seemed at first that she was giving me credit for doing these things, I always had the sneaking hunch that she really meant that in her eyes it wasn't quite right for me to be doing such things.

Eventually, I had a serious disagreement with Annie when some of us felt the co-operative wasn't meeting our needs. In particular, as a single woman, I wanted to have the possibility of bringing in one or two other women who might want to share in putting up a building with me. I had made a number of friends through my work in the library at the college in Salmon Arm. I couldn't continue living in the loft much longer, and I wasn't interested in building something for just myself. I had brought up the question of adding to our members, but Annie had been totally opposed. She felt there was no way we could allow more people to join us on the land. After many meetings a number of differing issues came up and we reached a crisis point. It was obvious that I was not alone in my dissatisfaction with the status quo, but the question became what to do about it.

In our early starry-eyed days we had decided that we would not allow the price we had paid for the land to be increased if and when we ever sold. This was an ideal we should abide by. But here we were at a point where some of the members wanted change, Claire had already left, and others wanted out. Someone said we should just get an assessment of the land so that those who wanted to stay could then either buy us out or find new members. Annie was horrified. She said that was not what we had agreed to originally. And in some ways she was right. Two of the members disputed this decision, words got very heated, and I began to get upset. Yes, it had been a stupid, idealistic decision; yes, we had made it. But somehow I got my back up, and when Annie looked at me and said, "You remember that, don't you?" I just looked straight back at her and said, "No," knowing that I was not answering her question either adequately or entirely honestly. She looked at me in disbelief.

I left the farm shortly after that, as did four of the others. The co-operative was officially dissolved and the farm sold. It was not an easy procedure; it was complicated, and there were meetings with lawyers, a lot of correspondence and many hard feelings. I lost touch with Annie and her family after that, but I wish I could have found a way to talk to her, to better explain my answer. It was like going through another divorce, but I had to get out.

Massage School

After the co-op I deliberated over what to do next. I'd been having problems with my back, and a friendly receptionist in a chiropractor's office suggested that I consider going to massage school. It was an intriguing thought; maybe I'd learn more about my body, which I had taken for granted, since it had always worked well. I might just find my feet—and my hands—at the same time!

At that time it meant going to Ontario, where the only accredited college in the country was located. I was ready for something entirely different, so why not go? I phoned and found there was still space for me to enrol in the next session, which started the following month, September. Norma said that her sister Hattie, who lived in Toronto, would be more than happy to have me stay with her until I found accommodation near the college. It all happened quickly.

For a while I was unlucky in finding a place to stay at a rent I could afford. Landladies didn't want single women renters. They said that boyfriends always presented problems, as they usually visited the girlfriend's residence—something I'd never thought about. It wasn't much use telling them that I didn't present a problem, because I would be busy studying and wouldn't have time or interest in much else. Eventually I found a "shared" house with four other people on Bathurst Street, a convenient location within walking distance of the school. I had met Pat on our first day of classes and was delighted to hear that there was still a spare room in the house that she and her partner, Mark, had found.

Also sharing the house was Vassilis, from Greece, who was in training as a Gestalt therapist. His intense and somewhat erratic behaviour never ceased to amaze us. Dennis from Saskatoon was a tall, blond, twenty-three-year-old sociology student at the University of

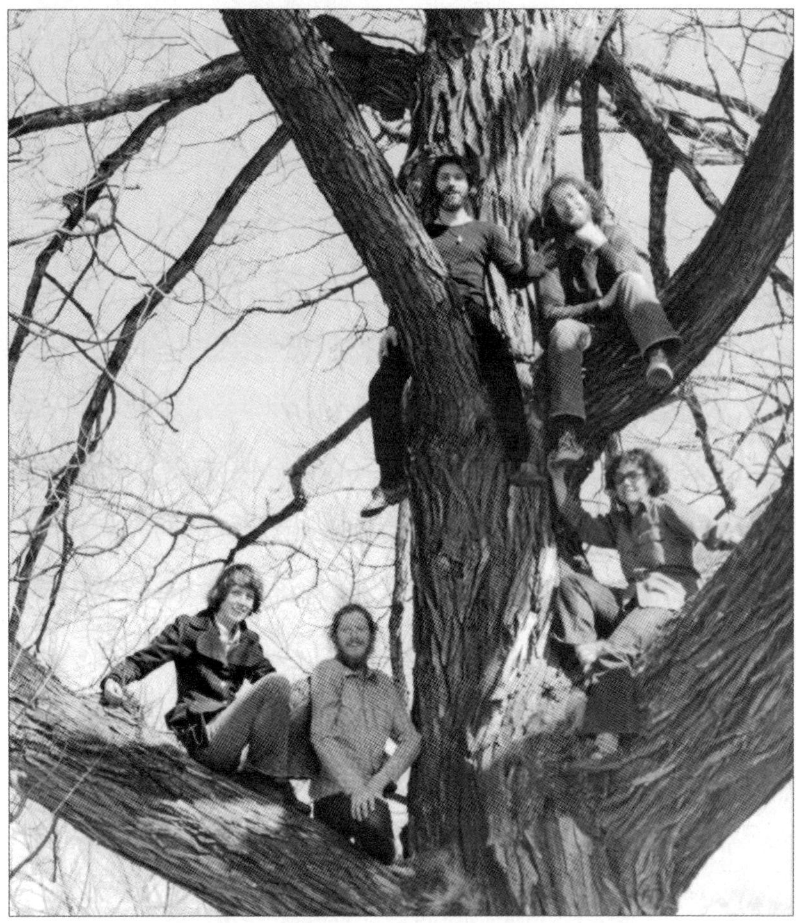

My Bathurst Street family in a tree.

Toronto. The shared arrangement brought many advantages: lower rental cost, bulk food buying, a varied supper menu, which we took turns cooking, and an opportunity for companionship.

I found it fascinating to learn about the systems of the body and the various functions of each of these. How could I have lived this long without knowing something about them all? Giving and receiving massage was part of the daily routine at the school, and gradually I found my hands responding to the tissues they were encountering. There was pleasure at first, certainly, but soon it became something more. In time my hands learned to encounter trouble spots that needed attention.

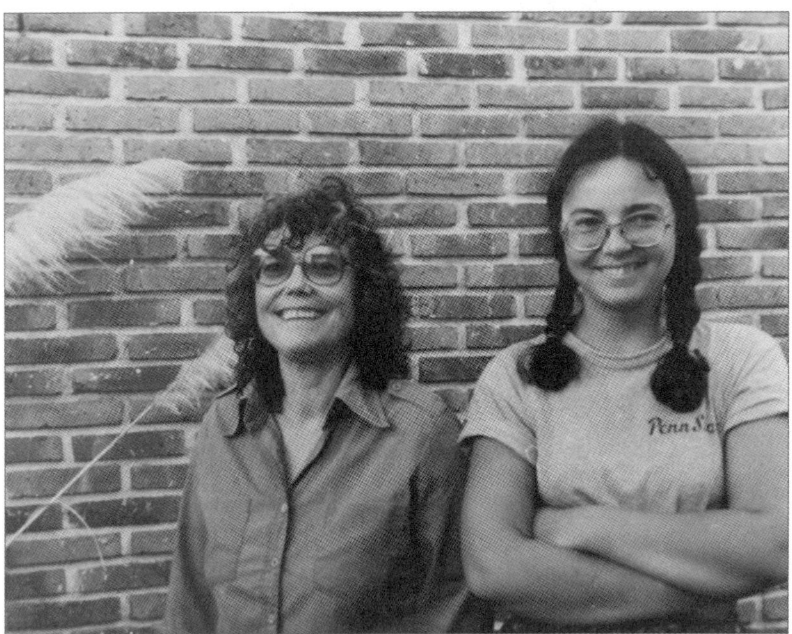

Claire visiting in Toronto.

We were a mixed bunch of students, and I became particularly friendly with a young woman from Japan who had practiced shiatsu in her own country before coming to Canada. She was having language problems, and I did my best to help her with the written work. Certification in massage was her only entry into legitimate body therapy at that time.

I should have been studying full-time, but I was enjoying the opportunity to go to pay-what-you-can theatre previews, foreign films, concerts and particularly jazz performances. I had been missing city life. I found a great jazz group that played frequently at the Brunswick pub that was within walking distance of our house, and Mark, who was also a jazz lover, would frequently join me there in the evenings. Vassilis decided he'd like to come with me when I went to international dancing classes each week, and Dennis enjoyed theatre and films, so I had no shortage of company. Pat was much more studious than I was and decided to spend all her evening hours at home studying, but she didn't make me feel bad about my different choices. It all turned out to be a pretty harmonious arrangement.

Vassilis was a very sociable creature, and he had constant overnight female friends. So much for those objections landladies had presented me with! He quite amazed us with his diversity and his energy. I remember that on one of our outings Dennis and I were talking about the interesting fact that we were the two "solos" in the house, and he simply said, "You know, we could change that." It took me totally by surprise, rather a pleasant one. He suggested I might like to join him that night. He was twenty-six years my junior and an interesting and quite delightful person to spend time with. I was happy to take him up on it and thereafter we spent alternate nights, depending on who felt like it, in either Dennis's or my bedroom, although my bed wasn't as comfortable as his, because I had only the single one I had built. I must confess that he was a very skilful lover for one so young, and I was totally taken aback. However, when it got close to exam time, we both became more prudent, studying conscientiously into the nights and forgoing this pleasure.

It came to graduation night at the college and Dennis had accompanied me. I was particularly upset by the director of our massage school, who made a point of stating that "the oldest" student in her class had remarkably passed all the exams. She greeted me with this comment as I came to the front to accept my certificate. It hadn't been easy, being the oldest woman in that class; it was shortly before my fiftieth birthday. I just wanted to disappear—where else, but to the washroom. I'll never forget how Dennis sent someone to find me, crying my eyes out in the washroom. He sent a message: "Ask Ann if she'd like to come for a walk with me; there's a magnificent moon out tonight." He was truly a thoughtful friend, something more important to me at that stage than being a good lover. His presence greatly enriched my year in Toronto. We did keep in touch for a while after I left Toronto, but our lives took their own ways. I wonder now if he married the blond, blue-eyed Saskatchewan girl his mother had picked out for him.

SELF-EMPLOYMENT

I was a little lost upon my return from Toronto. I had a diploma from the massage school, but each province has its own requirements, so I would need to pass a BC examination before registering to practice here. I hadn't really thought this out beforehand, but I knew I wanted to live in Vancouver. I enjoyed city life. I was presently sharing a small rented house with a friend, Janet, and wanted to find something more permanent. I needed a secure base for this new stage in my life; hopefully I could find something modest to buy. All I would need after getting my BC registration were clients and somewhere to set up a practice; it would be a whole new ball game. Building a massage practice would take time. I could no longer rely on finding work piecemeal as I had done for so many years.

The East End had quite a few offerings at relatively low prices and I liked the area, but I had very little money for a down payment and no income security. My local credit union couldn't offer a mortgage. Then a sale sign appeared on a very unappealing house, just kitty-corner from where I was living. It sat on a totally barren lot with three trees recently chopped off at the base. Who would want it? It was a basic square-looking house with peeling paint, looking utterly neglected. Nonetheless I phoned the realtor.

After viewing the interior, I realized it, too, needed immense work. Although poorly cared for, it had been solidly built in the early 1900s and had good stone footings. It had been subdivided, and inside the single outside front door there were two separate entrances so that upstairs tenants had their own access. The main floor had stairs down to a full basement that was currently filled with junk. This would give me enough space, with the advantage of renting the top floor out to help with a mortgage. But it wasn't the kind of house I ever thought I would buy.

The realtor said the owners had rented out the house for years but had recently moved to New York and just wanted to get rid of the house at any price. She could probably get them to carry a mortgage if I had difficulty getting one. With much trepidation I put in an offer and asked the real estate agent to do her best. She pulled it off for me. I had a mortgage from the owners on a five-year term, by which time I should be earning enough to satisfy requirements at the credit union. I gave the tenants three months' notice. They weren't pleased about this, and they made me pay for it by leaving the place shockingly dirty and filled with masses of junk. It took me seventeen trips in my little Datsun pickup truck to move all the garbage to the landfill in Delta.

I printed business cards and visited doctors' offices to advertise myself. I could put up a massage table in the house until I found a more suitable location. At this time, in the late 1970s, massage was still a questionable occupation. Registered massage, which was medically approved, had limited coverage under British Columbia's Medical Services Plan (MSP) but was struggling to assert its legitimacy. We were incorporated as the underlings within the physiotherapy association. I attended all meetings of the association as soon as I passed the exams and got involved in the practicalities of this new occupation. While canvassing doctors, I met one on West Broadway who had a keen interest in massage and he asked if I wanted to work out of his office. He had a spare room and would be happy to rent it to me for fifty dollars a month. What a piece of luck; I was delighted to accept his offer.

Being self-employed was going to be a new experience—more than a little daunting. Who knew if there would be patients booking appointments this week or next week? Massage therapists were still comparatively new on the health scene, but I found people who had been involved in car accidents or trauma at work quite often needed my services. These clients would often require written progress reports, which demanded careful attention to the wording, as they might end up in litigation if the Insurance Corporation of British Columbia (ICBC) or Workers' Compensation Board (WCB) were involved. I worked at first only from medical referrals and received payment directly from MSP, around $8.75 per treatment at that time. I had to

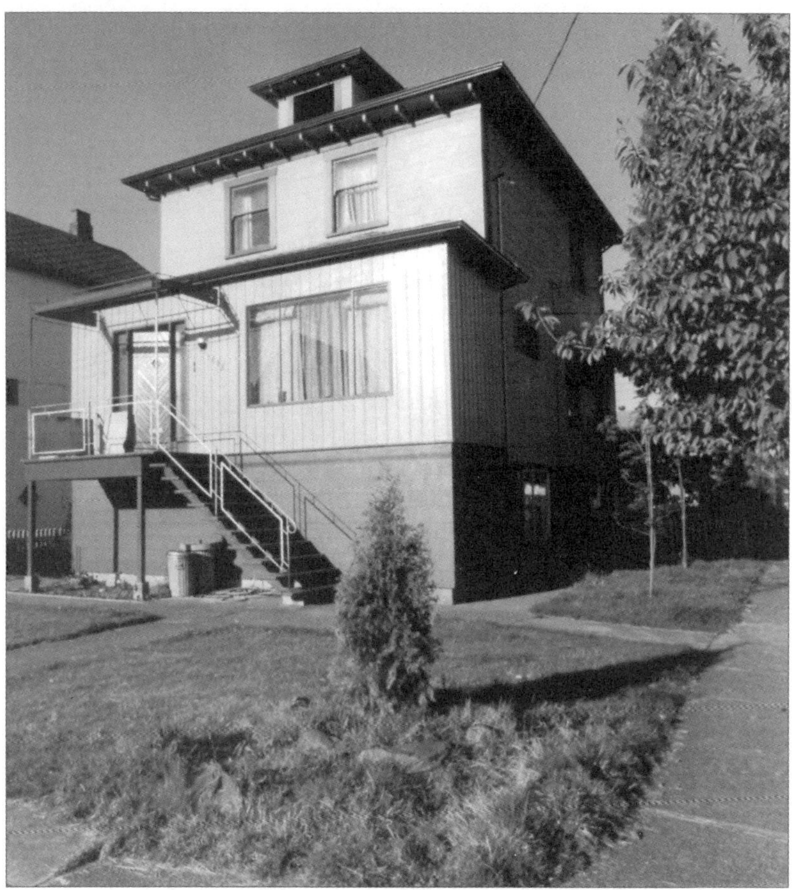

Salsbury Drive house, after being painted by Andy.

submit billing cards for each treatment and then wait for a cheque to arrive once a month after these had been processed in Victoria. There was certainly some insecurity in the scene, but I had plenty of experience living frugally.

I became intensely involved in our professional association. I found myself on the board, attended negotiations with MSP in Victoria and had to resign myself to the fact that instead of getting better pay for our work, we were expected to reduce the time we spent with patients. "Twenty minutes should be enough," we were told, and this was not likely to change. Surcharging or "opting out" of MSP was the only other way we could go. Our numbers were growing fast, and

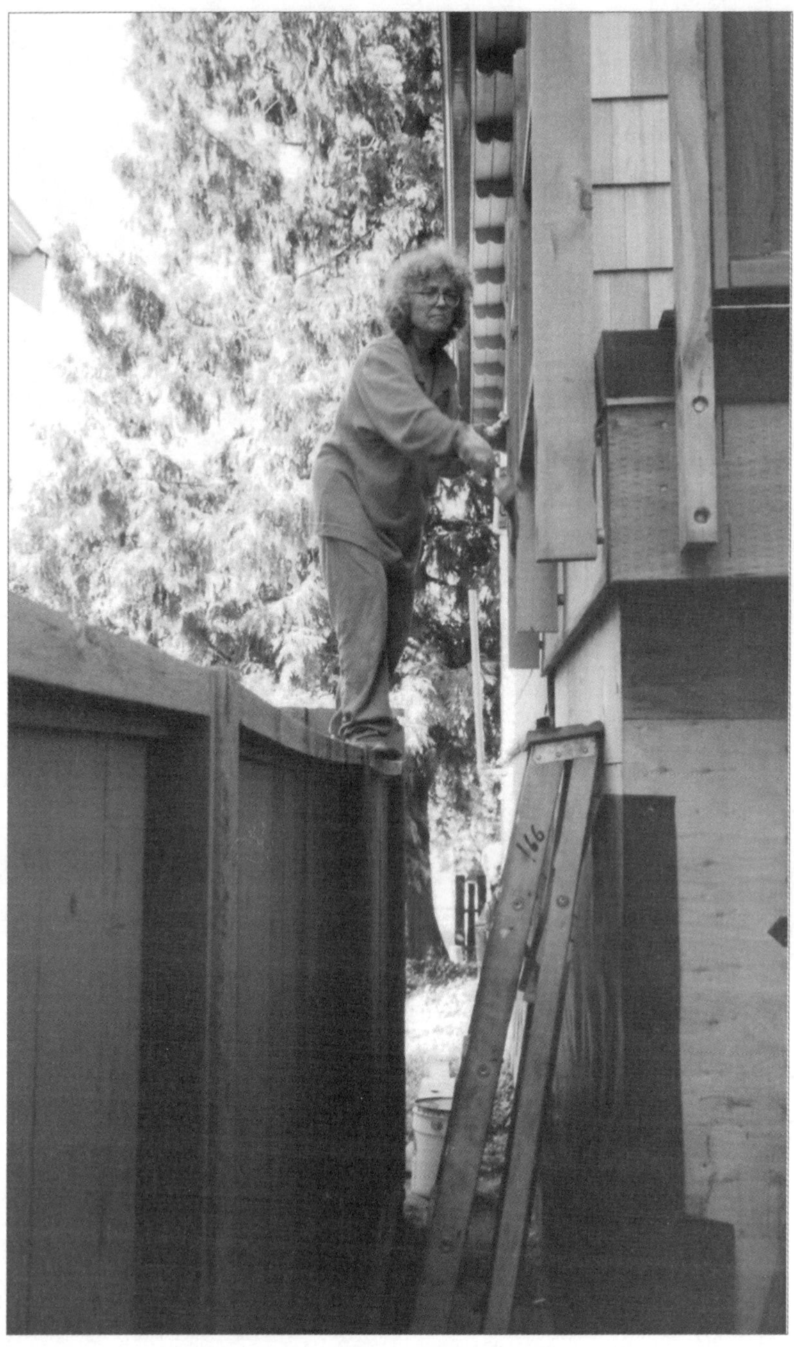

Working on new deck and siding on the Salsbury Drive house.

massage colleges were springing up all across Canada. Massage practitioners' views differed greatly, and many were calling themselves therapists rather than practitioners. As an East Ender I did not want to opt out; my patients who needed treatment would not have the means to pay for it and few of them could afford a surcharge. However, massage therapists eventually evolved into a separate grouping independent of the physiotherapy association, and many of the new therapists chose to opt out of MSP altogether.

Meanwhile, there was a lot to be done in my house before I could comfortably use it. As well as the many loads of garbage, there was soiled carpeting to strip from all the main-floor areas, wood flooring to be sanded and refinished and the big bare patch around the outside of the house to deal with. The electric supply was seriously inadequate and the plumbing was ancient. Luckily there were some federal grants available to first-time buyers, and as a single woman I was eligible. After form filling and obtaining multiple work quotations, I started renovating. I bought paint by the gallon; I'd become good at covering all kinds of wall surfaces, including flaws, with paint. I bought trees to plant. My Scottish roots chose a couple of rowans (mountain ash) for the north side, as these are traditional guardians, and I purchased a couple of evergreens to spruce up the front yard.

At the well-stocked Magnet Hardware store a block away, I could get almost anything that I needed in an emergency: odd items for repair work, tools and building materials. I was a frequent customer. One day, when I was asking advice about what I should get for a particular repair job, one of the two helpful Italian brothers who ran the store said to me, "What you really need is a man in your house." I looked at him and said, "Don't you think I have enough problems?" It was certainly a friendly area.

I lived on the main floor and continued to rent out the upper floor, so I didn't really have a lot of living space. I set up the bedroom as a massage room so that I could see patients who lived in the East End, as these were coming regularly and it avoided them having to travel across town to the West Broadway office. However, where to put my double bed? I needed to keep the living room clear and realized that the wall between those two rooms had originally held French doors, which had been replaced by wooden siding. If I made my bed lower by cutting down its legs and also sawed carefully through the siding between the two rooms, with just enough space to slip the bed through width wise, I could virtually have half a bed in each room during the day, and then pull it out either way to sleep on during the night. Half of a really low bed would not even look like a bed—problem solved.

I continued working both at the West Broadway office and out of my home until I found another massage practitioner, Eleanor Knight, who suggested we look for a location on Commercial Drive and open a clinical practice together. This proved to be a much better solution and we enjoyed working together for many years. We were successful enough that it wasn't difficult to find therapists to act as locums who were quite delighted to carry on our work at times when one of us needed a break.

Motherhood Should Be a Choice

I was invited to give testimony on January 25, 1986, at a public meeting in Vancouver in support of Dr. Henry Morgentaler, who was being charged with illegally operating abortion clinics in Winnipeg and Toronto. The Vancouver Women's Health Collective was instrumental in encouraging a group of us to present our histories in public; we met weekly to prepare ourselves for this event. It was hard to consider speaking out in public about something most of us had never talked about, even with our closest friends. But it was becoming clear that this was important to do, and my two daughters who lived within reach came over from Victoria to support me in person. This was my spoken presentation at that meeting:

> The reason I'm giving testimony today is that I want to break the silence that has placed, and is still placing, women in isolation around the question of abortion. I have no idea whether my mother, or either of my grandmothers, had an abortion. I do know, however, that my great-grandmother had twenty-two children, my paternal grandmother had twelve children, my maternal grandmother had eight, and my own mother had five. I would have eleven children today if I had not aborted. As it is I have five living children, all of whom I dearly love.
>
> I was married at nineteen, in Scotland, and gave birth to three children within the first four years of marriage. I hadn't chosen those pregnancies; no one talked about "choosing" pregnancies at that time. For me, one of the fears around pregnancy was that housing was very scarce. We lived in "rooms" and that was not easy with

small children…When I had asked my doctor what to do to avoid pregnancy, he was embarrassed, but he fitted me with a diaphragm. It didn't provide very reliable protection, however, because I kept on getting pregnant.

At that time I'd only read about women having miscarriages from falling downstairs, or from drinking gin and taking very hot baths. I tried the gin and scalding baths but only fainted and got violently sick. Then I read in the classified ads in a local newspaper about a remedy for "menstrual irregularities," which sounded a little odd, but I wrote away for it. The remedy turned out to be tiny silver pills that came in a little bottle with instructions: Not to Be Taken for Pregnancy. I suspected these might work. I took the dose; they acted as a strong purgative, and after extreme cramping and a feeling that I was losing my insides, I miraculously bled. I stocked up on those pills. The next time I became pregnant, they didn't work after a first dose, so I upped the dose and got the needed result. But the third time I had to use them, they didn't work at all. And when I told my doctor about the pregnancy, he said I probably should have had a new size of diaphragm fitted after my third child was born. His information was a bit late. My husband said that he'd heard about a knitting needle being used to induce abortion. With a lot of anxiety, we tried it. After two attempts, bleeding was induced, but it wouldn't stop, and after several days, I was passing bigger and bigger blood clots. I called my doctor and he told me to go into hospital right away.

This was my first hospital experience. My husband wasn't allowed to stay with me, and I didn't know what was going to happen. I was taken into the emergency room—it was incredibly cold—and given an internal examination. Then I was shaved and left there alone for the night…In the morning I was told they were going to operate, and I was taken into another room, where my stomach was pumped; tubes were put through my nasal passages and into my stomach, a very unpleasant experience, and then I was put under with ether.

I clearly remember struggling so hard to come out of the ether; it felt like struggling back to life, and it seemed to take the longest time. I could hear the nurses talking about me and the terrible thing

I'd done. I was put into the maternity ward for recovery; the nurses showed their disapproval by ignoring me, and I didn't feel I had much to share with the women who were there with new babies. I felt guilty and isolated. When I was told that I had an internal infection and would have to stay there until the fever went down, I felt quite frightened...I signed myself out of the hospital, against their authority, but I knew I couldn't get better in that environment. Just over a year later, I had another child.

Then we decided to emigrate to Canada. It took over a year to make the arrangements, and the month before we were due to leave I found I was pregnant again. I was too scared of messing up our travel plans to consider doing anything drastic, so my fifth child was born in a small town in eastern BC. I was still using a diaphragm; there was nothing else for protection at the time.

I know there were two more occasions when I induced abortion, and it was a knitting needle that we used again. I no longer had access to the silver pills. It was scary and I felt I was pushing the limits, but I also felt I had no choice. I pretended to be having a miscarriage when the hemorrhaging began, and I was taken to hospital each time and had good care. I think my doctor suspected, though, because I remember him saying, "You won't do anything foolish, will you?" when I told him I was pregnant again. I also worried that they might refuse to continue giving me care at the hospital.

After the birth of my sixth child the miraculous "pill" came on the market. Those early pills were a super-high dosage, and I do wonder now, when I experience mood swings that feel chemical in origin, whether those high-level doses, which made me feel remarkably good—"high" is the best description—have had a permanent effect on my chemical balance. But at the time it was a real lifesaver for me. I took the pill for five years, until I contracted hepatitis, after which I couldn't use it. I was then fitted with an IUD.

Unfortunately, after I was fitted, the duration of my menstrual periods increased from six days to eleven days and the flow became heavier. About nine months after it was fitted, and just after we arrived in Pennsylvania, where my husband had a three-month guest artist teaching appointment, the bleeding was profuse and wouldn't stop. Because we were non-residents and had no US medical insurance, I was refused entry at the local hospital, and I had difficulty in finding a doctor who would treat me. I remember eventually sitting in one doctor's waiting room and saying that I wouldn't leave until he removed the offending IUD. So much for safer birth control; I was back at stage one.

In summing up: as I said earlier, I don't know if my mother ever had an abortion. Certainly, I didn't tell her about mine. But I am thankful that my daughters have been able to choose, in a climate of comparative acceptance, whether to have, or not have, children. And I want that choice to continue. It's never easy to make a decision to abort. It's not any easier to make that decision now than it was when I made my decisions...And I do believe that women who choose abortion, rather than an unwanted pregnancy, should be given the dignity of safe, supportive medical care. Women will take dangerous steps when they have no choice. For myself, the worst thing was the fear that I might have damaged a baby that I hadn't succeeded in aborting. We don't need to subject women to that fear, guilt or blame.

I charge the abortion laws with violating the right of women to make decisions about their own bodies. I charge the abortion laws with violating the right of children to be chosen. I further charge that this violation has resulted in physical and mental abuse to countless unnamed women and children.

The public meeting got good coverage and had more impact than most of us expected. Breaking the silence eventually resulted in necessary changes to the law. It was worth the pain that most of us went through in contributing our voices.

Vancouver Years

I lived in my house on Salsbury Drive for over thirty years, by far the longest time I'd ever stayed in one place. I had no difficulty in finding people to share the house; most came by word of mouth, and many became valued friends.

My son, Andy, and his wife, Susanne, lived in the apartment above me for many years, and my third set of grandchildren was born during this period. What a delight they were to have around and how lucky I was to have that experience. However, I also remember my concern when I found two-year-old Josh poking a knife into an electrical outlet in the kitchen one morning, and another time when I found my prize rhododendron bush with all the branches denuded at its base, after he'd pruned it with the secateurs he'd been watching me use on some other bush that really needed them. There were surprises, always.

I loved the area, often referred to as the Italian area, and certainly most of the coffee bars and some of the restaurants and stores, including an outlandishly smart shoe shop, were Italian owned. I could walk to just about everything I needed in daily life; there was not only every kind of food available, but bookstores, a library, banks, a medical centre, a liquor store and even two small parks, all within a few blocks of my home.

Bit by bit, I became part of that unique community. I liked being an involved member of the East End Food Co-operative and seeing it move from being in a small building on Victoria Drive to an actual storefront on Commercial Drive. I sat at times on various committees of the co-op board and initiated questioning around the labelling of genetically modified foods. It seemed completely backwards to be forced to label non-genetically modified products. I attended a federally sponsored meeting about genetically modified foods in a prestigious West

End hotel, where most of the attendees came from large manufacturing or pharmaceutical companies and were promoting the values of genetic engineering. Brewster and Cathleen Kneen, publishers of the *Ram's Horn*, a monthly about food issues, and I had to practically force our way into this meeting, as we did not appear to have the

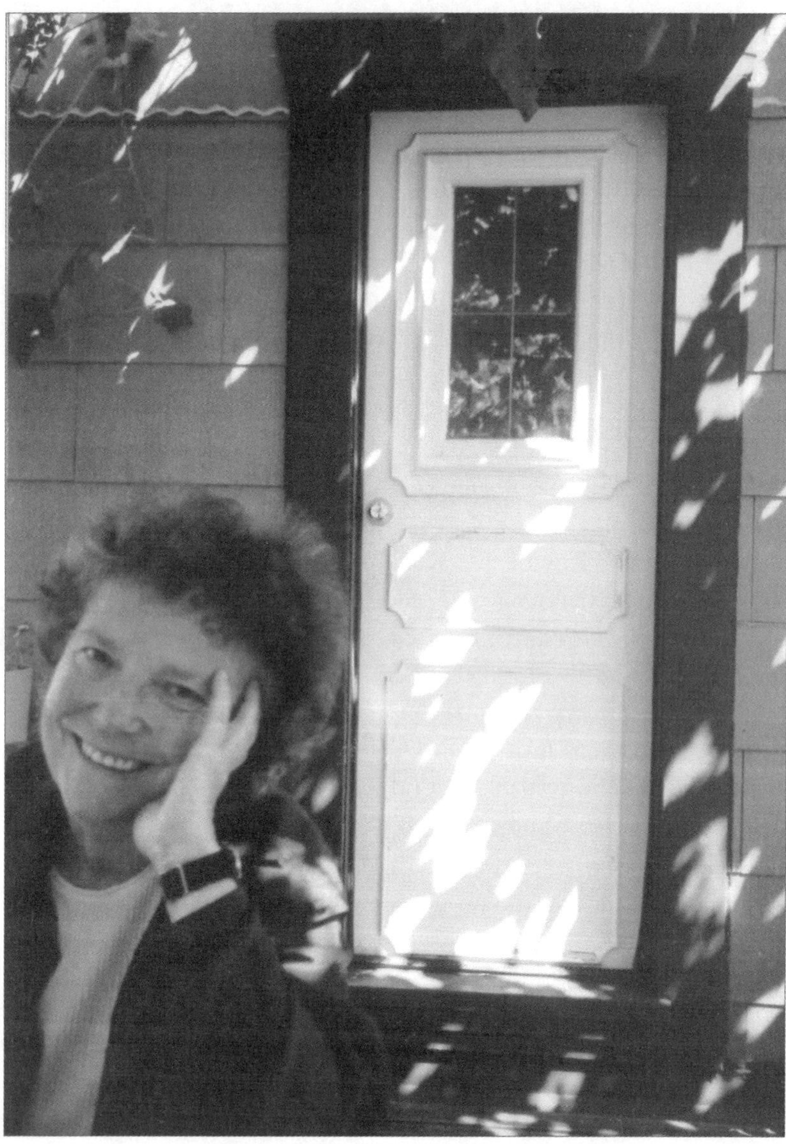

Under the grape arbour on the side deck, Salsbury Drive house.

expected credentials. This meeting had been advertised as "public," and yet it was difficult for us to get our questions and observations heard. After that, I distributed petitions on promoting non-genetically modified food to as many stores as would take them on Commercial Drive, the best I could think to do.

I also became a member of the board of the Reach Community Health Centre. This was a medical clinic of integrated facilities, including dental, which still provides valuable services to the area. In its earlier years there were many heated discussions within the board regarding pro-choice and other issues, and I remember valuing the progressive stand taken by its members.

Almost next door to the Reach Clinic was a unique café-cum-meeting-place called La Quena, which was largely operated by volunteers. It provided a venue for evening talks, political discussions and informal concerts, and it became a good place for immigrant Latin Americans to meet with others. My good friend Elena, who has since returned to Argentina, often shared duties with me at the counter. She also attempted to improve my school Spanish, but not very successfully! Pauline, one of my neighbours, brought her exuberant preschooler with her when she volunteered; she was happy to have other eyes watching him and actually giving her a break. Children were always welcomed.

During this period I attended various human potential workshops, but the rebirthing experience turned out to be less dramatic than I expected. There was a lot of searching going on, but most of it seemed to be only on a personal basis, which I found tiresome. Then Radical Therapy became the "in" thing and I became part of the response team for an Emotional Emergency Collective. We scheduled ourselves to be available on phone duty round the clock for people who felt they were in crisis. This seemed to be a more useful thing to do, but also rather presumptuous when I look back on it. How qualified did we think we were?

There was endless opportunity for political involvement. I joined the Raging Grannies, and one of the actions we undertook was going down to the military recruitment office, where we volunteered to take the place of the youngsters who were being encouraged to join up. We met with a very perplexed reception on that occasion; they just didn't know what to do with this gaggle of grannies.

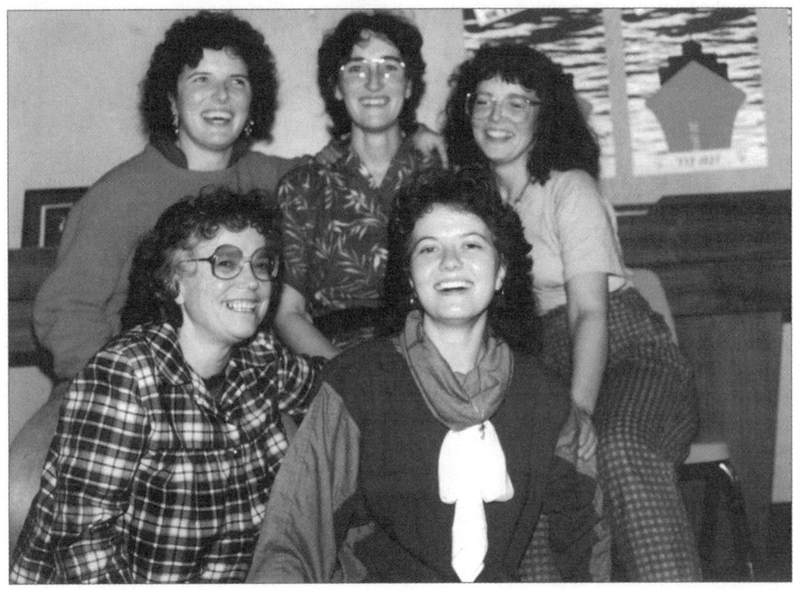

With Judy, Janet Lawton, Claire and Natanis at Claire and Bill's Nicaragua send-off party, September 1985.

For some years I was part of a non-violence collective. We met weekly to figure out ways of dealing with aggression, how to stand up for our rights when police got involved and how to access legal help. Within the group we needed to tackle the question of how to reach consensus and what to do if we couldn't reach consensus. The issue we were most concerned about was the establishment of a US nuclear submarine base at Nanoose Bay, north of Nanaimo; we wanted to figure out how to protest this effectively. A small group of us spent a weekend there, uncomfortably tenting on the rocky shore, trying to develop a strategy to house ourselves if a large enough group could coalesce. That was a very cold weekend and unfortunately we never became a big enough group to take this further.

There was so much else, in music, theatre and film. Jazz clubs came and went, but the Classical Joint and later the Alma Street Café were two of my favourites. One evening I remember hearing a very young woman playing piano and singing at Alma Street, just inches away from me in that small space, wondering if she was nervous, and thinking, *She's really good, this youngster from Nanaimo.* It was Diana Krall. Jazz moved around, clubs opened and closed, places changed

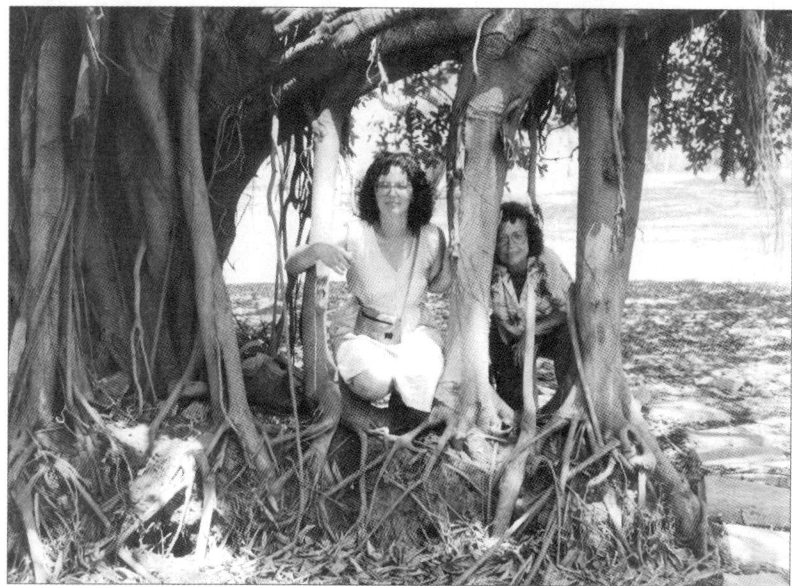

With Judy in Managua, Nicaragua, April 1986.

hands, and eventually the Cellar, on West Broadway, became the most long-lived location before closing after thirteen years. I enjoyed live theatre, too, particularly small theatre, and the early days of the Fringe Festival, when I was able to see all the events by volunteering.

I loved dancing. There were so many benefit dances for the numerous groups that were doing work for causes that needed funding, from Rape Relief to Co-op Radio, from Women's Resource Centres to Tools for Peace in Nicaragua, and many more.

On one occasion when I went to the Commodore Ballroom with a couple of friends and paid a goodly sum for entry, we were surprised when they came round to charge us for the second band. I refused and said this hadn't been part of the deal. I yelled at the bouncers, "Don't touch me! We paid for the evening." I wasn't normally a shouter, but this time I raised my voice and managed to force them to let us stay. I was proud of myself that night.

I loved to sing, yet not be conspicuous. I certainly had no interest in being a soloist. It was the shared singing and the harmony of "part" voices that I enjoyed. Mostly I sang alto, and it was only later that I found myself in the soprano section; quite surprisingly my voice had moved up somewhat. I joined a folk singing choir for a number of years and then became part of Bonnie Ferguson's choir, the Trouts, which would entertain at seniors' residences with old-time favourites. It was a great name for a choir, based on the Trout Lake Community Centre near her housing co-op. Eventually I joined Marcus Mosely's gospel choir, the first auditioned choir I joined. I nervously sang an old Gaelic song, the only one I knew, hoping to wheedle my way in; he graciously welcomed me.

Through all these different activities I cultivated a rich circle of friends. Twice a week I would meet with some special friends for coffee after taking aquatic classes at the YWCA, and we would ponder over current affairs and try to figure out how the world could and should be run. We would also share information about books we were reading, films we had seen and interesting events that were coming up.

The years went by quickly and retirement came sooner than I thought. I realized I had to slow down, but retiring was an odd thing to think about. Everyone told me, "You have to plan for it." I'd never really planned for anything much, so I didn't see the need for doing it now. I'd just do more of what I enjoyed doing and pick up some part-time work if I needed to supplement my small rental income. The garden could always use my time. It wasn't very large, but it was a bit needy, as it cornered three sides of the house. And as a senior I could always audit university classes for free.

When my friend and massage clinic partner, Eleanor, decided to move to Saskatoon, I knew I would miss her greatly. And after thirteen years of massage work I found my wrists feeling somewhat weak. As I was repairing and recovering an old chaise lounge, I found myself having trouble using the hammer; my wrists were just not working well enough. I had to decide whether wielding that hammer—much needed in an old house—or continuing to work physically on bodies would make most sense. I loved my work as a therapist, but the hammer won, and I slowly retired from working five days a week, to four days, to three and then two days, gradually working my way out of the clinic. Our practice was quickly taken over and it's still going strong today, more than three decades after we first opened its doors.

I was happy when I was offered some occasional work as substitute manager at two subsidized housing units in the East End. The

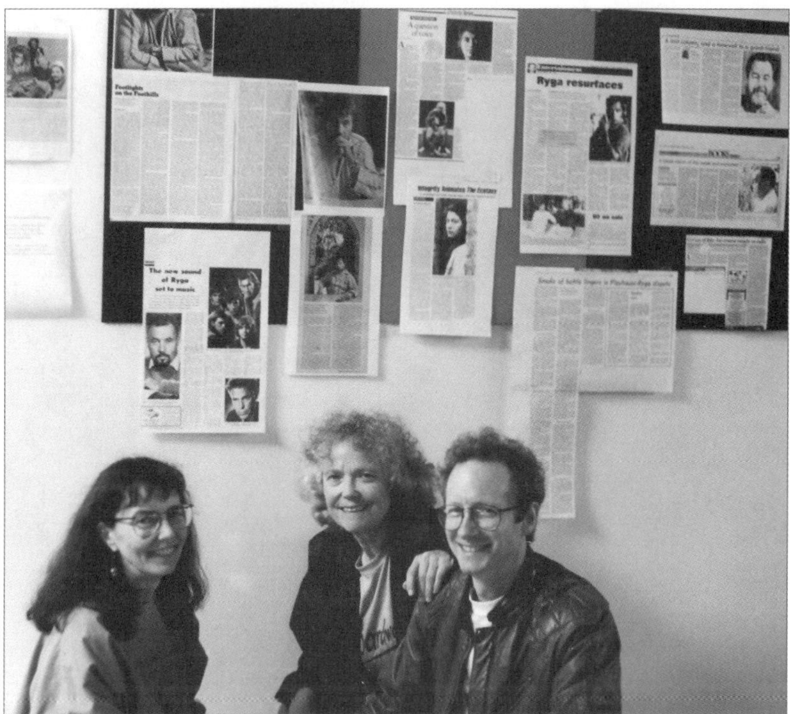

With Claire and Bill at a Ryga Centre benefit in Vancouver, April 1996.

work was interesting and there were always some problems to be addressed. Tenants dealt with their financial distress in different ways—some permanently behind with their rent, others finding where to get the best prices on groceries or clothing, and a few who had constant grievances that couldn't always be met. I sometimes felt a bit bad about being paid for this work, but it was modestly paid and I could be a good listener, so it was a fair enough exchange.

For a while I took on some part-time office work at CRS, a wholesale workers' co-operative that was operating close to Burnaby. I liked taking the SkyTrain there and enjoyed taking down orders by phone from small communities in outlying areas of the province. It reminded me of the importance of food co-operatives as a way of ensuring that food growers could have more direct access to consumers, benefiting both growers and consumers in the process. Years later, I was delighted to hear of their reunion party to celebrate the co-op's fortieth year of operation.

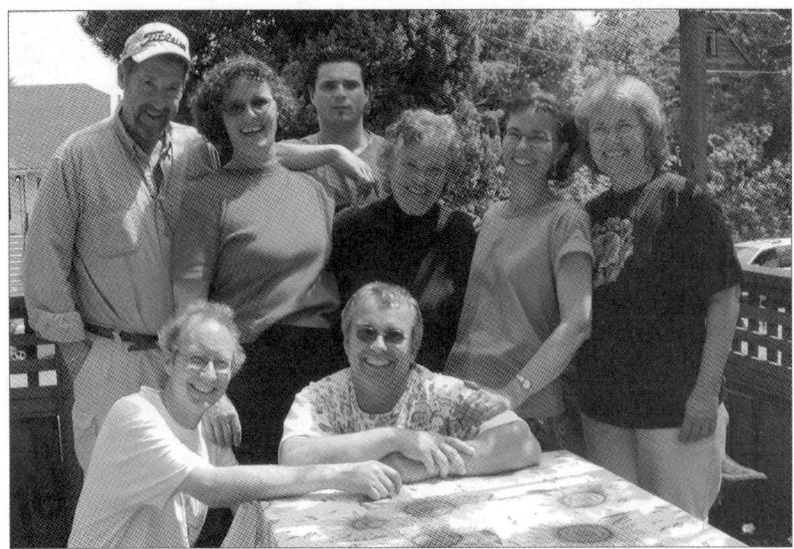

Jerry, Judy, Shane, Claire, Kate, Bill and Andy help celebrate my seventy-fifth birthday.

I could now travel more often to visit family and friends who lived in other parts of BC. I already knew both the East and West Kootenays thoroughly, having travelled those parts frequently and explored many rough mountain roads in my little Datsun pickup truck that I had set up with space to sleep. I'd had some awkward experiences after getting stuck on logging roads trying to find alternate routes from Merritt to Summerland, as I always preferred the unknown route. But now I could explore some of the Cariboo, where my daughter Claire was living with her partner, Bill, in Wells. They were creating the Amazing Space Studio and Gallery in a deconsecrated church.

I later took my grandson Josh with me, at an early age, to expose him to rural life, including several visits to my herb specialist friend, Dianne, who lives high above Balfour, in the West Kootenays, about one kilometre from the highway. He would always be surprised to find no TV in this home, but he would greatly enjoy finding an egg in her henhouse.

I have loved going there at the end of the summer, helping her gather and process all the garden produce, which always included picking her own bountiful crops, as well as from neighbours who had more than they needed of apples, plums, pears and sometimes even some

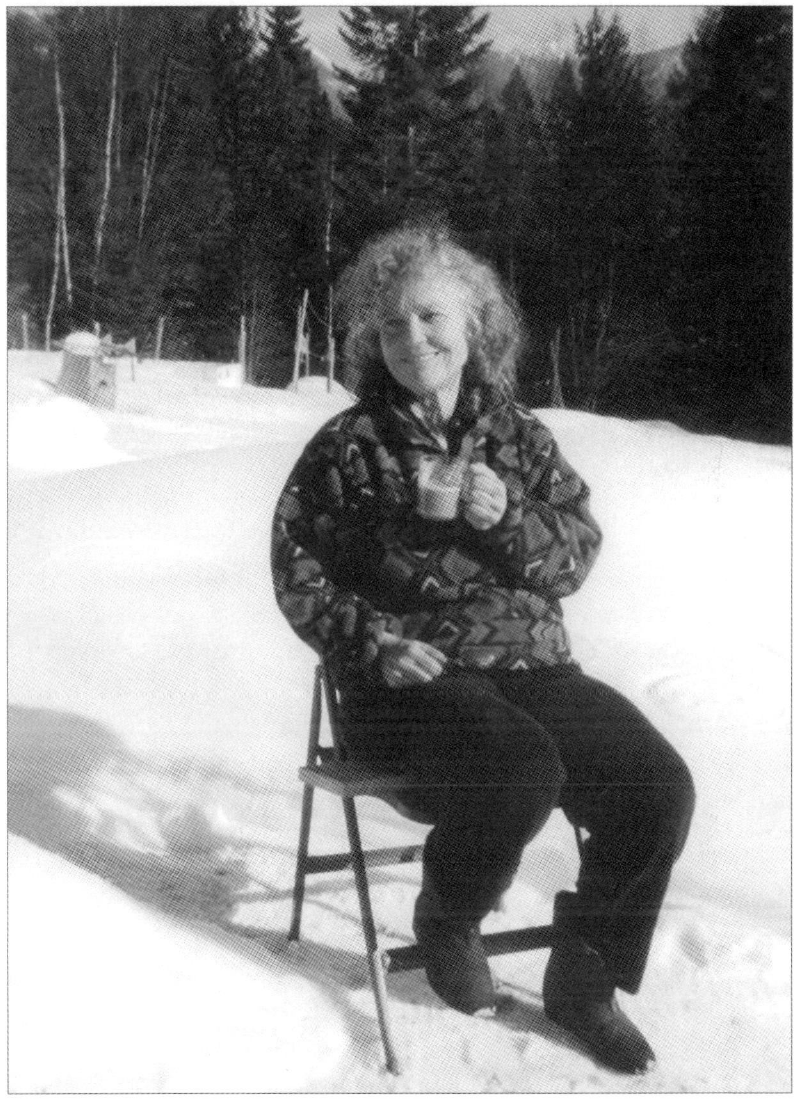

Coffee at Dianne's place near Balfour.

late raspberries. She and her blind husband are almost self-sufficient. They take great joy and delight in growing enough for the winter and sharing what they have. They have a rich life with very little, which inspires me. Canning and drying fruit, trudging up the mountain to find special herbs and roots, watching her process her ointments and tinctures, I have learned a lot from Dianne.

Josh's Birth, 1992

I couldn't sleep. At about three o'clock in the morning, I finally got up and put my clothes on. Then I dithered, debating with myself, and finally got into my car and drove to the hospital. My daughter-in-law, Susanne, had gone into labour late that afternoon, and we had walked together round a few neighbourhood blocks in the early evening. She had stopped every six or seven minutes, stooping forward, groaning a bit, and then in a minute or so she'd straighten up and walk on, saying, "Boy, that was a good, strong one." She was feeling confident, but seriously tired, when Andy took her into the hospital around 9:00 p.m.; she'd been having contractions on and off for two days. Her closest friend, Michelle, was going to be her labour coach, and Andy had gone to prenatal classes with her so that he, too, would know what to expect and how to help.

I was well aware that I might not get news from the hospital till early morning, as this was Susanne's first baby. My own experience from having given birth six times led me to expect that she might still have another few hours of labour ahead of her. But I hadn't really wanted to tell her that when she left for the hospital. She was so sure she'd give birth within a couple of hours, and I didn't want to discourage her optimism. I wasn't sure it would be helpful.

I wondered what the regulations were regarding those allowed to attend a hospital birth. Because Susanne already had her husband and her closest friend attending her, I had hesitated to ask if she'd like me, her mother-in-law, to be there, too. I could be one too many. Her own mother lived in New Brunswick; she couldn't have been farther away.

Even though Andy had lived in the upstairs apartment of my house since I'd moved into it twelve years earlier, I somehow never felt the same ease with him that I shared with my daughters. He led a different lifestyle from mine and had made it clear that he neither expected nor needed me to look after him, nor to be involved with his affairs. Susanne had moved in with him just over two years earlier. I liked her and they seemed delighted and ready to be parents. I was more than happy to see the changes that her presence brought about in Andy's life. But I was cautious in pushing my friendship on Susanne and reluctant to take our relationship for granted, knowing that a mother-in-law is never chosen; she just comes as part of the package. So I didn't know if either of them would really want me to be present at the birth.

Despite my uncertainties, at around 3:30 a.m. I arrived at the emergency doors of the hospital, where a nurse was having a cigarette break outside. I thought it must be hard to have to leave the building when you needed a smoke, but I was puzzled by this thought, because I'm an avid non-smoker. I asked her where the labour ward was and she told me to go round to the other side of the building to the night entrance. Then she gave me specific directions as to where to go once I was inside. I had already parked the car and I was cold, not having dressed very thoughtfully, and a slight flurry of snow was falling. I felt a need to hurry. It was a relief to know which corridor to take when I went in, as there was barely a soul about. It also meant that I was able to find my way to the labour ward unchallenged.

Some homing instinct took me straight to the right room. Susanne was being attended by her doctor and by a nurse, both of whom, at that moment, were looking at a screen that showed dense, uneven, zigzagging graph lines, obviously of some importance. Susanne was half lying, bolstered by pillows, on a narrow hospital bed, looking worried and exhausted. Michelle was standing beside her, holding her hand. Andy was sitting close by, also looking exhausted. It had been a regular workday for him. He worked long hours at a physically demanding job, and he had had no preparation for this long night. He looked up when I came in, and I'll never forget his words, "Thank goodness Mom's here; it'll be all right." It was such a relief to hear that and to know I really was welcome.

Neither the doctor nor the nurse seemed bothered by my presence. They were far too concerned with Susanne's condition, as it was obvious that things were not going well. She was at the pushing stage, but every time she pushed, the baby's heartbeat weakened and slowed down. The harder she pushed, the worse it became. Her doctor was now asking her to stop pushing altogether; she wanted a second opinion from the gynecologist on duty that night. But as he was presently performing a Caesarean, they would have to wait. The nurse said it had been a very busy night for him, as there had been an unusual number of C-sections to deal with. He came in shortly afterwards, carefully assessed Susanne's condition, looked over the monitored data and said it looked as though it would be wise to schedule her for surgery. He would get her in as soon as possible, but he had another emergency birth to deal with first.

Andy looked troubled and anxious, asking, "Can I still be with her for the birth?" The surgeon, without answering his question directly, said that he would equip Andy with a gown and cap, perhaps to let him down easily. I was now formally introduced to Susanne's doctor and to the nurse. There was going to be some waiting time, which meant that Andy could lie down for a while, and Michelle could take a break.

Susanne's contractions were fortunately coming less frequently, and I was able to take a turn by her side. It gave me a chance to ask her about the various contraptions that were strapped to her and about the different monitoring devices she was hooked up to, for I knew nothing of these modern and complex mechanical birthing attendants. In turn I told her how it had been for me, giving birth at home in our living room with a midwife and a nurse, and she was as bemused by my experience as I was with hers.

Although she was disappointed, she was also relieved by the decision to do a C-section. She'd been sensing for a while that something was wrong, and that they'd given natural birth as good a chance as possible. For some reason the baby wasn't coping. I couldn't help but wonder if the baby was at risk while we were waiting for the operating room. I cautiously asked the doctor, and she assured me that the baby's heartbeat had revived since Susanne stopped pushing with the contractions.

Around 5:30 a.m. the surgeon put his head round the door and tossed Andy a green gown and cap. "Time to dress up!" Susanne was wheeled out of the labour room with Andy beside her, and Michelle

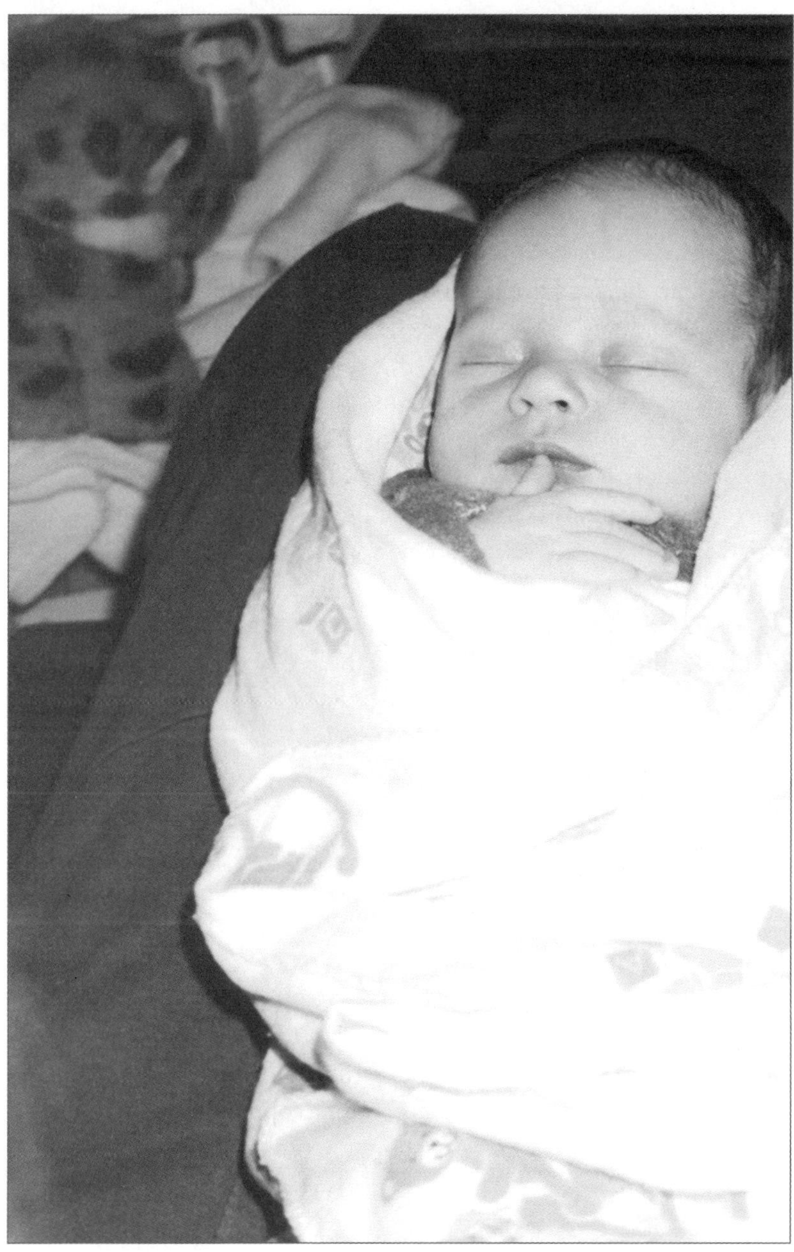

Newborn Josh.

and I were shown a corridor area where we could wait. About fifteen minutes later Andy joined us, crestfallen. "They only allow medical staff to be present for the operation, but they let me stay with her till the last minute." And then he confessed, "I don't know if I could actually have managed to watch them cutting into her anyway; I wouldn't want to faint on them!" The minutes ticked by slowly. The corridor was bare and totally silent. We felt we had to whisper, tried to make jokes, but it was hard going and none of us had much to say.

The surgeon finally appeared, bouncing down the corridor toward Andy with a huge grin. "Well, you're a father now; you've got a lively young baby boy. You can go in right away, but perhaps the other two of you would wait a few more minutes. She's still a bit groggy from the anaesthetic." Susanne was more than a bit groggy when we finally saw her; she could barely hold the tiny bundle and immediately passed it over for one of us to enjoy. Andy had got his video camera out and was doing his best to capture those first moments. Susanne's doctor came over to us and quietly said, "It was good we made that decision—the baby's cord was wrapped three times around its neck. It would never have made it on its own."

WANDERLUST

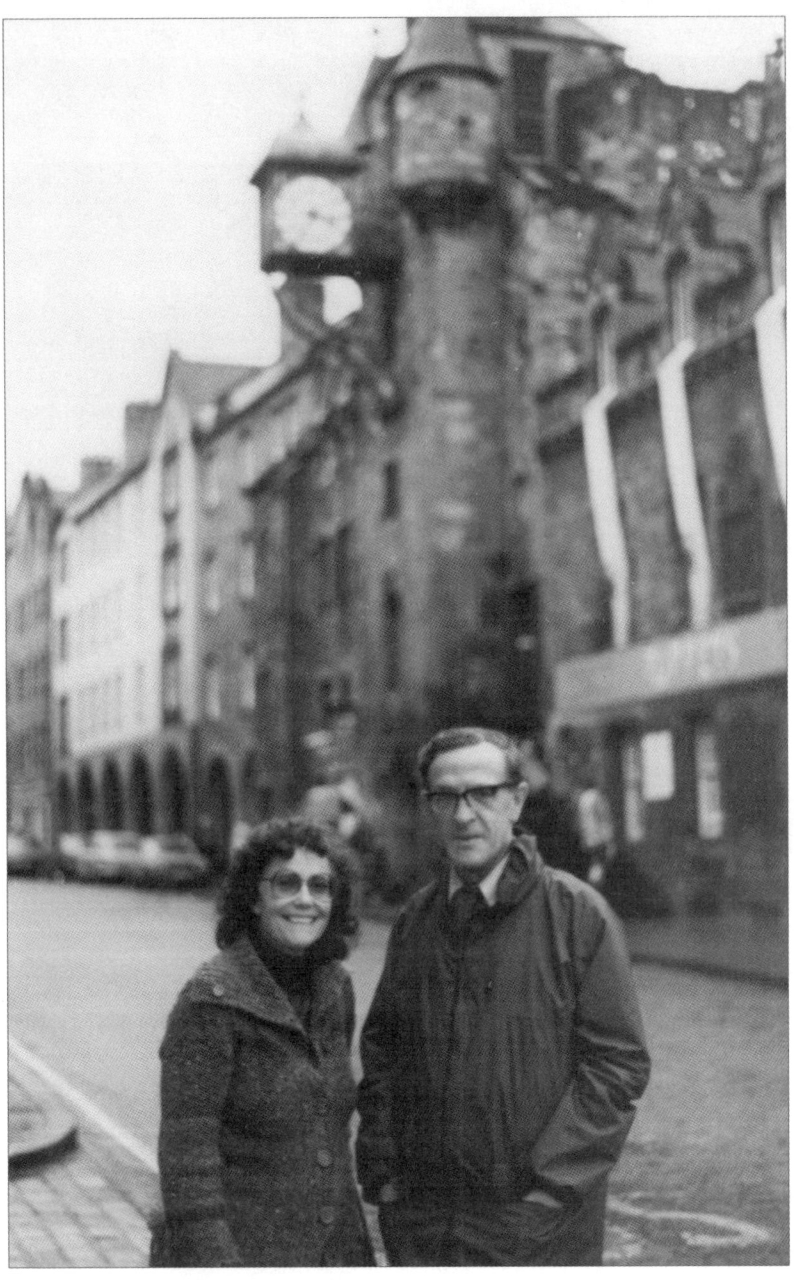

With my uncle, David Murray, in Edinburgh.

imagine, a view like this when you get up in the morning,
said a visitor to the stony mesa

this small village perched on narrow ledge of ancient outcrop
on cliffs exposed in all directions
to heat, cold and winds that sweep these plains

this village does not have water, says our Hopi guide
in quiet voice
we choose to live like our ancestors
we grow our corn in the desert below with dry farming
we must wait till the rain comes
testing the ground till there is moisture
enough to plant the seed
there has been drought for two years
but maybe this year there will be rain

we pass a mud brick oven
hot charcoal is being raked out by the woman tending
she does this with care,
making sure the coals are pulled from all the corners
a second woman stands by with shovel
to catch the ashes
and now another woman appears with trays
of rounded pita bread, already risen, ready for the oven's heat
in preparation for a ceremony
that will take place tomorrow

No photos allowed on this land
they take the spirit
No soliciting allowed on this land

visitors are guests and must not be harassed
Would you like to see my Katsina dolls
a large man shyly asks as we pass his door.
behind him a woman, small child in arms
looks at us anxiously

We look below us at the footsteps worn into the long, steep cliff path
by centuries of women carrying water to their homes

We came by car
and think the view is beautiful
–1969

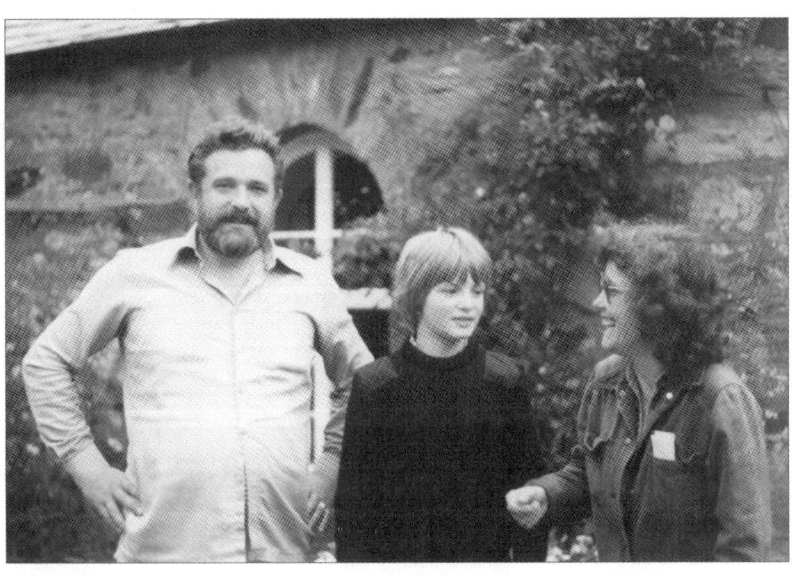

In Scotland with my brother Jervis and nephew Dougal.

I have greatly enjoyed travelling for much of my life, in large part because it involves an escape from routine. Going alone, as I have often done, would require me to connect with strangers—an effective antidote to shyness. However, for me its greatest appeal has been meeting a larger world, entering new situations and being challenged in some way to recognize the common ground that we all share, as well as the very different ways in which people live.

I have always travelled modestly; youth hostels provided the best accommodation wherever I went. They varied quite a bit from country to country, but they always welcomed elders. Nowadays couch surfing offers opportunities for others, mostly younger. But regardless of one's mode, travelling offers rewards that no amount of web surfing can provide. I feel immensely grateful for having been able to taste so many places. The following chapters, taken directly from my journals, describe some of these trips.

A Bulgarian Bus Trip, 1981

We had been waiting for the bus for over two hours. This was a part of the city that was obviously poor—a northern suburb of Istanbul, an area that we had not previously visited. Only a few scattered shops, meagrely stocked: no hustling and no tourists. We were waiting on the sidewalk with our backpacks and assorted bags, somewhat of a curiosity to the young children on the street, and we couldn't help but wonder if we were really in the right place. It was not a bus depot, just a street location that we had been given for the bus that would take us to Belgrade.

I was travelling with Norma's sister, Millie, and Janet, whom I had known from our Summerland days. We had been companions for the last four weeks through France, Italy, the Greek islands and Turkey, by rail, bus, large steamers and small boats, while staying in sparse rooms, tiny pensions and barrack-like hostels. Millie was revisiting places she had already lived in and loved, while Janet and I were filled with the wonder of first-time observers.

It had not been easy for us to get information on buses travelling out of Istanbul. Later we would understand why. As we waited, we thought of phoning the agency that had given us the information, but we were not able to communicate well enough to either find a phone or ask for the use of one. We realized it was unlikely that there would be many phones in this district.

A few other people joined us, apparently waiting for the same bus. Although we lacked sufficient Turkish to communicate at ordinary street level, we became quite adept at improvisation. The others did not seem perturbed by the long wait. Around 5:30 p.m., the bus arrived, four hours late. The driver, a harried-looking, officious man, hustled us unceremoniously aboard.

The bus was tightly packed. We found seats at the back, though mine was only a partial seat, as I was sharing it with a very large man in military uniform whose body needed more than his ticket allocation. My two travelling companions found seats that were reluctantly emptied of overflow baggage. We settled in, in our separate places, relieved to be on our way.

Taking a prominent place on the bus was a large, multi-generational Iranian family with several small, lively children; they were refugees from persecution who had all their worldly belongings with them, hoping to find a safe home in Italy. Two young Yugoslav women, both students, were returning home from their studies in Turkey and were delighted to act as interpreters for us and to practice their English. The military man sitting beside me turned out to be from Egypt, and later he graciously shared his small supply of dried fruit with me. He was travelling to Germany, but he politely declined to discuss his assignment or politics.

There was a surprising lack of services. Instead of the usual vendors we had come to expect and rely upon during our journeys, who would come to the windows of the buses with food and drink, we found that we were on a very different kind of trip, with some unexpected confrontations. Our driver, who turned out to be Yugoslav, was anxious to get to the Bulgarian border before darkness fell. We had hoped there would be a meal break, or at least an opportunity to pick up food from stalls at a washroom stop. With some high-speed driving we made it to the border by dusk, near 7:30 p.m. However, the customs official on duty decided that the daily allocation of buses allowed to cross the border had already been met. This seemed to be a somewhat arbitrary decision, and our driver was furious. The well-armed official told him that our bus had a choice of either paying a "head tax" for each passenger or remaining at the border until the following morning.

What we had forgotten was that in 1981 Bulgaria and Yugoslavia were not on speaking terms. Yugoslavia had remained independent of the communist bloc since the Second World War, and its neighbours were still making it pay for past insubordination. After a long, extended and mostly incomprehensible shouting match, the Yugoslav girls translated, explaining to us that we would have to sit in the bus for the entire night, exactly where we were. The driver would not allow any of us to pay the head tax, which he said was illegal and would just disappear into the customs officer's pocket. He thought it was obvious that some of the passengers could not pay this. Moreover, the official was demanding that it be paid in US dollars, a further insult.

Since there was no customs building at this crossing, just a small concrete box-like structure with a bright floodlight blazing the breadth of the road and a couple of sentries on duty, and as there was no toilet on the bus, most of us relieved ourselves alfresco after stumbling out into the darkness during the next ten hours. We had been careless in not bringing some food for the journey, because until this time we had always encountered an abundant source of food: the rural population made a meagre livelihood by supplying food to tourists. It was the middle of a hot July, and we had been looking forward to stopping at a local village café for a simple evening meal and a cool drink. This bleak situation was quite a disappointment. We couldn't help but be a little envious of the Iranian family, who brought out a small cooking stove, placed it in the aisle of the bus and proceeded to cook themselves a modest dinner. But in due course, we all settled down as best we could in our cramped seating to sleep away what we could of the night.

At dawn, our driver began tooting his horn. After some altercations and another shouting match, the bus finally moved forward across the border. Then our driver informed us that the bus would not make another stop until it had crossed right through Bulgaria and reached the Yugoslav border. This was a little alarming: no food, no toilet, no leg stretching or fresh air.

By now we were beginning to get to know some of our fellow passengers. I didn't converse as much as I would have liked with my military companion. When we were travelling in Turkey we had been unexpectedly addressed in German many times. We discovered that there were many German tourists in Turkey, and any faces that looked Anglo-Saxon were assumed to be German. It was rather refreshing for us; in other parts of Europe we had to battle against being labelled American. Also, a large number of Turkish people sought work in Germany and learned the language. The Egyptian seated next to me seemed to speak German, but very little English. My German, however, was limited, as I hadn't spoken any since my teen years. And although I had by now acquired a Greek phrase book and a Turkish dictionary, I could not communicate with him in his own Arabic language.

The two young women from Yugoslavia were delightfully talkative and friendly. Skodja, who sat directly in front of me, was tall, blond and quite ambitious. She wanted to work in the diplomatic service but had some reluctance about joining the Communist Party, which would be a requirement for such a position. She had total admiration and respect for Tito, but she had reservations about the party itself. Her friend Mila was a complete contrast: short, with dark curly hair, and with little interest in the political scene, which bored her. She quizzed Millie and Janet, who sat across the aisle from her, about the pop and fashion scene in North America; these were much more interesting to her.

After Skodja and I had talked at some length about politics, about women's issues, about the great opportunities for education that Yugoslav students were offered, she hesitantly said she had a favour to ask me. She had bought a fur coat in Istanbul, where she had been living for the last two years, studying Chinese, Arabic and Turkish, and she didn't want to have to pay the exorbitant duty levied at the Yugoslav border. Would I be willing to take it across for her and say it was mine? As a Canadian, I would not be subject to any levy by Yugoslav customs. Because I'm someone who has few qualms about such matters, I shrugged and agreed. My companions, Millie and Janet, looked very bothered, though, and expressed their anxiety at my being so cavalier and naive.

The trip through Bulgaria, as seen from the window of our bus, took us through large expanses of tidy and seemingly rich agricultural land, light industry and rather charming and typical eastern European villages. It would have been interesting to stop at some of these, but our bus kept going. We did manage to persuade the driver to stop at a public washroom in the early afternoon only to face the wrath of the elderly woman who was the attendant. She insisted that we pay for the use of these facilities and that we pay in Bulgarian currency, which of course no one had! By this time, I was frustrated enough to adopt the shouting techniques of our bus driver, and I remember demonstrating that if we couldn't use the washrooms, the attendant might have to clean up the floor. I'm somewhat embarrassed to recall that incident, because we were visitors and I would like to have dealt with the situation in a more conciliatory manner. It is not the way I like to act, especially in a foreign country.

After this one and only stop, we reached the Yugoslav border in the early evening, with growling stomachs. For some strange reason, I expected we would be given a red-carpet welcome. So I was more than a little surprised to find that we were all taken off the bus, with strict instructions to leave all our bags and possessions on the seats. Then we were herded into a customs building, lined up for interrogation and separated into two groups. Meanwhile, the bus was driven off into a large warehouse. Word of mouth informed us that the bus would be searched microscopically, ostensibly for drugs, but other sources said it was for gold. I was wearing the fur coat that Skodja had asked me to take across the border for her, and it looked not only a little incongruous in the heat, but also rather large for my small size. I confess to having had some rather uneasy moments, wondering if she might possibly have hidden some drugs in the lining. However, once more I found how privileged I was as a Canadian: one look at my passport and I was nodded on, without a look or query about the large coat I was wearing. It really wasn't fair.

One Iranian family was harassed, even though they explained they did not want to stay in Yugoslavia, but were only in transit to Italy. Iran was still in a revolutionary crisis after the shah's departure in 1979, but the officials suspected them of carrying gold. Most Iranian women own some gold jewellery, and they would certainly need to bring whatever valuables they had with them if they were starting a new life from scratch. Also, Middle Eastern currency has always had little value in European countries.

While the bus was searched with a fine-tooth comb for suspected contraband, we had to wait. We were told there was a restaurant up the road and many of us went to investigate. Because we had not yet been able to exchange our money, the young Yugoslav women immediately offered to buy us food. Mila, in fact, insisted. Over supper, Skodja asked us where we were staying when we reached Belgrade, which would not be for another ten or eleven hours. Great—another night on the bus! We told her that we always looked for a youth hostel or any low-budget accommodation. She immediately insisted that all three of us stay with her; it would be an honour, she said, to offer us hospitality.

When our bus appeared again, we seemed to have lost a few of our passengers, including the Iranians, which was quite distressing. Skodja explained that sometimes people had to be detained until their stories could be verified. There were many Iranians on the move at this time, and although a lot of them were genuine fugitives from political persecution, there were sometimes others with different motivations.

I sensed a certain relief in the uniformed Egyptian man once we crossed the Yugoslav border. He became a little more talkative and now admitted to knowing some English. Perhaps he had drunk some Slivovitz, the region's apricot brandy, at the border restaurant, which could have contributed in part to his greater expansiveness, but could hardly account for his sudden acquisition of English. He now spoke about having some apprehensions over his assignment in Germany, but he would at least take advantage of it to take some leave and travel to other European countries.

With a reduced number of passengers, we were able to spread out a little and use the empty seats to stack our luggage, which freed up our cramped limbs. The bus continued on its journey overnight and did not stop again till we reached Belgrade, bathed in misty grey colours, the following morning. Skodja was as good as her word and insisted that all three of us stay with her in her mother's apartment, located in one of those standard, nondescript concrete buildings for which proletariat regimes are famous. Her mother was visiting relatives at the time, and Skodja assured us there was plenty of room. She was a gracious host and gave us a wonderful introduction to the city. We were more than amply rewarded for the small favour I had undertaken for her.

An Unexpected Trip to China

In early May 1991 I realized I'd been working pretty solidly at our massage clinic in East Vancouver over the past year and felt it was time for a break. One of my patients told me about a courier service that provided cheap flights to the UK in return for the use of luggage space, meaning you had to travel lightly with only on-board baggage. It sounded interesting, so I called this company and asked if I could book a flight with them for a visit to Scotland. They said, "We have nothing for the UK until November, but I have a cancellation next week for China if you're interested. It will only cost four hundred dollars." I was a bit stunned—I hadn't thought about China; it was one of those places people went to in organized groups. But what a bargain! She added, "You'll have to get a visa, but you have a week to get it; the plane goes to Hong Kong." I immediately phoned my partner, Eleanor, at the clinic and asked if she could manage if I took off so soon. She said she'd be able to get a locum if necessary. I should go.

Packing enough into a small backpack to go on board with me was a priority, as was getting a *Lonely Planet* guidebook and a dictionary. I bought a small, thin phrase book, and although the pronunciation and inflection of Chinese words were beyond me, it would have to do. Hong Kong was still a UK protectorate at that time, so I would be able to manage there for the first day or two before going into mainland China, which is what I really wanted to see.

The plane was completely full; many Chinese families were returning home to visit. It was a long, wearisome journey, but with a spectacular fly-in: skimming over and through the immense high-rises, then landing—as if on a pontoon—on a narrow strip with water on both sides, with a surrounding maze of small boats, ferries and fishing vessels lighting up the water with reflections. This remarkable airport has now been replaced with one outside the city limits, which is probably better for those vulnerable to heart attack. A mass of friends, relatives and others—many holding signs held high—were waiting, surging in on those of us struggling to get out into the main waiting hall. I held my courier package high, and within minutes a young man came toward me with a smile to retrieve it from me.

I went to a taxi queue, but my driver didn't understand where I wanted to go, a student hostel called the STB. He knew all the hotels that English speakers normally used, but he eventually managed to find the hostel in the back streets. My grey hair surprised the staff; they apologized for having only a top bunk available that night. I was in a room with five double bunks, but welcoming faces peered from the other beds. Ivy from Kuala Lumpur said she worked for seven years to make this trip to Hong Kong, and she wanted to practice her English. She suggested that we go out to the night market. I had regained energy, so we walked for two hours through the markets and side streets, and then down to the ferry terminal. Streets everywhere were crowd ed with people jostling, but it felt safe and friendly. The poor had their night spots on the sidewalks, some of them holding packed plastic bags, others huddled on piled-up newspapers, and one had a little camp cot against a building.

The next day was blustery, with a wild hurricane-force rain that sent people scurrying for shelter. I found that I had to get a ticket in advance for the train that would take me to Guangzhou, formerly Canton. That presented its own problems—amazing how bureaucracy is the same the world over—and I was told that lineups for the train started an hour before departure, even though a ticket allocated the coach and the seat number.

We left exactly on time the following day. The people in the coach smiled at me, but no one spoke English. I brought out my phrase book, but it offered little for conversation. I showed it to the others, who looked politely but shook their heads. Only later did I realize that many of them could not read and that student-aged youngsters were my best bet; they were delighted to have any opportunity to try out some English, which was being taught in schools.

Kowloon —— Guangzhou
(Soft Seat Express Through Train)
Fare H K $ 138.00
Valid for Train No...... Coach No......
Seat No...... on......
Issued by Kowloon Station

When I left the station in Guangzhou I felt the full impact of being in a country where I could not read anything around me: signs, notices or information of any kind. Moreover, I couldn't read numbers—something that had never occurred to me. How would I know which bus to take or where to find a washroom? I found myself facing one of the widest streets I'd ever had to cross, jam-packed with bicycles, bicycles and more bicycles weaving amongst each other perfectly, avoiding the odd hand-pulled cart or the occasional bus. I was startled by it all. My *Lonely Planet* guidebook was certainly a blessing to have; I knew where the hostel was—the only problem was how to get there. I must have looked a bit uncertain, because a young man on a bicycle with a sidecar came up to me and said something that sounded like "change." I was pretty sure he wasn't asking me for change, but I finally realized he meant "exchange" and was offering to take me somewhere. I understood I needed to get some local currency, as Hong Kong had its own dollar, so it seemed a good idea to do what he indicated, get into the sidecar and go with him, wherever.

He took me down a side street to meet a woman outside her house; she was offering me paper money that I believed was yen and asking for Hong Kong dollars. Why not? This would get me started. I showed my bicycle man the hostel on a map in the guidebook, and he offered to take me there for some of my new yen. I enjoyed this unexpected travel mode; it was a great way of seeing a fair part of the city—after all, I was now in a city of over five million people. We rode past a remarkable market with caged birds, small cats, chickens, turtles and eels, all apparently for the pot, and one woman walking out with a live, wriggling fish hanging from a string tied round its middle. And then a big spice market with wares open to smell and touch; how bland our food stores appear in comparison. Washing was strung out high across the streets, or was some of it clothing for sale? I would have liked to have been able to ask about this.

I was the only woman that night in the five-bed room I'd been assigned to in the hostel. There were two other English speakers: Fred from Glasgow and Sean from Edmonton. We went out together to eat; they'd both been travelling for a while and knew how to get around, but they were surprised that I was on my own. We had an excellent meal, but I found that it wasn't possible to get a glass of wine or a shot of brandy; one must buy a bottle, and as Chinese wine is 35 percent proof, that's not a good idea. At the table next to us, there was a young Moroccan woman, Sandrine, with her aunt. Sandrine and I conversed in French, and she suggested that I take the #5 bus to a much smaller place, about five hours north of Guangzhou; she said it had interesting surroundings and I would get a feel for rural China. She loved travelling and suggested we keep in touch.

The bus depot was a little intimidating, but I finally got a #5 bus ticket to Zhaoqing—though I'd have to wait five hours, as they didn't run frequently. The bus drivers and conductors were mostly women. The way to get them to stop was to slap the side of the bus; the conductors would yell out destinations as we went. The drivers were amazingly patient, never an inch of space between vehicles—bicycles always scraping through—and the buses were so old the gearshift often got stuck, but everyone had equal rights on the street, and everyone managed. I don't remember seeing a single road accident during the entire time I was there.

I arrived in pouring rain in Zhaoqing. Someone pointed out a big, dull hotel, air-conditioned and swanky. I explained that I wanted something less costly and the receptionist told me of a seven-star place about three kilometres out of town. She phoned to set it up for me and suggested I take a taxi. The taxi wouldn't start; either the battery was dead or the heavy rain had got to it, but with another taxi driver's help, it was pushed to start.

I enjoyed a beautiful drive across a narrow avenue over the lake, looking over to the Seven Crags, for which the area was renowned. We skirted the lake and then came to a handsome building with a grand entrance that looked as if it could have been a noble's residence, with beautiful tiled roofs and high ceilings, all signs of opulence. The driver asked me to pay in Hong Kong dollars, which surprised me, but I couldn't figure out how the exchange worked, so I agreed. I was given a huge room with twin beds, a bathroom and a veranda, slippers, a toothbrush and paste—but no towel!—and the usual large Thermos of hot water with a teacup and tea bag. I used the mosquito net that night; the extreme humidity brought them out.

Staff directed me down the road to eat at the Songtao Hotel, which was filled with Chinese tour groups who had come to see the Star Lake and the Seven Crags. As always, it was a problem to get a table for a single person—often a group would wave and welcome me to join them. Tonight there was the usual large menu, but a lot of the items were "not available." A family invited me to share what was already on their table; they just handed me chopsticks and a bowl and encouraged me to help myself; hand signs worked wonderfully.

The area was rainy and I needed a raincoat, so the next morning I asked how to get into town. I was told to ask one of the men with motorbikes to take me; I'd find one in the village just beyond the Songtao Hotel. I walked through the village, surrounded by water and paddy fields, and sure enough, there was a young guy standing by his bike, ready to offer me a ride. I indicated I wanted to go to a store in town where I could get a raincoat. He seemed to understand and showed me what the fare would be. His name was Wei; he loaned me his jacket and, when we got close to town, a helmet. Washrooms were hard to find and infrequent, but he made a toilet stop. In the country it was fairly simple; you would just go behind a little stone dike and squat over a ditch; in a park you might straddle a little tiled ditch with water flushing down automatically every now and then. But in both cases it was bare bums alfresco and don't forget to bring your own toilet paper. The motorbike ride was great, very comfortable, and Wei took me to a department store, where I bought a large waterproof cape, similar to what I'd seen women wearing on their bicycles.

I spent the next day exploring the Seven Crags, an island of caves and grottoes of sculpture-like formations. Stairs had been built into the rock, discreetly leading to a Buddha-like figure where people lit incense, with numerous little kiosks along the pathways offering packages of candied fruit, biscuits and drinks. A swinging metal bridge

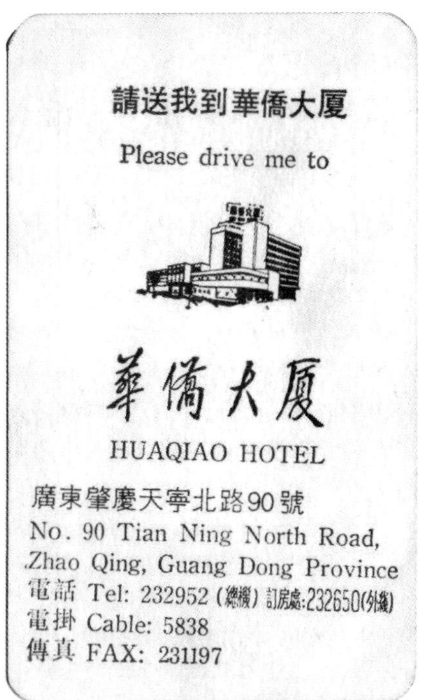

across the lake took me to the entrance; young people took great delight in swinging this to its limit. This resort-type attraction brought in many visitors, but few children. I seldom saw more than one child with a parent—the effect of state policy.

It was dark when I returned to my majestic lodgings. With my poor night vision, I found the walk a little scary; the few little strings of light along the way did not illuminate much. I got under my mosquito net again, but there were more mosquitoes inside it than outside! The next morning I took a pleasant walk into town, noticing the rice paddies with frogs croaking musically, and saw people gathering algae from the lake and putting it into large plastic bags or into baskets for yoke carrying.

A large number of buildings were being built along the way, probably for housing, with bamboo scaffolding used everywhere. A little stone house nearby turned out to be a place for collecting garbage, which was burned every now and then. One day I saw a pig sleeping in one corner.

Many services were offered on the streets: a man in medical uniform sitting with his stethoscope and blood pressure equipment on a table on the sidewalk; a woman with her sewing machine and fabric; another doing shoe repairs. I saw no police anywhere, or perhaps I didn't know how to identify them. All used an abacus for calculating, at speeds that appeared faster than a computer, but most of the stores required a lot of paperwork even for simple purchases.

I found it disconcerting to be the centre of attention whenever I ordered food or bought some produce. I had become conspicuous with my backpack, and many smiling, curious faces would talk and laugh with each other about how to explain things to me. A few young children would run up to say "Hi," having seen me pass before.

I enjoyed staying there for several days, but had to figure out how to return to Hong Kong. I thought it would be interesting to travel by boat down the river. I went early to the embarkation waiting room and saw my first notice in English, Made in the Committee of the Patriotic Sanitary Movement of Zhaoquin, but had no idea what it meant. Crowds of women arrived with packages and large blue, red and white plastic bags filled to the brim. They inspected each other's "bargains" and soon there was standing room only. Someone passed around a bag of peanuts to share, followed a little later by a woman collecting the shells. The people I waited with were in good humour. We had to go through customs and change our money back into Hong Kong dollars, but fortunately, I had kept all the right papers.

The ship we boarded was a little daunting. It was obviously ancient, with heavy-looking lifeboats, unwieldy contraptions that looked rusted in place. I was shown my cabin, a tiny four-bunk room, with no sign of another occupant. I watched our departure; it was still misty and overcast, almost dark, even though it was only 6:00 p.m. I wandered around but did not find much free space or many available seats. I found my first cockroach in the toilet—such a healthy-looking brute, I hadn't the heart to kill it.

Shortly after returning to my cabin, I heard a knock. An elderly gentleman looked quite startled to see me. "Sorry, sorry," he said. I said there was no problem and indicated which bed was mine. However, he left immediately and returned a few minutes later to show me he'd got another bunk upstairs. He bowed his way out.

After supper I returned to find a rather delightful Frenchman, with an open bottle of cognac beside him, occupying the second bunk. We talked politics, social issues and internationalism for over two hours. He was a good observer who worked for a non-hierarchical industrial company outside Paris. He didn't like the US, said money doesn't bring happiness and washed out an empty glass with cognac before pouring me some. We shared the opinion that the Right and the Left are both stuck in their thinking, that dialogue is essential and that there are good points in both. In the morning he offered me the rest of the cognac: he didn't want to carry it around. I couldn't let it go to waste and crammed it into my backpack.

We arrived at the boat terminal in Hong Kong at 7:00 a.m. It was too early to hunt for a room, so I sat in a McDonald's for a while. Then I tried a hostel run by a man from India. It was the homeliest place I had seen for a while. Young westerners were sitting around a table with coffee mugs and a package of bread while pails of soaking laundry sat in the corner. A wall was plastered with old notices and new For Sale ones. But the man couldn't let me know whether he would have free space until later in the day, so I wandered down Mody Road, the most likely place to find something, but without luck. I considered splurging for the YWCA, but only doubles were available, which cost far too much. However, at least I could find a good coffee there.

I decided to take a ferry to Lantau Island instead. Everything in my pack was now damp and reeked. How did travellers do their laundry? I had given up wearing my money belt, which was simply too hot. So I just carried my bank notes and traveller's cheques in my bag of dirty clothes. But I wanted somewhere to drop my backpack to let everything air. For the short trip to Lantau, I bought a first class ticket, which proved to be a mistake, as the air conditioning was excessive.

On landing, I took a bus to the Po Lin Buddhist Monastery, where I found accommodation, a two-person room with another woman. It was a peaceful place, quite large and set up to host large groups. The price was modest and the office well organized, with a computer that determined the table at which to sit for each meal. The monks wore grey gowns and there were many older women, also monks, working as caretakers in the dorms. Food was simple and adequate; plastic bowls and wooden chopsticks simplified the washing up—we just rinsed out our bowl to use it for tea.

I met many others in the dining room, most of whom were Chinese. I heard differing opinions from them about the changes they expected to happen: Hong Kong had been a colony of the United Kingdom since 1841, and the handover of control to mainland China was to take place in June 1997. One young woman didn't expect much good to come from it: "China is dictatorial; we need choices and also to have a chance." But she talked about her long days working over twelve hours in promotion. Another, a young mother who worked as a saleswoman in an emporium, said that regular workers did eleven-hour shifts and figured things would not be much different when the new government took over, but hoped "maybe it will be better."

I met Peggy, a nurse from Liverpool, who suggested we climb up the mountain to meet the sunrise the next morning, which would mean leaving around 3:00 a.m.; she said she'd come at that time to my room. But when I knocked on her door at 5:30 a.m., there was no response. I walked alone up the path behind the monastery in search of the large, thirty-five-metre-high bronze Buddha statue for which Lantau is renowned. I climbed and climbed some more, becoming quite dispirited to see no sign of it. At a turn in the path, thinking I'd missed the way, I was startled to find it towering over me from behind. It was spectacular, stunning and overpowering—a huge golden-coloured "Buddha in the sky." Then a beautiful black dog came walking past me, quietly, the only pet that I had seen during my trip.

This trip gave me insights into the welcoming spirit I experienced so often. I'll never forget the groups of young women who sometimes surrounded me, wanting to talk, asking me my age, asking why I was alone. They were as curious about me as I was about them. I was never hassled and never felt in any kind of danger. I suspect I was occasionally overcharged, but I can make allowances for that. I was fortunate to have the opportunity of going there; to my knowledge, courier flights are no longer available.

On my return to Vancouver I wondered, as I drove home from the airport, how I would be feeling, as a traveller from Asia who didn't speak a word of English, when looking at our large billboards and seeing sidewalks here that looked so empty? It was a sobering thought that made me realize I was experiencing culture shock.

BAFFIN ISLAND

In June 1995 a free flight offer from Air Canada started me looking at Baffin Island. I'd never been to the real North, and I might not have another opportunity; this offer could fly me anywhere in Canada, so I booked a ticket with my long-time Quaker friend, Lesley. My first stop was in Yellowknife, where I first heard the phrase "some idiot from the South." We stayed for a few days with Lesley's daughter Heather Ann. Our second stop was in Rankin Inlet, where I saw no signs of a community anywhere near that tiny, informal airport, but many people were eagerly awaiting packages and foods that had arrived with our plane. Flying over such huge blankets of snow was quite intimidating. Where did people live here and how did they live?

When we reached Iqaluit, our bed-and-breakfast host had not yet arrived to pick us up, so we had time to talk to those waiting for the next plane to leave. One of them, James, a teacher in Cape Dorset, was carrying a frozen duck with him to Newfoundland. James had become a courier between his new neighbour in Dorset and an old neighbour in his home community in Newfoundland. He was desperate to get away for a bit, as he was missing his own family, even though people could not understand his leaving during summer, the finest time to be on Baffin. June is spring, July is summer, August is fall; the rest is winter.

We also met Diane and Michel, from Saskatchewan and Quebec, who were teaching in Iqaluit on a five-year contract. They had four years of teaching and a leave of absence in the fifth year, prepaid by docking 20 percent off their salaries during the first four years. They had two adopted Inuit children, both of whom seemed large for their ages; one was three months and the other three years old. Babies tend to get their teeth very young up there; some are even born with teeth. Rent for their government housing was deducted from their paycheques. They said that the housing was squalid: it hadn't been painted in thirteen years, and costs for heating and electricity were phenomenally high.

Our Swedish-born host, Jens, from whom we rented, took us to his house in Apex, a small community at the end of the road, five kilometres from Iqaluit. It stood out: a beautiful custom-built house that contrasted the sparse boxes in which most of the locals lived. Jens was proud of his building; he had settled here and hoped to build more, but he wasn't sure if he'd be able to sell them.

The next morning we decided to walk the shoreline to Iqaluit and found ourselves looking out over an inlet of ice chunks, many of them smudged black, some of them looking like big, jumbled blocks of dirty Styrofoam. Beyond strips of water and ice lay the west side of Frobisher Bay, which rose a little more steeply to an endless terrain, north and south, of snow patches and bare tundra. The clouds were low that day—the wind was howling—and there were few bodies to be seen out of doors.

On reaching Iqaluit we talked to the woman who served us at the Komitilq restaurant; she was originally a teacher in one of the more remote communities. In her time teachers were supplied with provisions for a whole term: canned goods only, nothing fresh at all and no choices. She, too, had come from Quebec and was scathing about the new, recently built school there in Iqaluit. The lack of windows and its huge size were intimidating for the students. "Yes, idiots from the South designed it," she said, adding that the old schoolhouse in Apex was much more friendly and comfortable.

At 2:10 a.m. I listened to the wind whistling, increasing in its noise, around the small hill that our windows overlooked. There had been no real darkness, only a slightly duller light. Low clouds hid the sun or moon, but a little brightness began to appear on both horizons. These windows, all eight of them in a semicircle, faced south; the ground rose from under them so that the beautiful tiny flowers of the tundra could be picked from inside—if the windows could only open.

We went to the Anglican church service in Apex, but we could not find the entrance (as with many buildings there). We opened a door to find ourselves behind the choir, which felt odd, but as we walked a second time around the building we realized there was no other way in, so we quietly took our places behind the singers. The service mixed ceremony with informality. All the speakers were women and they spoke in Inuktitut. The priest introduced the service, played the organ for the hymns and then gave the final words. Children came and went, small ones occasionally looking for their mothers who were in the choir. And the children, being children, were fairly noisy, playing games with one another, having fun until being told to stop. The choir members wore gowns; they sang with strong, beautiful voices. I would love to have been able to record their one unaccompanied piece.

We got to know the little girls who lived close by, watching them turning over small stones in the mossy ground. They were looking for beetles, and I asked one of them if she'd mind me taking a photo of the beetle in her hand; she smiled and nodded. They were sisters: two, three, four and five years old. They found some more beetles and came running to me. "Would you like to camera these?"

Lesley and I were invited to an elder's luncheon in Iqualuit in a care home, the only facility of its kind on Baffin Island, a huge expanse of territory. One of the residents, Mary, wearing amazing antelope boots, told me she was 'hungry for lunch and became my friendly shadow, hugging me over and over when we left. We heard that young people in the community sometimes adopted elders who had no local family.

We decided to travel beyond Iqaluit and were told about "homestays," where one could lodge with an Inuit family. After an awkward phone call to Jeannie, who spoke little English and lived in Lake Harbour (now known as Kimmirut), we arranged to stay with her. Her community was reachable only by plane, and the flight was decidedly informal: a Twin Otter with room for fifteen people, with two in the cockpit that was open to the body of the plane, folding seats and extra seats that could be removed to carry supplies. Looking at the pilot and co-pilot riveted me throughout their takeoff, as they registered, watched, and then pulled on handles above them. Flying over a vast expanse of lakes with greenish tinges around their edges and rockscapes that rolled and rolled, then ending with a very smooth landing on a tiny, narrow landing strip just above houses at the top of the hill at Lake Harbour, filled me with sheer delight.

Eliya, Jeannie's husband, met us at the landing strip. About 350 people were living in Lake Harbour at that time, and it felt like a happier place. Many houses with steep roofs, in better condition than those in Iqaluit, nestled into the hillside. Jeannie was at work when we arrived, so Eliya made us coffee and we met their daughter, Pitsy, her friend Uta and young Tommy, whom they had adopted. We went out for a steep walk down to the harbour. Then I continued to the co-op store, where there were carvings and a buyer from Winnipeg who had just bought a crate-load of them. She was meeting with the carvers to talk to them about what would sell, which left me feeling conflicted. Lesley later pointed out that they might as well make what sells, but I couldn't help remembering how frustrating it was for Zeljko whenever people pressured him to make artworks that would sell.

Jeannie was one of a family of twelve; two siblings had died, and six brothers and three sisters were left. Her daughter Martha, who worked at a treatment centre in Iqaluit, was home for a few days. She worked shifts and said the courts were not good; sentences were too soft, especially for physical and sexual abuse. Jeannie made muffins for us on her return from a meeting after work and said we would have dinner together the next evening. Eliya would make us a "South" breakfast of bacon and eggs in the morning.

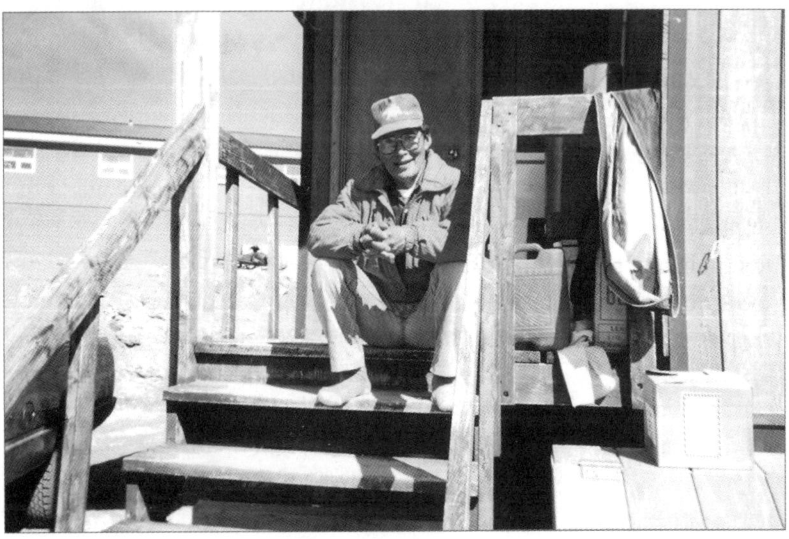

Eliya on his front steps.

I wanted to stay up and photograph at midnight on the longest day of the year, but the sky was overcast and grey. The next morning, I asked Eliya how he had managed to shoot a wolf when he was travelling at 140 kilometres per hour on his snowmobile; he had painstakingly described this to us in his limited English. He said he would rest his rifle on his shoulder and shoot when the wolf was on a rise, and he demonstrated this with a drawing.

In Lake Harbour people drew lots for who could hunt for a polar bear. The winner would have two or three days to hunt one. They shot a total of thirteen bears that winter and all were shared in the community. Martha told us there was a lot of sharing, especially of native food, and a co-operative storage plant facilitated this. Polar bear had a short season, while caribou were available all year; Arctic char were ice-fished most of the year, seal whenever they were around, and during our visit there were eggs, as well as down, from eider ducks. "Help yourselves to anything," Jeannie said. We enjoyed endless muffins, bannock and coffee but were aware that the refrigerator was very sparingly stocked.

We climbed the hill behind the house, where the magnificent view north over Soper Lake and River reminded me of the north of Scotland, but intensified and extended: bleak, rugged, ancient, haunting, compelling and a little scary. The opposite direction led to the new water dump, past the old one and onto a new road. Back at the house we found Martha and her friend, both friendly and talkative. Martha explained that the family's adopted son, Jimmy, was the birth son of the youngest daughter, Pitsy, who had just finished grade eleven.

Early in the day we heard shots from the seal hunters. The harbour was in breakup, so the rifles were ready as the seals popped up for their first taste of fresh flowing air after a long winter. Carvers were out, too, working outside their homes, some with electric equipment and others with only simple hand tools. Lesley bought a seal carving from an older man who stopped her in the Northern Store, and I bought one from a younger lad who stopped me outside the co-op. Both were simple, traditional pieces.

Many of Jeannie and Eliya's extended family came to share a caribou stew dinner that night. We all helped ourselves to a small bowlful, and as guests, we were offered seconds, which we declined. It was delicious and served with bannock and a grape drink. We all had coffee before dinner, reminiscent of dinner with the Rygas. Coffee helps to fill you up. The eleven of us ate most of the modest pot of stew. Jeannie's sister, Emily, took the few leftovers home with her.

Jeannie's brother worked for the housing department. We learned that the federal government and the Canada Mortgage and Housing Corporation put up the money for construction, heating and water, but Inuit had to rent housing. Although houses built before the seventies could be purchased, newer homes could not. Why? Bit by bit the government was opting out of these subsidies.

Jeannie went out again after supper for another meeting. An energetic person, she had an ambition to hike from Lake Harbour to Iqaluit, through Katannilik Park, before she reached age fifty. We heard it would take at least ten days to do it.

We saw very few white faces in Lake Harbour: the new manager at the co-op store, the Parks manager, the RCMP representative; that was all. Inuktitut was spoken everywhere, and many Inuit did not speak English. Children learned English in school, but those under five didn't speak it. Most children seemed to have a bicycle. ATVs were the only vehicles, but they could drive almost anywhere: up steep, stony or sandy hillsides. Large items such as vehicles, equipment and furniture were brought in once a year by sea.

We flew back to Iqaluit, a little sadly. Instead of walking the five kilometres to Apex we took a small, decrepit taxi, with doors difficult to open or shut, no seat belts and up to six people crammed in. With no roads beyond this five-kilometre range, everyone paid a standard fare of five dollars a trip. Many drivers were quite taciturn, but the ones who spoke French were more communicative. Quite a few Québécois lived on Baffin Island. Some of the young women who came up for summer work stayed on. There were also immigrants from Nova Scotia and Newfoundland who loved the dry climate.

At the exclusive Frobisher Inn we found a deluxe Sunday brunch. One could return as often as one wanted for the buffet of roast beef, baked ham, baked mushroom chicken, waffles, omelettes, eggs Benedict, sausages, bacon, French toast, cheeses, pâté, shrimp, Arctic char (better than salmon), turbot, mussels, crab, prawns, fruit

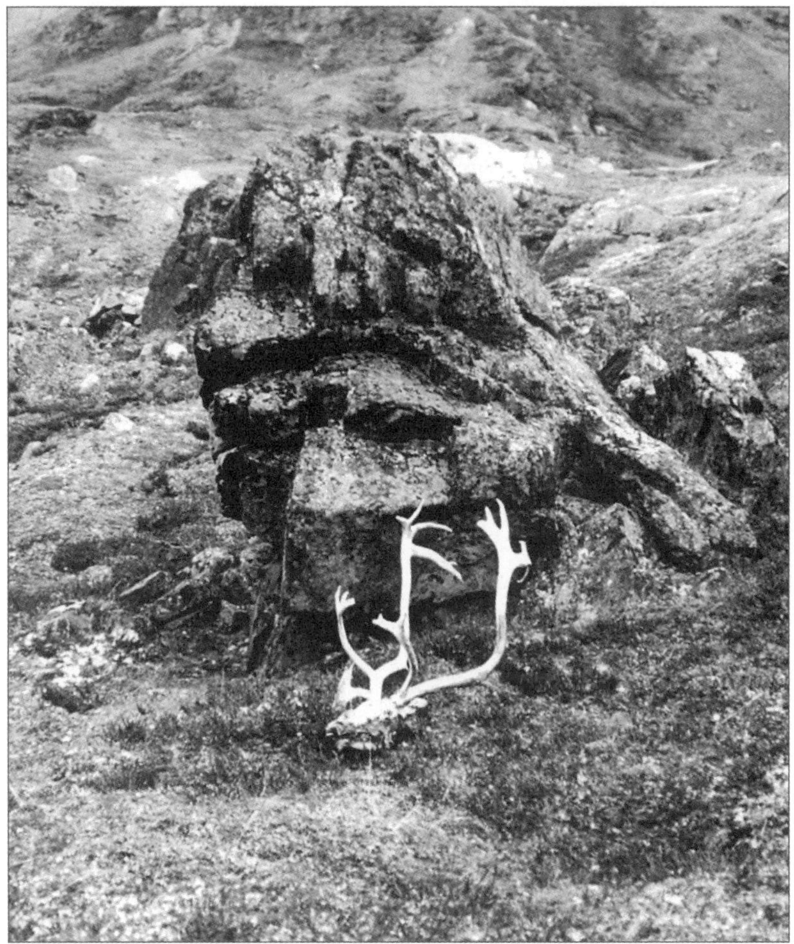

Caribou antlers on the tundra.

platters, vegetable platters, croissants, muffins, pies, tarts, baklava, trifles and strawberries covered in chocolate. I thought of our homestay hosts, their meagre food supplies and Martha's anger at the price of an apple at four dollars and wondered how this hotel, which catered to privileged visitors, could put on such a feast. It was a complete contradiction to what was available in the local restaurants.

Later we hiked to Sylvia Grinnell Park, but we nearly got lost on paths that became bogs or ended in rocky areas. We found our way after meeting a solitary mountain man who directed us over the hills.

Wild seventy-kilometre winds kept mosquitoes away but made walking difficult. We encountered lots of marshy bog wherever snow had melted, and remnants of caribou carcasses, beautiful antlers and bits of hide, but the ravens left little. The terrain was full of surprises and rich with brilliant colours of every hue from the tiniest of flowers that filled the tundra at this time of year. The gorge behind the metal dump had a beautiful rock face on one side and a hillside on the other, with a small river tumbling down. Its clear water dissipated once it reached the flats. A team of a dozen beautiful husky dogs tied up by the stream howled when they saw us. Being needed very little in the summer, they were kept tied together and fed a seal every week or so. I felt bad to see them tied up and howling, but there wasn't much we could do.

This journey has been my only trip to the Far North, and it more than met my expectations. It made me aware of the rich history that precedes "our" Canada, and I appreciated seeing this community, with its sharing, in practice. Although I caught only a glimpse of Inuit culture, I felt strongly that more of us would benefit from connecting with it.

Australia

I might never have gone to Australia if my sister didn't live there. But it had been nearly thirty years since we'd seen each other and I felt a visit was long overdue. Susie lived near Adelaide, in South Australia. Her eldest daughter, Barbie, had just accepted a job in Darwin, an outpost in the North, but Barbie didn't want to drive her car there in early January, the hottest month of the year. She asked if we (my daughter Natanis and I) would like to take a trip north, through Alice Springs, taking her car and leaving it with her in Darwin. She added: "But it's old and doesn't have air conditioning, and I don't know if you could handle that—cars here all have air conditioning." Well, it would probably take three or four days of driving, but we were up for the challenge. What better way of seeing that immense expanse of outback, and driving on the left side of the road again, which I hadn't done for thirty years? It might be fun.

I had no idea that the only road north would be so quiet and remarkably narrow. It was quite disconcerting to drive for hours and see so few vehicles, and it was very easy to drift over to the right side of the road when there was little or no traffic for mile after mile. Occasionally a very large produce truck (called a road train), which took up most of the width of the road, would appear in the distance, and as it came hurtling toward us I would have to remember which side I should be on. In such flat country, you could look into the distance in every direction and find very little growth of any kind. This was desert we were travelling through, with very little life—animal or vegetable.

Coober Pedy, with its advance notice of smallish mounds of dirt concealing opal mines, was our first overnight stop. This was a town that was built mostly underground; our bunks in the youth hostel were literally dug down and shaped into the ochre-coloured earth—raw, earthy bunks, somewhat uninviting for the thin sleeping bags we carried with us. We entered some small stores that were many steps below ground. There was one megastore in town on the ground level, which had fierce air conditioning; the extremes, both inside and out, were not easy on our bodies.

The heat was burning through our shoes, and roads could not be stepped on barefoot; we had to move swiftly across them. On finding an outdoor swimming pool we gasped with delight, but we were horrified to see that Aboriginal children were denied entry. We decided to give it a miss. This was the eighties, and I believe things have changed since then.

Ayers Rock, Uluru, was our next stop, and because this is sacred to the Aboriginal people of the area and is listed as a UNESCO World Heritage Site, it is given generous attention. This red monolithic sandstone formation dominates the landscape, and visitors have an opportunity to talk to Aboriginal guides who are hired by the tourist industry.

We met with a delightful elder who showed us how to find witchetty grubs, a great source of protein in this barren (to us, anyway) land, but not exactly an enticing food. I remember asking her how they dealt with thirst in such a dry land. She looked around, to make sure nobody was close to us, and said, "I'll show you, but you mustn't tell anyone—I could lose my job." This friendly woman hunted for a little tuft of grey-green, looking for a particularly shaped leaf in it, and said, "If you chew this very, very slowly for many minutes, your thirst will disappear. Try it." We did. It worked, and I trust she didn't lose her job, since jobs were hard to come by for Aboriginal people.

It got hotter as we drove farther north toward the equator. We got used to starting our driving at 5:00 a.m., carrying wet cloths to put around our heads, taking a break of several hours midday and driving again into the evening. We always found a place to eat along the way, though they were rare, with few food options. I never expected that I could actually eat the famous Australian meat pie day after day, but it was always reliable and filling. I found the humidity in Darwin unbearable; I simply couldn't handle the muggy heat and made my way over to the east coast as soon as possible, travelling by bus.

Natanis joined me at Magnetic Island on the east coast, and then we travelled south to Sydney where Natanis had to leave for home. I continued on to visit a friend, Jenny, whom I had met in Canada some years before. She and her partner looked after the progeny of roadkill. There are many kangaroos and wallabies killed on the road, and often there is a baby to be found, still alive, in the pouch. Those who volunteer to find and care for these infants must take special training. They return them to the wild when they have recovered well enough to survive.

Jenny said I'd be more than welcome to stay with them for a few days, but I would have to share my bed with one of those babies, as they would only survive if they were kept closely against a heartbeat. It was an awkward night for me, but a precious one, and at some point I managed to feed my tiny companion with a dropper. And although I'd slept close to my own babies when they were small, this tiny creature was a great deal smaller, and I was fearful of rolling over, of suffocating it. I never thought I'd sleep with a baby kangaroo!

CHIAPAS

On a solo trip to Mexico in 1985 I met up by chance with some students from Vancouver's Emily Carr University of Art and Design, who were touring archaeological sites. Their guide, Sally, was one of their teachers, and she wanted to visit the remote ruin of Bonampak that was built between AD 200 and 400. The only way to get there was to charter a small private plane; no roads entered that area. Only two of the students wanted to share this charter with her, and Sally offered me the fourth seat at a very reduced price. Of course I took it.

I'll never forget that little plane. Held together in some places by string and ropes, it looked homemade. The pilot was actually tying some knots together when we met up with him on the field where it was located. I did wonder how well it would fly! I got into it with some trepidation and had to hold the door closed, then hang on to my seat, with fresh air blowing through the open windows. I knew it wasn't a long trip and that we weren't dealing with mountains; we were going into tropical forest. The pilot said we would never fly much higher than the trees; mostly we would fly through them. What an unusual journey it was, navigating through the jungle, dodging densely forested areas and looking down over a narrow canyon with a swiftly flowing river. It took well over an hour to reach our destination close to the Guatemalan border.

There was only one guard to greet us at the Bonampak site itself, which unfortunately turned out to be a bit of a disappointment. There was no information about where the various parts of the old city were located; the guard wasn't able to tell us anything about it. His one job was to provide "security." I wondered how many people were really likely to make it here? Trudging through the rainforest to find the famous painted city walls was beyond our ability; heat, overgrowth

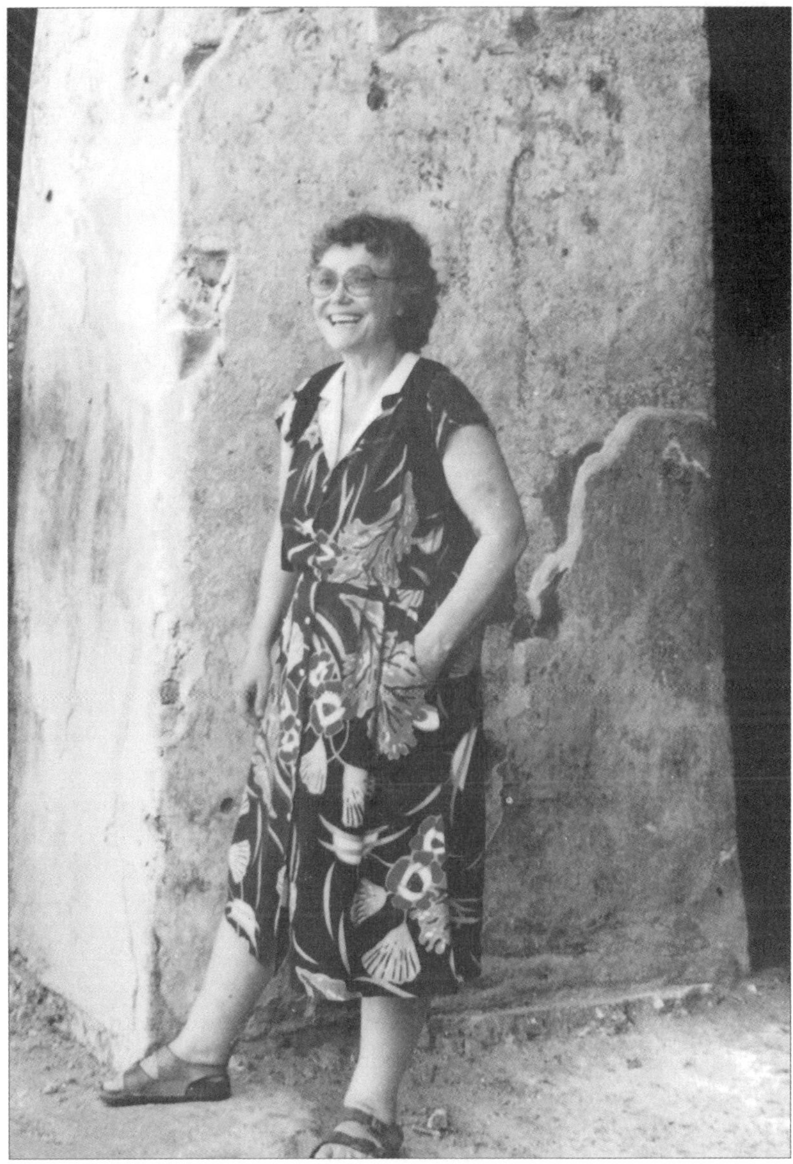

In Palenque, near Bonampak, in Chiapas; Candace Parker photo.

and terrain were tough obstacles for which we weren't adequately prepared. But the flight itself was a memorable experience, never to be repeated.

An Oriental Christmas

The highway to Jerusalem
runs through a valley of craggy hillsides
that saw the war of independence
shed blood in plenty
rusted vehicles, skeletons of war lie
abandoned on the rocks, red-ochre graveyards
memorials to the dead

The highway to Gethsemane
is narrow, winding between
high stone walls that climb the Mount of Olives
with branches of eucalyptus weeping
casting a shadow of sorrow

The highway to Jericho
winds down through smooth, rounded
hills of brilliant limestone
with sand-coloured awning settlements
of Bedouin families, nestled in clefts
the living history of a vanishing era

The highway to Bethlehem
is lined with flags of black, white and green
that hang like streamers
criss-crossing the road
images of Arafat, billboard size, at every turn
celebrating today, another birth
a new independence
The highway to Haifa
lies through red, stone-scarred landscape
from which emerge ancient buildings
piece by piece, arch of a viaduct
and a sea of white plastic shelters strawberries and peppers
while waves come crashing to the shore
from deep blue Mediterranean Sea

The highway to Nazareth
wanders through a valley of fruit
and ancient catacombs
and a crusader fortress towering
over a McDonald's, run by the local Kibbutz

In December 1995 Palestinians in Bethlehem were granted limited self-rule. "Would you like to go to Bethlehem on Christmas Eve? They say the midnight Mass is quite an event." I was quite taken aback, firstly because I don't profess to be Christian and secondly because my friend, Amos, an Israeli Jew, has little patience for religious ceremony; he calls it "crap." And here I was being offered an opportunity that would thrill many people. I thought for a moment, and then asked Amos if he would feel comfortable going there. Amos and I had met at an Israeli folk dancing event back when I was starting my massage career and he was just finishing his training as a Rolfer; we had shared a common concern about how much work our new skills would bring. Also, we were both unattached, and we began a friendship that remains, despite his paranoia and my optimism (which he calls naïveté), until the present day.

I was his guest here. I had never seriously thought I'd ever come to Israel; it was a place that harboured too many unresolved questions for me. In fact, Amos and I were often deadlocked over the plight of Palestinian refugees and what I considered Israel's inflexible position on settlements. But somehow our friendship had managed to survive our opposing viewpoints, and that was something we both valued. I was sharing space in his modest cottage on the coast, midway between Tel Aviv and Haifa, visiting places in the Middle East that had been remote but nonetheless familiar names to me for as long as I could remember. "It's a once-in-a-lifetime chance for you," he added.

I had to agree and thought it might give me a new perspective on Christmas; I could certainly do with that. For many years now I had been experimenting with ways to escape the external hysteria and the internal depression that Christmas brought. Boycotting the event didn't seem to work, because neither my friends nor enough of my family did that, and I always got pulled into the chaos if I stayed around them. So the only alternative was to get away from it by removing myself physically from the scene. I had gone on fasting retreats several years in a row, but these turned out to be boring. I had even house-sat in a remote area of the Kootenays one December, but power cuts had further isolated me. This year I was in Israel, because Amos had generously given me an airline ticket.

To get to Bethlehem for the evening's activities meant going through Jerusalem, and although Bethlehem is only some fifteen minutes south of the city, we knew there would be heavy traffic that evening. Amos, mostly a mild-tempered man, nevertheless had some very definite rules. He would not drive through any part of the West Bank territory in the dark, and as darkness falls early and with unexpected suddenness here, it meant planning trips quite carefully. In this instance, it meant that we would drive through the Bab al-Wad, which is part of the valley highway that runs from Tel Aviv to Jerusalem, in the late afternoon.

This is a narrow valley, not strictly speaking in West Bank territory, but it is an area haunted by war memories for all Israelis. So we travelled that section of the highway, a craggy, winding valley, in full daylight. This was my second trip through this area, and I felt a historic ghostliness pervading this derelict-looking gash. Rusty military vehicles had been left abandoned near the roadside, stranded in awkward positions—skeletons of war that recall the attacks that came from the hills above. They had been there since the Israeli War of Independence, fought some fifty years ago. It was not comfortable to see these constant reminders of the insecurities that still existed.

In sharp contrast to its desolate surroundings, the highway is always busy, and rush hour starts just before 3:00 p.m. It seemed busier than usual that day, and I began to sense a feeling of anxiety coming from Amos, who was driving. I had wanted to take on my share at the wheel, but I wasn't sure that I could handle it. I've driven in places like Mexico City and rugged terrain like flooded, deep-rutted logging roads in the backwoods of British Columbia; none compare to rush-hour traffic in Israel. The drivers go berserk, cutting in and out of lanes without warning, driving on the embankments to overtake on the wrong side, honking if you're not driving at least twenty kilometres above the speed limit, all of it rendering the thought of terrorists quite tame. I would be risking both of our lives to try to drive in this chaos, so I didn't insist.

We had been getting snippets of news all day. Palestinian self-determination for Bethlehem, which had now become part of the West Bank territories, was originally scheduled for December 18, but it had been postponed to allow the completion of an alternate highway, which

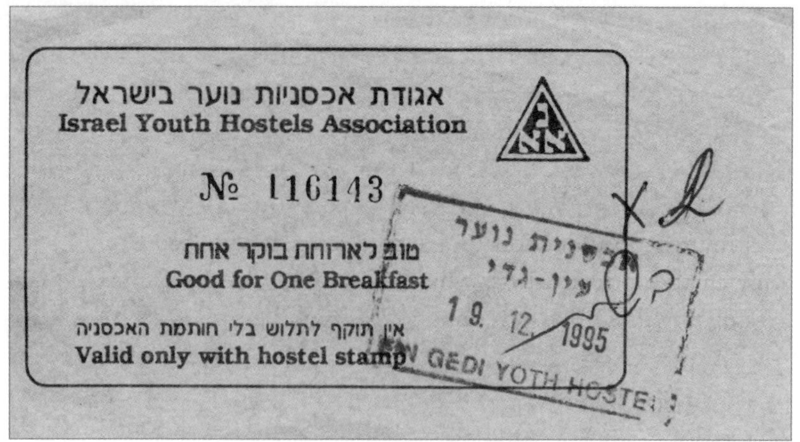

אגודת אכסניות נוער בישראל
Israel Youth Hostels Association

№ 116143

טוב לארוחת בוקר אחת
Good for One Breakfast

אין תוקף לתלוש בלי חותמת האכסניה
Valid only with hostel stamp

19. 12. 1995

would allow Israeli vehicles to bypass the town. Self-determination was actually taking place today, December 24, and Yasser Arafat would be in attendance for the ceremonies. One information source said that Israelis would not be allowed into Bethlehem. So when we reached Jerusalem, Amos decided to phone a friend of his who lived there. Gideon was a travel guide who grew up with Amos, and he would know the latest on the situation. More importantly, Amos could trust his advice. He suggested we meet him in the King David Hotel, where he was organizing a tour for Japanese visitors.

The King David Hotel is a landmark in Jerusalem: big, important, expensive and central. Amos knew it well, but on this occasion he could not find it. He was nervous and anxious, so I asked him if he was sure he wanted to continue, provided there were no glitches. He angrily said yes, and he didn't want to discuss it further. We found a parking spot for the car and walked to find the hotel. Gideon was there, waiting for us, calm and assured. Of course it would be perfectly safe for us to continue on to Bethlehem. He gave us the name and address of an Arab friend of his, Kosta, who owned a well-known tourist store on the outskirts of Bethlehem. We could leave the car safely with Kosta and walk on into the town. He assured us that security arrangements were in place and that busload upon busload of pilgrims, visitors and tourists would be en route for the celebration of the midnight Mass. Of course Israelis could go; he thought it should be an exhilarating evening.

It was a cold evening. Jerusalem is at quite a high elevation, and there was an unusual chill in the air. It was already dark and neither of us was dressed warmly enough. We looked for a place to eat on our way back to the car, but there was not much choice, and we didn't see anything that appealed to us. We went into a supermarket to look for some ready-to-eat food but were appalled at the prices. It was my first introduction to a supermarket here; I had been buying only in the local markets, where food was fresh and unpackaged. I was disappointed that this one looked exactly like a North American supermarket, where everything is prepackaged. All that "insulation," as I call it, makes things twice the price they should be. "Should be" is not quite right. Here, as everywhere else I've ever been, the price of food doesn't reflect the work and labour of production; the farmer never receives a fair share. Here, produce from the West Bank, which is labour intensive, is sold at far lower prices than produce from the highly mechanized kibbutz farms.

Despite our hunger pangs, we made our way out of Jerusalem. Nearing the edge of the city, we noticed a sign, Oriental Food, on a rather ritzy-looking restaurant to our right, and Amos stopped. I thought, how strange to find the first Chinese restaurant I ever saw there. Then I wondered if I really wanted to eat Chinese food here, tonight. Amos parked the car and I suggested that we look at the menu before making a decision. Hee was usually quite agreeable to looking at a place and discussing its merits, but tonight he just grunted, which I took to be some form of acknowledgement. We went inside, and I was stunned by the decor: Persian carpets, weavings and wall tapestries, bowls of fruit and delectable-looking trays of Middle Eastern pastries. I gazed in total surprise. Amos asked me what I expected, informing me, "Oriental food is what we eat here." I was a little embarrassed and told him that I always thought of Oriental as Chinese! It was one of the few laughs we had that evening.

Over dinner, which offered us warmth and a good respite, I asked him again if he really wanted to carry on. I assured him that I would understand if he changed his mind. "It will really be quite in order to go back if you aren't feeling comfortable about going to Bethlehem. I won't hold it against you! I know you never enter West Bank territory." He said he didn't know, but thought it was okay. I repeated my offer, but again, he said he was sure. Eating the complimentary pastries delayed our return to the inhospitable outdoors, but I had a strong Turkish coffee to keep me going.

Back at the car, Amos was first convinced that someone had vandalized it, groaning, "The bastards!" Although rocks were occasionally thrown at Israeli-owned vehicles, I didn't see any damage, and I wasn't sure how he would know unless it were very obvious, as his car was already quite dilapidated from traffic mishaps. He muttered, walked around the car a couple of times and then decided he was mistaken. All was well.

Traffic was becoming heavy on the Bethlehem highway and we edged our way into it. There were frequent roadblocks with alert Israeli troops standing guard on the side of the road. We were frequently slowed, scrutinized and then flagged on. But we were not questioned—we had Israeli licence plates. Those with Arab plates were being pulled aside. Highway lights were infrequent, but the roadblocks were well lit. Some groups of tour buses had come to a halt, and other Israeli vehicles passed them. However, Amos decided not to pass the buses and waited for their movement, so we were considerably slowed down.

Eventually, we came toward the last blockade before the strip of no man's land. On the Israeli side, there were small groups of religious protesters bearing placards, cordoned off to the side of the road. I wanted to see the placards, but without Hebrew I couldn't read graffiti, posters, newspaper headlines or any "people's information"—everything was in Hebrew or Arabic. Amos explained that these were Israeli fundamentalists protesting Arab self-determination. It looked as though they were not being allowed through; the Israeli police were holding them back. We edged forward; all traffic was now crawling, and for a short distance there was no military presence, no police. This no man's area was in total darkness. Then we saw lights and the navy-black uniforms of the Palestinian traffic control police. We were entering the new self-rule territory of Bethlehem.

These Arab traffic policemen looked so young, but I realized they were the same age as most of the Israeli soldiers we had seen, barely out of childhood. They were more lively, more excited, moving around in and between the vehicles wherever they could, gesticulating and waving everyone on, trying to get the congested traffic moving. But it was a hopeless task. Vehicles were squeezed in on all sides; there was no attempt at lanes. I thought, fleetingly, of what would happen if there were to be an incident. We were totally trapped.

Then, unexpectedly, there was some movement and freedom. I felt a sense of physical relief, as if I had left a claustrophobic confinement and could breathe again. I noticed a well-lit group of green-uniformed military to the right of the road—Israeli soldiers. I wondered aloud why they were there inside this new "free" territory. Amos said they were there to guard Rachel's Tomb, a Jewish heritage site. Of course! We were in a part of the world where three major religions converged, each claiming historic and heritage rights. Land encroachment, territory and self-determination were political issues that could not be resolved without an understanding of the Muslim, Christian and Jewish traditions. If I gained nothing more from this trip, I welcomed the experience of seeing the complexities that underlie decision-making in this part of the world.

We were close to Bethlehem; it had taken us an hour and a half to cover just a few kilometres. Earlier we had discussed the pros and cons of taking a bus instead of the car, and at one stage I had even proposed walking. But Amos, despite his fears of rock throwing, said he felt safest in his car; he probably felt more in control. I had a very different history, and I want to ditch my car when I sense trouble.

We had to find Kosta's store so that we could park the car and do the last lap on foot. Gideon had told us that we should take a left fork after passing Rachel's Tomb, and ahead of us lights indicated buildings to the left, but we simply couldn't move left; we were blocked in by at least three sets of vehicles on that side. Black uniforms appeared again, moving nimbly between us, intent on directing our section of the road to take the right fork. There was no choice. Amos cursed, "I knew we'd get into some fucking mess like this. God knows where they're sending us!"

There was no point in trying to calm him or to suggest we go back; the traffic was flowing in one direction only, but at least it was thinner from dividing into two streams. I quietly suggested we take the first road to our left to see if we could find a way onto the other fork. Suddenly, Amos made a quick U-turn in a narrow section, hugging the edge of the road and facing a flood of headlights on the inside of the fork, moving against the traffic going the other way. His manoeuvre stunned me, but no one stopped him. I had forgotten this unnerving Israeli habit of doing U-turns, anywhere, any time, despite the fact that they are illegal.

We managed to sneak behind the police dividing the traffic and saw tourist stores on both sides of the road; most had Kosta written above them in English as well as in Arabic or Hebrew, perhaps for the benefit of the many Christians who travel here. Amos recognized the store we were looking for. "Kosta" and his son were standing outside, watching the entertaining traffic jam. When they saw us they waved and directed us to park our car up on the sidewalk. Gideon had phoned to tell them we were coming. Amos anxiously asked if his car would be safe. They laughed uproariously and said that nobody would bother stealing a car that looked like his. He didn't find that very funny.

I thanked them for giving us a parking spot, and we began walking, hugging the edge of the road. The paving was uneven, with chunks of sidewalk missing here and there. The few street lights were dim. But store lights were blazing and helped us to see our footing. The strange assortment of goods in these tourist stores amazed me: inflated Disney-style Santas side by side with mournful pastiches of the Virgin Mary in sweet rose-adorned gilt frames and droopy plastic crucifixions. I saw numerous olive-wood carvings of doves, crosses, manger scenes and the Last Supper, and identical yet individually carved replicas.

Ahead I could make out the magical outline of Bethlehem above us, a dense silhouette of churches and mosques against a background of lights. I wanted to get there quickly, as I was finding the stores difficult to look at. Amos decided to walk in the middle of the road in the midst of the slow-moving traffic, which made me uncomfortable. Why should we compete with the vehicles? He wanted to be fully visible, away from doorways and alleys that may have hidden dangers. However, I stayed to the side. I was less fearful of hidden dangers than of the evident ones.

The traffic slowed as we climbed the hill up to the main square, and the number of pedestrians kept increasing. The congestion made me want to keep closer to Amos. It would be almost impossible for us to reconnect if we lost sight of each other, so I walked beside him, gently holding his arm. He said, "Don't do that. You're hurting my back." I knew from this reaction that he was isolated in his own world of fear and wanted to remove himself from any physical contact. I explained that it would be unwise to lose each other and asked again if he wanted to go back. He replied that we hadn't got there yet. I knew he couldn't really hear me.

More vehicles were diverted into side roads, presumably to areas where they could park. Others just parked haphazardly on the sidewalks as we had done. The crowd was converging from alleys and side streets, and as we got closer to the centre of Bethlehem the atmosphere became happy and noisy. From the voices around me I could tell there were many nationalities present; Scandinavian, French, German, Spanish and Hungarian were just some of the languages I recognized. Arabic, Hebrew and Japanese had already become familiar. The youngsters of this neighbourhood were having a great time. "Happy Christmas," they shouted as we went by.

We seemed to have left the area of tourist traps. Good smells wafted from some of the little open kitchen doors we passed, and some form of table ball game was being played behind some of the other doors. As we moved round the last bend in the uphill road, we came to a complete people jam. An ambulance with a red crescent was facing us, surrounded by police shouting and gesticulating, trying to clear a way as it attempted to inch its way through. I had never been in this kind of tense situation before and knew little of crowd behaviour or management. How lucky I was that paranoia is not one of my problems. I didn't really mind the crush of so many people; the evening was, after all, quite cold. I managed to keep beside Amos, trying not to jostle him, though I felt his rigidity and knew he was having a very different reaction than mine.

The square, when we finally reached it, was floodlit, and there were sounds of choral singing coming from several directions. The Church of the Nativity, which is on the south side, had a mass of people in front of its gates; they were holding up pieces of paper in their hands. These gates were holding back those who wanted to enter the large, walled enclave outside the church itself. I began to understand the problem as I listened to those around me. One would have needed to apply for admission to the midnight Mass at least a week before.

These pieces of paper were permission slips, and without one it was impossible to enter. Even with a permit, it was going to take some time to push through the crowds and gain entry. I turned my attention to the activity in the square.

Manger Square: the name struck me as extraordinary. People were milling around and I couldn't identify any focal point. There were tight groups of Palestinian male teenagers. The only women were visitors and tourists; local women were not in evidence. I heard bottles rolling on the flagstones and immediately thought of beer bottles. Then I remembered I had not seen any drinking. Muslims don't drink, and few Israelis drink either. There was a certain swaggering in the way some of the young men moved about. But I also heard one of them chide another for not making way for me—likely a visitor, since he had spoken in English.

I watched the Palestinian police moving through the crowd. One of them appeared to have something in his hand that he was directing toward people in the crowd. I saw him taking someone aside, quietly checking him out with what turned out to be a metal detector. As I was watching this little scenario, I was startled to hear loud firing noises. Before I had time to be alarmed, the square was brilliantly lit by a shower of fireworks exploding over our heads. I had never been directly beneath a fireworks display before; it was magnificent.

In delight, I turned to Amos. "Isn't this wonderful: fireworks, floodlit buildings and the sound of so many choirs!" He looked as if he'd rather be anywhere else than here and muttered something about Vancouver having better fireworks than this, then added, "What do you want to do now?" I felt quite sad and said, reluctantly, "I think we should go back." Again I tried to take his arm, because as we turned to go out of the square and back down the hill, we were battling the increasing numbers still arriving. But again he said, "Don't do that." By now he was very angry. I felt the leaden weight of all the fear and anger roiling beneath the surface of this celebration. While the Arab population was rejoicing in a return of old territory, Israelis were terrified of their new independence. And Christians were celebrating—not only here, but also all over the world—an event that has caused untold centuries of oppression for both of these peoples and for this land. The sadness of all those wrongs overwhelmed me. I sobbed uncontrollably as we stumbled, separately, through the jostling and noisy crowds to make our way back to the car.

At the foot of the hill, I found myself turning once more to look at the floodlit silhouette of the remarkable domes, minarets and spires piercing the sky behind me. As I stopped to catch my breath and stem my tears, I noticed that directly above us the clear dark was filled with a myriad of tiny, sparkling stars. I realized that this deep and silent sky, with its enduring magnificence and magic, could be shared by us all—in every corner of the world—without the need of a Christmas to celebrate it.

Aswan Hospitality

He follows me, with anxious face
– The program is not finished yet
– I know, but I am tired
– You like the music, yes?
– I liked it very much, I'm sorry I must leave
– I will accompany you a little way
– Thank you—no
I am used to travelling alone

He takes my arm
– It is no trouble, I like to
I gently disengage

This young man of twenty-four
tells me he works for the Nubian dancers
whom I have just been watching
– You like disco?
– Sometimes yes, but not tonight
– Why not? Disco is fun, we could go together
– I am tired, I was up at three o'clock this morning
to catch the train to bring me here
It has been a long day, I will not go to disco

– How old are you?
– I am old, very old
He peers at me
– About a hundred?
– No—not quite that much

– How much—how old—how much?
Wearily, I ask him to leave me
to go back, to go home, to find someone else,
...some other woman
I catch myself in horror

– It is no trouble to be with you
–You have a wife?
I do not answer
–Your wife, he repeats, your wife?
– Husband—I say, in spite of myself
No, I like travelling alone
We near my hotel, I am relieved
I wasn't sure that I could find it
He seems anxious
–You give me tip
– No—I say it clearly
– Please, you will do one thing for me?
– What—I ask
– Please, one kiss
I laugh, and say
– No, goodnight my friend
and mistakenly offer him a handshake

– Please, only one kiss
He moves suddenly close to me
brushing his hand with accomplished movement
over my breast
and whispers "give me a chance"
I move swiftly away
I am too old
I have forgotten the rules of this game
– No, goodbye!
I say it angrily
I like travelling alone

A Train to Venice

Following the trauma of the terrorist attack on New York's Twin Towers in September 2001, airfares dramatically decreased in North America, as many people developed a general fear of flying. This gave me another opportunity to visit my long-term friend Amos, who was staying with friends just outside of Rome. I'd never been to Rome and it would cost me less to get there than a flight to Toronto!

We spent several days visiting the many sites for which Rome is famous, including the Vatican, where we saw the pope and where some nimble fingers lifted my wallet out of my purse—a common occurrence, I heard later from the police.

I wanted to visit Venice and decided to take the overnight train there. Amos was a bit put out. He was keen to see Florence, which I had already seen on a previous brief trip through Italy, but he wasn't interested in Florence. His anti-Muslim rhetoric and paranoia, stirred up by 9/11, were getting to me. I decided we needed a break from each other. Getting my ticket to Venice was complicated, but getting to the train station was even more so; all bus drivers had gone on strike that evening. Taxis were in high demand and I had to be extremely pushy to get one or I would have missed the train and lost my ticket.

My seat was in a shared compartment with five others. I settled into a corner and waited for the other passengers to arrive. I knew there were no empty seats; all tickets had been sold. Eventually, five men joined me who all appeared to be Arab, as well as friends. I wasn't uncomfortable—just surprised to be joined by a group of men only. As the lights were dimmed for the night ahead, the man seated bedside me turned to me in a friendly manner and quietly said, "You are quite safe. We are all Muslim." I have never forgotten those words and never will.

Life in Victoria

Although I have covered them only briefly, my three decades in Vancouver merit a book of their own. I lived in a lively neighbourhood and loved having grocery stores and espresso bars within walking distance. An extensive community of friends and a diverse range of organizations enriched my life. However, the tasks of being a landlady and a homeowner became progressively draining, and I eventually decided it was time to sell. The house sold quickly.

My initial plan had been to purchase a smaller place in Vancouver's East Side or West End, but I couldn't find anything suitable. For a couple of years, I rented a basement suite in Andy's house in East Van, and I was also offered space in Judy and Ian's home in Victoria, located several blocks from where Natanis lives. I alternated my time between both cities to test out these new locations. As I progressed through my eighties, though, I began to face some unexpected health issues. My daughters in Victoria could offer needed support, so I stopped commuting and settled in Victoria.

Moving from Vancouver left a social hole that I have not yet filled. However, Victoria offers plenty of film and theatre, as well as live music—jazz being my favourite. The city has a wealth of accomplished musicians whom I am happy to be able to hear live. I also get a lot of joy from going to Daniel Lapp's choir every Wednesday at the Victoria Conservatory of Music with Judy, Ian and Natanis. I tried several choirs here before finding this was the perfect fit.

I had taken jazz piano classes back in Vancouver with the late Kathy Kidd. I would have gladly continued with them if she hadn't moved to Paris. She founded the Jazz Vespers at St. Andrew's-Wesley United Church in Vancouver, which continues to this day. She was a wonderful woman with such delightful energy—so inclusive of other

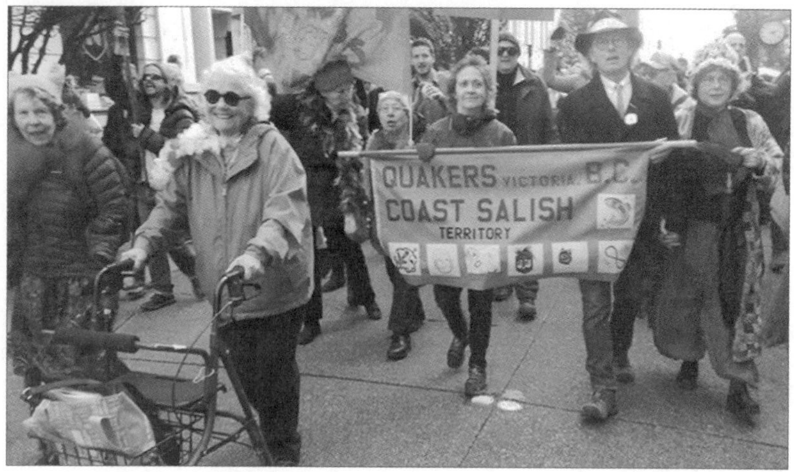

At a demonstration with the Raging Grannies.

people, and the kind of spirit that makes the best music. To follow up, I took classes at the conservatory in Victoria for one term. I quickly learned that it wasn't just about playing jazz, but also about listening differently, and I realized that it would take a lot more work than I had anticipated. If I had stuck to folk or popular music, I might have continued, but the loss of my eye increased the level of challenge; I will discuss this health issue in the next chapter.

My most fun and rewarding political activity in recent years has been with the Raging Grannies. We meet here once a week, and although I don't have the energy to participate in all of the group's actions, it's heartening to be with others who share a political analysis and desire to do something to bring about change.

As an individual, I continue to write several dozen letters to MLAs, MPs and government ministers every year. Recently I have started to write them by hand, because I understand it may be more effective. I can't yet tell if I get more responses from handwritten letters than from printed letters, but I have sometimes received personal responses instead of nondescript, standardized replies.

The Eye

I've been blessed with good health for most of my life, but this last decade has presented me with a lot of medical terminology that I didn't learn about in my training as a massage therapist. I've had the benefit of cataract removal, hip replacement and dental implants—great surgical services that were not available in earlier times. But as time goes on, I find unexpected limitations, both in energy and in physical movement. One thing I didn't expect was to lose my right eye.

For two weeks in October 2012, while visiting family in Scotland and my friend Sonia in Paris, my eye was irritated. Upon my return home, my optometrist diagnosed conjunctivitis, which seemed an innocuous enough problem. I used the eye drops he prescribed for a few weeks. Then one morning I noticed that vision was hazy in the right eye, and by the afternoon the eye was totally without sight. I rushed to the optometrist who, upon examination, said that he couldn't find the lens; it had disappeared. It just wasn't there! He sent me to the hospital's emergency ward, and my daughter Natanis took me there immediately and stayed with me throughout the night.

I saw four different ophthalmologists over the next several days, but there was no hope; the lens had gone for good, and my eye was useless. I was now taking five different types of eye drops, interspersed at various intervals during the day out of concern for the other eye, in case an internal infection had caused the disappearance of the lens. Removal of the eye would probably be a good idea and was scheduled for three months ahead. I felt like a zombie for those three months. My body did not react well to the medications; I had very little energy and constant nausea. I relied on Sudoku puzzles, book after book of them, to keep my mind active.

After surgery came the option of either getting a prosthetic or using an old black eye patch that I had colourfully embroidered some twenty years earlier to protect my eye after cataract surgery. I was advised to see an ocularist in Vancouver and was quite admiring of her ability to create a facsimile of my eye. She showed me how she used single-strand embroidery thread to replicate the tiny blood vessels. I liked this use of natural fibres! However, learning to remove the prosthetic eye for cleaning, then reinserting it into the socket, was tricky. Sometimes the prosthetic has a mind of its own and can leap out quite unexpectedly—twice this has happened at the dinner table, which was quite disconcerting to those around me.

I almost lost it in a dimly lit coffee shop in the Royal Museum in Edinburgh. When the waiter brought my coffee we both heard a little clink on the floor. He said, "I think you've lost a button." I knew I didn't have any buttons on me and suddenly realized my eye had popped out. I said, "Oh, it's my eye that's down there." He bent down, picked it up, looked at it and thoughtfully asked, "Would you like me to wash it for you?" He brought it back on a little serviette and disappeared before I could properly thank him. No doubt he hasn't forgotten this event. A prosthetic isn't attached to the eye socket with needle and thread.

I contend with other unexpected issues as well. Sometimes while I am pouring cream into my coffee, the cream misses its mark and finds another home. I may reach for something only to find that it's farther away, and other times I can miss seeing that small step that can lead to a fall. But I'm very comfortable driving, though I no longer go the speed necessary for highway driving and I don't risk night driving; those are both a loss. When I took a refresher course, shortly after losing the eye, my instructor told me that one-eyed drivers tend to have an excellent record, no doubt because they have to be, or choose to be, especially cautious and attentive. I have little depth perception now, but I can parallel park with one eye, and I have learned how to manage a newer computer operating system.

I've definitely had to retain my sense of humour to contend with these new challenges. I did wonder, when I got my last pair of reading glasses for the computer, whether I should have paid half price for the lenses. I didn't think of it at the time, but only one of those lenses had a prescription in it. There ought to be some compensations! I had hoped to get help from the CNIB, but the branch here seemed really overworked. When I asked about a support group, they said they were stretched to capacity and couldn't take on anyone struggling with one-eye problems; I was lucky to have one good eye left. They had a point. As with so many situations, I could be a lot worse off.

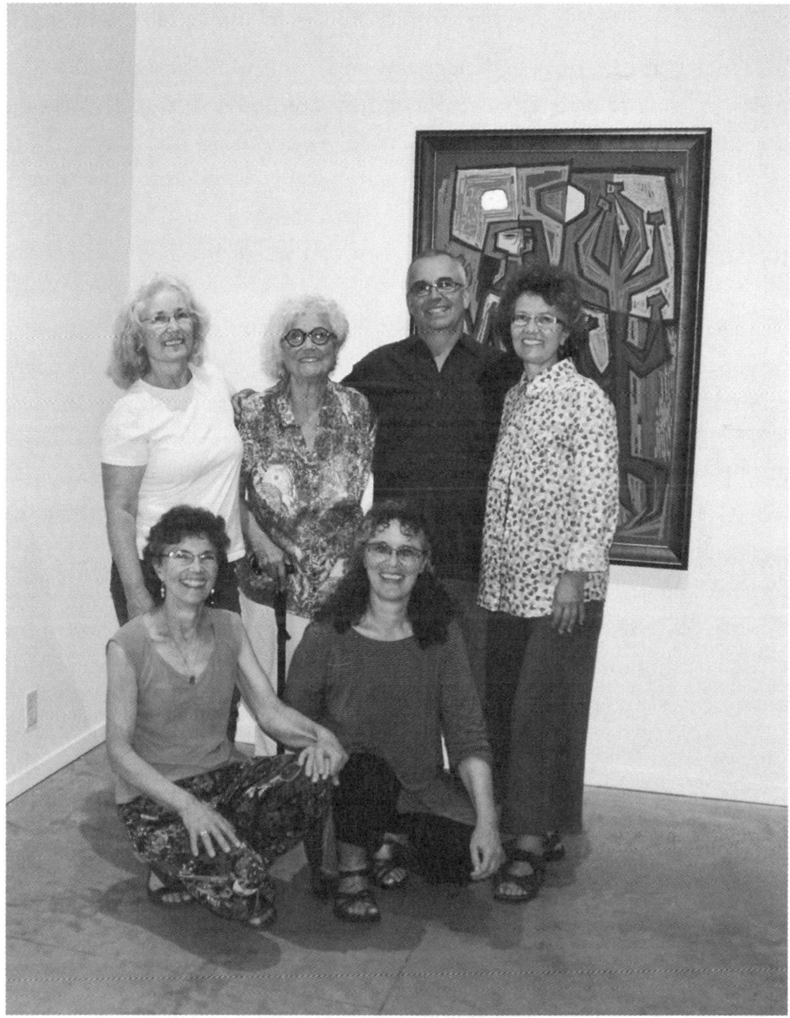

With Kate, Andy, Natanis, Claire and Judy at the opening of Zeljko's work at Touchstones Gallery in Nelson, 2014.

AFTERTHOUGHTS

So what is it like now, as I near the end, both of a memoir and of a physical body that struggles to keep functioning? I find myself facing the unexpected change in "time" itself—something that I never anticipated. As a youngster, a day was incredibly long, and now a year is fearsomely short. A day that disappears almost before it has started, together with my diminishing energy, can make life somewhat of a challenge.

Even in times that were hard for me, though, I never really felt there was ever anyone else in charge of my life. I knew I ultimately had to make my own decisions, for good or bad; no religious persuasion offered me any answers. I felt I had to figure things out the best way I could and take full responsibility for what happened. I allowed my life to take its own course and I am grateful to the fair winds that blew in my direction.

Whatever spiritual forces may exist beyond my understanding, I hope to remain open to embracing whatever comes my way. This sense of unpredictability makes life more interesting. I was blessed with an adventurous spirit that I trust will always remain with me.

My sense of social justice only gets stronger as I witness more of the struggles our world faces. We need to retool our individual and collective behaviour to respect the earth, which provides our most basic needs, and share our diminishing resources to make our society work for the benefit of all, not just the privileged few. Although I feel blessed to live in a country where we have the freedom, as well as the responsibility, to vote, we cannot wait for governments to make such changes for us.

Difficult, uncomfortable and immense efforts lie ahead, but positive transformations are always possible on every front—political and personal, in action as well as in ideology. This gives me hope. That is the message I would like to leave for my family, for my friends and for all those who read this: to never give up, to keep hope and keep pushing creatively for change. And enjoy yourselves while doing this with others!

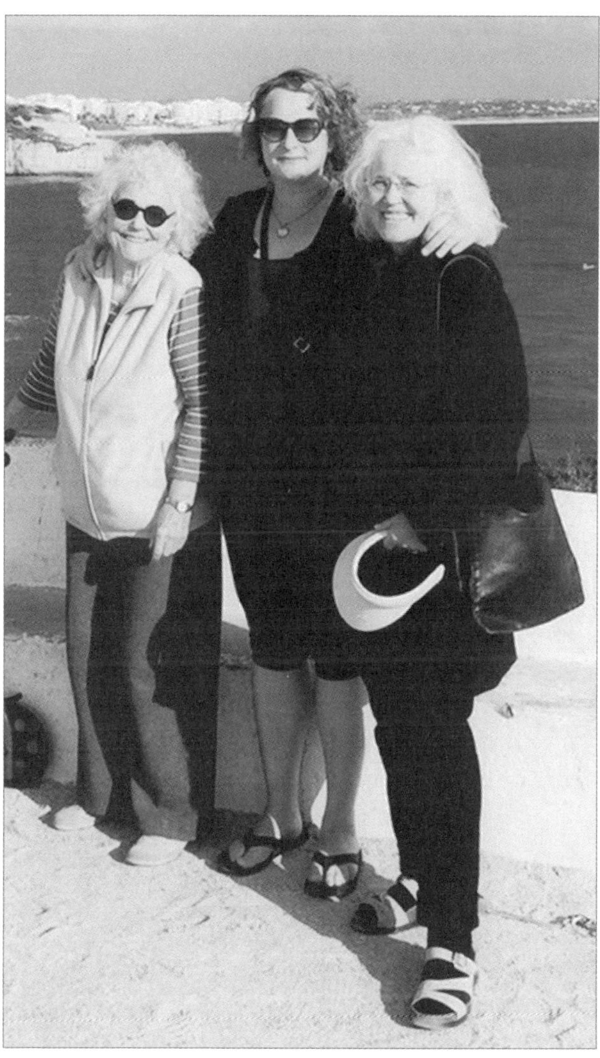

Three generations on the Algarve, Portugal.

Acknowledgements

I would like to thank all those who gave me encouragement in writing this: my daughter Claire, who got me started and kept prompting me from afar; and my granddaughters, Narisse, who from an early age kept asking me for another story from my past, and Jadzia, who constantly rescued me when I landed in computer chaos. Many friends read earlier pieces and offered appreciative comments that kept me continuing: in particular, Grace Golightly, Cady Williams, Arlene Weaver and Zandrika James. Also Monika Ullmann, who brought some initial structure into it.

I'd also like to acknowledge Buffy Cram's writing workshops, which kept me focused, and I'm most grateful for her considered and thoughtful suggestions for editorial revision. Susie Hudson Forbes kindly converted the original design file for Caitlin Press. Ian Crawford used his photographic skills to make some of my old photos discernible. Bill Horne used his remarkable ingenuity in dealing with my data management challenges and final editorial needs. He also laid out and designed all the material for publishing. His invaluable assistance has made this project a reality. My warmest thanks to all of them.